MARTIN LUTHER

A Biography for the People

DYRON B. DAUGHRITY

Abilene Christian University Press

MARTIN LUTHER

A Biography for the People

ACU PRESS

ISBN 978-0-89112-423-8

Printed in the United States of America

LIBRARY OF CONGRESS CATALOGING-IN-PUBLICATION DATA
Names: Daughrity, Dyron B., 1973- author.
Title: Martin Luther : a biography for the people / Dyron B. Daughrity.
Description: Abilene, Texas : Abilene Christian University Press, 2017. |
Includes bibliographical references.
Identifiers: LCCN 2017027574 | ISBN 9780891124238 (pbk.)
Subjects: LCSH: Luther, Martin, 1483-1546. | Reformation—Germany—Biography.
| Lutheran Church—Germany—Clergy—Biography.
Classification: LCC BR325 .D38 2017 | DDC 284.1092 [B] —dc23
LC record available at https://lccn.loc.gov/ 2017027574

Cover design by Greg Jackson
Interior text design by Sandy Armstrong

For information contact:
Abilene Christian University Press
ACU Box 29138
Abilene, Texas 79699

1-877-816-4455
www.acupressbooks.com

17 18 19 20 21 22 / 7 6 5 4 3 2 1

Praise For

Martin Luther: A Biography for the People

"Nobody disputes the importance of Martin Luther in world history, or in the development of Christianity. It's a pleasure then to have such an accessible guide to the man and his thought, with a judicious assessment of his impact. Daughrity deserves all praise for this readable, and reader-friendly, account."

—**Philip Jenkins,** Distinguished Professor of History, Institute for Studies of Religion, Baylor University

"I wish this book had been available when I was a student! Daughrity's biography of Luther brings alive the Reformer's life and work, presenting it in an exciting yet scholarly way. While demonstrating Luther's great contribution to the Protestant Reformation, the author is not afraid to acknowledge his darker side, discussing his hostility towards Jews and Muslims."

—**George D. Chryssides** York St John University, UK

"Counting myself among the 'common people' for whom this book is written, I am deeply grateful to Daughrity for this splendid, highly readable biography of Martin Luther. There is so much to learn from and to be spiritually edified by it."

—**Peter C. Phan,** Ellacuria Chair of Catholic Social Thought, Georgetown University

"It is a massive challenge to produce a comprehensive 'biography for the people' on the complex personality of Martin Luther. Daughrity, however, well up to the task. His extensive reading, but more so the passion for the man and the subject shine through in every line."

—**Herbert Quelle** Consul General Consulate General of the Federal Republic of Germany

"Daughrity offers a riveting portrait of the reformer as pastor, theologian, and Biblical translator, whose passion for communicating the gospel of Christ brought him into contact with men and women from all walks of life. Deeply researched and beautifully written, this biography for the people is a story about the people who were central to Luther's life and work.

—**Christine Helmer,** Professor of German and Religious Studies, Northwestern University

"Seminal characters like Augustine, Benedict, and Martin Luther remain fountainheads of Christian life relevant to the present day. Daughrity returns to the wellspring of the Reformation and narrates a personal encounter with the riches of the Christian tradition, but also it stands as a creative, hermeneutical exercise in which Martin Luther is re-interrogated with the Church's present situation in mind."

—**Enrico Beltramini,** Department of Philosophy and Religious Studies, Notre Dame de Namur University

With gratitude and deep respect, this book is dedicated to three close friends who have been unfailingly supportive and encouraging to me during my first decade at Pepperdine University:

Randy Chesnutt

Tim Willis

Dan Rodriguez

Contents

Acknowledgments

I am deeply grateful to Jason Fikes and his staff at ACU Press. They are a joy to work with. I could not ask for a more supportive press.

I am thankful to my fellow Faculty Seminar participants who visited Luther sites with me in the summer of 2016. We had great fun and lots of robust conversation. My presentation on Luther's attitude toward Jews fed into my chapter on that topic in this book. Hans-Dieter, Sara Thögersen, and Bill Hopkins put together a thrilling and enriching experience for us. We enjoyed lovely conversations in stunning settings while chasing Luther's ghost. Thanks for the good memories John Williams, Ed Meadors, Terry Carter, Robert Goebel, Emily Gray, Glenn Jonas, Scott McGinnis, Herbert Quelle, Bob Shaffern, Buz Myers, Carl Hughes, Carol Loar, Charles Lockwood, Sandra Kohler, Darek Jarmola, and Michael Hammett.

I would like to thank the undergraduate research assistants who helped me with this project: Katie Kawachi, Yvonne Ramirez, and Sarah Park. Sarah, you deserve particular mention here; you were relentless in tracking down wonderful little facts about our man Luther! I also want to single out Michael Gaston, my graduate assistant over the last year. It has been a pleasure working with you. I look forward to seeing what you do with Clovis and Clotilde.

To Pepperdine's Religion and Philosophy Division, thank you for your collegiality and encouragement through the years. Here's to many more years together.

To my incredibly supportive wife Sunde and our four children: Clare, Ross, Mande Mae, and Holly Joy, you make life so beautiful. I am so proud of all of you.

> *Now to him who is able to do immeasurably more than all we ask or imagine, according to his power that is at work within us, to him be glory in the church and in Christ Jesus throughout all generations, for ever and ever! Amen.* (Eph. 3:20–21)

Dyron B. Daughrity
Malibu, California

1

Introduction: "I Will Not Recant Anything"

Martin Luther was as surprised as everybody else that the following words on October 31, 1517, would cause such an explosion in the Christian world, ravaging the Roman Catholic Church. Truth be told, the words here are rather boring: a professor is announcing a theological debate about penance, and how Christians should understand it. What follows are the actual words, translated into English, of the opening of the *Ninety-Five Theses*, along with the first two of the ninety-five:

The Ninety-Five Theses
Or
Disputation for Clarifying the Power of Indulgences

> Out of love and zeal for bringing the truth to light, what is written below will be debated in Wittenberg with the Reverend Father Martin Luther, Master of Arts and Sacred Theology and regularly appointed lecturer on these subjects at that place, presiding. Therefore, he requests that those who cannot be present to discuss orally with us will in their absence do so by letter. In the name of our Lord Jesus Christ. Amen.

> Our Lord and Master Jesus Christ, in saying, "Do penance," wanted the entire life of the faithful to be one of penitence.
>
> This phrase cannot be understood as referring to sacramental Penance, that is, confession and satisfaction as administered by the clergy.[1]

How did these rather blasé words make such an impact? They set in motion the Protestant Reformation. They opened the floodgates to literacy. They marked the beginning of the end of the medieval world and the dawning of the modern age. They caused the biggest split in the history of Christianity. They set in motion a sequence of events that would lead to religious freedom. They blazed the trail for individualism. They set the stage for modern democracy. They spurred the rise of modern capitalism. They were a prelude to modern secularization—both of the state and of the individual.

Could it be true? Could these academic words—an invitation to a debate—have caused all of that? Scholars continue to debate these matters, but one thing is certain: Luther's public invitation to a debate on penance represents a pivot in the history of Christianity, and, consequently, in the history of the world. Nobody doubts that Martin Luther, at that time a thirty-three-year-old German monk and professor, is one of the most significant lives in history.

Probably more biographies of Luther have been written than of any other individual in history, save Jesus Christ. Thousands upon thousands of books have been written to explain him, his theology, the Protestant Reformation, the split with the Catholic Church, and so on. The material is overwhelming. Even Luther's own writings are too numerous to inventory. The German edition (Weimar) of his writings is now at 120 thick volumes. The American edition is currently at fifty volumes and still is expanding. Do we need one more?

Obviously, I think so. Let me explain why.

Passing on What I Received

I prepared this biography of Luther for the 500-year anniversary of the beginning of the Protestant Reformation—when Luther posted the *Ninety-Five Theses* on the Castle Church door in Wittenberg. However, I did not write this book simply to add to the party. No, I have other reasons.

I am making my own journey with Luther, and I felt it was time to investigate the man properly. This was my best chance, as we approached the big anniversary. Never again in my career would I be as motivated as I am at this moment. So, I decided to make my humble contribution.

I did not grow up knowing much about Luther, other than the few paragraphs written about him in my high school history book. The proper introduction came when I was taking a History of Christianity course in college. I knew I was not a Catholic, but I did not understand fully why there were Catholics and Protestants. When my professor started talking about this strange, conflicted, frustrated monk in Germany, I leaned in to listen. And I read. And read. Eventually, I decided to give my academic life to this topic. I finished my bachelor's degree in religion and started a master's program in history and theology. And I still had a deep thirst for more. I decided to do a PhD in church history. After that, I was offered a professorship teaching church history at a college. Now, I spend virtually every day of my working life writing church history, and no individual has impacted me more than Luther. So I want to share that piece of myself—immersed in Luther all these years—with others.

Today in my courses, I lecture more on Luther than on any other individual. He comes up time and time again. Grasping his ideas, his motives, and his self-understanding is critical to comprehending the history of Christianity. I would argue that by studying Luther we are studying our own intellectual history—why we think the way we do. Luther's life, thought, and career shaped the modern mind in profound ways. As the great Danish theologian Sören Kierkegaard described him, he was "the master of all masters."[2]

Luther's courageous confrontation at the Diet of Worms was truly a moment for the ages, especially when he looked straight at his high-ranking accusers—those who could easily consign his body to the flames—and clearly uttered the words: "I will not recant anything." These nobles and princes could easily have said, "Tie him up." But something strange happened that afternoon in 1521. Luther's defiance attracted some of those elite officials to his cause. Most people would wither when faced with life or death. But Luther was at his best at this moment. He defied them. *Fine, burn me.* He was willing to deal with the consequences of his unyielding convictions. They urged him to recant. They placed his books in front of him and told him the price he would pay if he openly defied the church. They gave him ample opportunity to backpedal and escape certain punishment. Luther looked right back at them and said:

"I will not recant anything."

My professor told us that story, and my palms sweated while he lectured. I was nineteen years old, and I did not know how the story ended. Who was this person? What kind of recklessness would lead someone to commit such an act? This was the medieval world, where people were burned routinely. Opposition to authority was dealt with summarily. Life was so easily extinguished. Luther was a lone monk against an army of rulers. He represented himself. It was pitiful. The crowd of nobles looked at him intently. Who is this man, this defiant priest? How dare he oppose the dictates of the church? Bring him closer and force him into submission. Nevertheless, Luther did not blink.

"I will not recant anything."

I could not get these words out of my head. This was a life worthy of consideration. This was courage. This was true independence. This was inner strength like none I had learned about before. Since then, I have continued reading and learning about this man, Luther. I teach about his life every semester now. While I must admit that my students are probably more familiar with the story than I was at their age, I take great delight in simply telling it with raw emotion—the way it was told to me—allowing it to penetrate their young minds as it did mine.

For the People

I wrote this book because I feel there is a need for it. It was not written for academicians. It was written for the people. I took my cues from Luther. Early in his career, Luther decided to aim his writings at the common person rather than always trying to write exclusively for clergy and professors. Luther realized something that many scholars never fully grasp: writing your ideas for the people rather than for the elite can unleash great power.

So Luther decided early to write mostly in German—the language of the people around him, the people whose opinion he really cared about. This was deliberate, since the ecclesial and academic language of his day was Latin. Luther made it a point to write in the language that would be accessible to the common man and woman. And this may be what saved his neck.

When Luther traveled to Worms to appear before the officials of the Holy Roman Empire, he was treated as a hero. People felt he was somebody they could touch and talk to. When Luther translated the Bible into German, he realized, deep down, that he was winning people to his cause. If they could read the Bible for themselves, he believed, they would take his side in the debates that were sure to come. And, indeed, many of them did.

This biography of Luther is an attempt to take general readers on the thrill ride I have been on my entire career in reading Luther and discovering more about him. I try to tell the story and tell it well, with clarity and concision. The book moves rapidly through the various stages of Luther's life, distilling the most important events without burying the narrative in the finer details of theology. Of course, I discuss theology throughout, but it is always contextualized within the man Luther, his times, the events going on in his life, and his relationships. I hope academicians will read it, but my primary purpose was to write a compelling story for the people.

Readers will likely enjoy encountering the "big ideas" coming from Luther, but there is another side of the story that this book presents as we place Luther in his socio-cultural context. He was a man utterly fixated on his salvation, but so was everyone else in his day. He truly believed that Jesus was present, actually present, in the bread and wine of the Eucharist. He expected the second coming of Christ at any moment. He believed Satan caused trouble outside his window. He cursed at the Jews. He feared the Muslims. He condemned the other Protestants who broke away from him. Tragically, he turned his back on the German peasants when they became overly zealous after reading his liberating ideas—and they paid the ultimate price for his rejection. He scoffed at the pope and openly insulted him as the antichrist. He was aware of the political dynamics of his day and knew how to play smartly in that arena. He wrote letters to his children when he traveled. Luther loved kids and realized that the future of his movement depended on them. Thus, he wrote lessons specifically for them. Lutheran kids still memorize his words.

And while Luther was a man of his age, he was also the turning point of his age. His socio-political context changed dramatically after his life had been lived. He is that interstice separating the medieval and the modern. After Luther, most things changed. Sure, people still ate and married and went to church, but changes were everywhere. Fasts were less frequent and lost their spiritual potency. Clergy married. Convents emptied. Women looked at priests as potential husbands rather than as men to whom they must bow. Churches became places where the word of God was preached in the local language. The lay people sang, not just the choir. Rome was no longer the center of the churchgoer's religious consciousness. For much of the Christian world, things were forever changed. And Martin Luther had everything to do with that shift.

Finally, I should point out the obvious here in this introductory chapter. Many books have been written about Luther, and many more are coming onto the market now that the 2017 anniversary has arrived. Biographies by Scott Hendrix, Lyndal Roper, and Heinz Schilling are among the best. I have used the first two, but Schilling's did not quite make it onto the market in time for me. This book is my humble attempt to add to the conversation. Hopefully, my version of Luther's life will be one that is readable, concise, fresh, and updated to account for recent research. As a younger scholar, I hope that my version of Luther's wonderfully rich life will usher today's students into Luther studies as Roland Bainton and other scholars did for me in the 1990s. It is my hope that this book will whet the appetite for religious studies, theology, and history in all liberal art students so that they will explore for themselves how this one man made such a difference in the world.

Notes

[1]This is the official introduction and first two theses of Luther's *Ninety-Five Theses*. I have used Timothy Wengert, *The Ninety-Five Theses*, in *The Annotated Luther*, vol. 1: *The Roots of Reform* (Minneapolis: Fortress Press, 2015), ed. by Timothy Wengert, 13–46.

[2]In Hans Hillerbrand, "The Legacy of Martin Luther," in *The Cambridge Companion to Martin Luther* ed. Donald McKim (Cambridge: Cambridge University Press, 2003), 238.

2

Luther's World

Martin Luther was born in 1483 during what was already proving to be a pivotal age. Europe was ascending onto the world stage as the premier cultural, military, and economic power in the world, and it was beginning to assert itself, especially in matters pertaining to religion. The Iberian Peninsula was ground zero for this push, evinced in the establishment of the Spanish Inquisition.

In the 1480s and 1490s, as Christianity was turning the tide against eight centuries of Muslim rule in what is now Spain and Portugal, Jews were caught in the crossfire. While Muslims were expelled in 1492, Jewish expulsion had already begun in the 1480s. Grand Inquisitor Tomas de Torquemada was given the reins to the Spanish Inquisition in 1483, the very year Luther was born.[1]

Luther's anti-Semitism has been roundly condemned by historians, but he came by it honestly. Anti-Semitic feelings were rife all over Europe, especially during the era of the Reconquista. Muslims were the enemy, but Jews were hardly appreciated. Beginning in the 1300s, pressure was building against Jewish and Muslim civilian populations as Christian kingdoms began to win battle after battle against Muslim armies in the Iberian Peninsula. Fearing the outcome, many Jews responded by removing themselves to the relatively safe harbor of Ottoman lands. Many more chose to convert to Christianity and became known as *conversos*. Even after conversion, however, their struggle for recognition continued, since many Christians believed that Jews had turned to Christ strictly out of self-preservation.

An Expanding World

At the time of Luther's birth (1483), Portuguese imperial ambitions were rising fast, and Christianity's fortunes were improving as well. Portugal's astounding period of expansion began with Henry the Navigator (1394–1460), a wealthy prince who was fascinated with Africa and the expansion of Christian influence there. Henry's father, King John I, put his son in charge of conquering the North African port city of Ceuta, just across from Gibraltar. Henry proved up to the task and made a name for himself, even in Rome. Henry was thus able to lead and finance a series of successful expeditions that kept him occupied for more than forty years. He began by establishing colonies on the islands of Madeira and Cape Verde off the west coast of Africa. In time, he worked his way to the mainland, reaching Guinea in the 1450s. Henry set up a Portuguese base in Lagos, in modern Nigeria. As early as 1441, the Portuguese were buying and selling African slaves.[2]

In Luther's day, Africans were associated with Islam. Today, however, sub-Sahara is mainly associated with Christianity. It was the Portuguese who began to change that perception. Their motives were mixed. They thought that by colonizing West Africa they could gain slaves, but they could also plant Christianity.

Luther's childhood—the 1480s and 1490s—was a rich time for Catholic missions along the coast of West Africa. In 1492, another world opened to these Catholic explorers when Columbus encountered the Americas. Nevertheless, the work in Africa was for many years extremely fruitful for the cause of Christ as well as for Portuguese commerce. The triangular relationship between Spain and Portugal, West Africa, and the Americas exposed Europeans to new worlds, increased Europe's standard of living, and introduced Africans and Native Americans to an unprecedented era that would forever change their way of life.

The story of the Portuguese in Africa is a complex one. Some Africans were taken as slaves to Europe; others were educated in Europe and transported back to Africa to help evangelize. Some Africans welcomed the Europeans, while others, obviously, feared them. The picture became very mixed. For example, "Juan Garrido (1480–1550), a conquistador who participated in the conquest of Tenochtitlan in the 1520s, was a free man of African descent."[3] Some brave European missionaries traveled to the rather sophisticated empire of Mali to engage in debates with Muslim scholars there. Most of the Portuguese travelers, however, made their way south, down the coast of West Africa, in search of gold, slaves, and souls.

In 1482, the year before Luther's birth, in present-day Ghana, a priest celebrated the Mass, the first one ever celebrated in West Africa.[4] By 1483, the Portuguese had established a bridgehead at the mouth of the Congo River, not far from modern Kinshasa, the capital of today's Democratic Republic of Congo—still today a nation with a strong Catholic presence. Throughout the 1480s, the Kingdom of Kongo became largely converted to Christ as the royal house became Christians. The king's son, Afonso, became a zealous Catholic, often forcing his people into the church.

The Kingdom of Kongo—encompassing parts of the modern nations of the Democratic Republic of the Congo, Angola, Gabon, and the Republic of the Congo—established extremely good relations with Portugal. Most of the people in that region became Christians, if only in name, due to the pressure by the royal family as well as the missionary labors of European priests. There are examples of Africans who went to Portugal to study for the priesthood and returned home to lead their people. For example, one Kongolese man named Henrique (1495–1526) was even elevated to the rank of bishop after having an audience with Pope Leo X, the same pope who became embroiled in controversy with a then-unknown German monk named Martin Luther.[5] Henrique was a rather exceptional case, however. Most Africans did not travel abroad for education or ordination. Indeed, the vast majority of them headed out on a quite different journey.

By the end of Martin Luther's life (1546), the slave trade was big business. "Some three to four thousand Africans annually" were being loaded onto putrid slave ships, going from West Africa to work the fields and plantations of the Americas.[6] These developments, for the most part, escaped the notice of Martin Luther. Using his pen as a weapon, he was preoccupied fighting theological battles in the north of Europe. His knowledge of the greater world around him was slim, and his gaze was fixed on reforming the church he knew. Indeed, Luther mentioned the Americas only a few times, describing them as "newly discovered islands in the West" and the source of a "new disease" (syphilis) that had been introduced into Europe. For him, the European discovery of the Americas was one more sign that the old age was nearing its end.[7]

Muslim Conquests

Luther interpreted major cataclysms as signs that the end was near. For all the talk of Luther opening a new epoch in history, it must always be kept in mind that he thought like a medieval man.

Portugal's unbridled ambitions ended neither in the New World nor in Africa. Its empire quickly expanded east when Bartolomeu Dias rounded the Cape of Good Hope—southern Africa—in 1488, when Luther was only five years old. When Luther was a teenager, Vasco da Gama reached India, linking Europe and Asia. Also during Luther's teenage years, in 1500, Pedro Alvares Cabral became the first European to set foot on the vast territory we now call Brazil. The Portuguese are typically known as the first global empire in history due to their continued advance under the famed explorer Afonso de Albuquerque (1453–1515). General Albuquerque expanded the Portuguese Empire beyond anyone's wildest imagination, into Malaysia, Indonesia, Thailand, Southeast Asia, China, and many places across Oceania such as Timor and New Guinea. When General Albuquerque died in 1515, Luther was a young man rising through the ranks of his Augustinian monastic order as well as serving as a professor of theology at the University of Wittenberg.

By 1512, the Portuguese controlled a huge empire. They proceeded to make good on their discoveries by establishing trade with these far-off nations and planting the gospel on these distant, exotic shores. When the Jesuits (Society of Jesus) were established in 1534, a new era of global missions began. It was led by a priest who was perhaps the greatest missionary in history, Francis Xavier (1506–1552), who was also a contemporary of Martin Luther.

While southwestern Europe was thinking in terms of expansion, it was quite the opposite for the southeastern side, the old region known by most as the Byzantine Empire. The Eastern Roman Empire had collapsed in 1453 when the Ottomans, led by Sultan Mehmed II, invaded, conquered, and plundered the city of Constantinople over an eight-week period. For many, it was unimaginable that the great epicenter of Eastern Christianity had fallen to the Turks. For others, it was a long time coming. Indeed, over the course of centuries, Muslim empires had taken their turn at reducing the once vast Byzantine Empire to a shadow of what it had been. Since Islam's rise in the seventh century, three Christian cities were deemed as particularly strategic—Jerusalem (it fell to Islam in 637), Constantinople (which in 1453 became, essentially, the new capital of Islam), and Rome. For many centuries, Constantinople was the big prize, and the Turks got it. But the way they got it cast a blanket of fear over Europeans, especially on the eastern front, for many decades.

On May 29, 1453, the ancient Christian capital, Constantinople, was overwhelmed and its residents subjected to "murder, rape, and looting" by Ottoman troops. "The Emperor's head was stuffed with straw and paraded around the cities of the Muslim world; his dynasty was scattered from the city of Constantine." Mehmed "had achieved that dream of Muslim conquerors since their first expansion out of Arabia" in the 600s.[8]

Luther was not oblivious to what was going on in the Americas, but he gave more attention to the Turkish threat coming from the east. And this was for good reason. The Ottoman Empire had no intention to stay put in Constantinople. Their sights were now fixed on the West, and their expansion continued, little by little, well into Luther's life.[9]

It is interesting to note that some historians believe the Ottomans may have been the chief reason Luther's movement was able to grow so quickly and flourish in northern Europe; the emperor's plate was simply too full.[10] The Ottomans had relentlessly advanced on western Europe, and for decades it seemed a *fait accompli* that Christian civilization was nearing its end. The greatest gains were made under Suleiman I (the Magnificent, who lived 1494–1566), arguably the greatest sultan/caliph in the history of Islam. His long reign lasted forty-six years and was the apex of Ottoman civilization. During his reign, the Ottoman Empire conquered Belgrade (Serbia) in 1521, the powerful Mediterranean Christian stronghold of Rhodes in 1522, and Buda (Hungary) in 1526. Historians generally consider the defeat of the Ottomans in the Siege of Vienna (1529) to be a turning point in history, as it stifled the great Ottoman advance. For 150 years, the Ottomans attempted yet failed to take Vienna. Finally, in 1683, the Christian world, led by the Hapsburgs, managed to push the Ottomans back once and for all.

New Science, New Ships, New Books

The Italian Renaissance commanded far more attention from Luther, however, than did the Turkish gains to the east, the discovery of the Americas, or the Iberian expansion to the ends of the earth. Luther's childhood took place when the Renaissance was reaching its apogee, and Luther's focus remained fixed, to the end of his days, on what was happening in Rome and, by extension, in western European civilization. Indeed, there was much to take in. Michelangelo was eight years old when Luther was born, and there is a chance they met each other when Luther traveled to Rome in 1511, during the time Michelangelo was painting the Sistine Chapel ceiling. The great Italian painter Raphael, also born in 1483, could have met Luther in 1511. Leonardo da Vinci—the quintessential "Renaissance man"—was thirty-one years old when Luther was born.

Luther was far from alone in producing groundbreaking written works during the first half of the sixteenth century, as several truly epochal texts were published during his lifetime, including Erasmus's *In Praise of Folly* (1508), Machiavelli's *The Prince* (1513), Thomas More's *Utopia* (1516), Erasmus's *Greek New Testament* (1516), and Copernicus's *On the Revolutions of the Heavenly Spheres* (1543). Martin Luther's *Ninety-Five Theses* (1517) and his publication of the Bible into German—often known as *The Luther Bible* (New Testament in 1522, Old Testament and Apocrypha in 1534)—must be added to this list.

Luther was born into a sumptuous era of Roman Catholic history. The magnificent art and décor, opulent building projects, ubiquitous renovation projects, and extravagant pomp and grandeur—all of this was impressive, but it required money. The Catholic Church was growing but not in the direction Luther envisioned or favored. He began to react against it, and this reaction is what set in motion the Protestant Reformation.

Luther's life took place during a rare and seminal age, an era of boundless opportunity. Europe was beginning to attain its long era of "unrivalled ascendancy."[11] The collective European mind was expanding geographically, scientifically, and astronomically. The fact that Luther disagreed with him did not change the fact that Nicolaus Copernicus was on to something important when he began to propose that the center of our physical reality was the sun rather than Earth. Western Europe's borders were expanding exponentially as Spain and Portugal capitalized on the new land and handed to the church millions of souls. The long era of Islamic dominance was slowly grinding to a halt as Christian civilization finally was proving itself a capable and worthy opponent.

Western Europe's growth was immeasurably promising during Luther's era. Its borders were becoming more secure due to the tremendous gains made in shipbuilding. Indeed, the Portuguese and Genoese had developed the carrack and the caravel, making European expansion possible. The carrack was a large ship capable of sailing around the world, withstanding the strongest of winds and carrying hundreds of tons of cargo from one continent to another. The caravel, however, was quick, deft, and maneuverable, even in shallow waters. Without these naval innovations, the Iberian Peninsula would not have been able to dominate the seas and propel western Europe to such heights.

Erasmus's publication of the New Testament in Greek allowed literate people to think about God's dictates in the original language, and it empowered them in unpredictable ways. Erasmus published this important work in 1516, just a year before Luther's *Ninety-Five Theses*. Across Europe, people were rethinking religion due to this landmark achievement. Martin Luther used Erasmus's Bible heavily, especially the second edition, which served as the basis for Luther's German translation. Luther was one of the early scholars who made use of Erasmus's herculean achievement, and he was not idle. Erasmus's work enabled people, like Luther, to compare the teachings of God with the rules of men. The Roman Church had great control over Latin, but it did not have the same power when it came to Greek or to the local vernaculars. For complicated reasons, the church had privileged the Latin Vulgate, translated by Jerome (347–420). However, for many centuries when scholars began tinkering with the word of God (Jerome's version), it became clear that nothing was off-limits. The most primary source of Christian orthodoxy—the Bible—now was subject to scrutiny. The leaders of the Renaissance had a great fascination with returning to the most primary sources, and capable scholars took notice. This empowerment—this putting the Bible into the hands of the people—was critical to Luther's success. And Erasmus played the leading role in that story.

But the great figures of the early Renaissance were typically southern Europeans, with some notable exceptions, such as Erasmus, who was a Dutchman. Luther seemed to come out of nowhere. He did not have the financial backing, the political connectedness, or the illustrious family pedigree that many other outstanding men of his day had. His parents were hardworking Germans. And despite Luther's great fame and international prominence five hundred years later, during his lifetime he was earthy, rugged, and crass.

A Hard Life in a Tough World

Luther's life, however, takes us back to an era when the average life-span was in the thirties, maybe forty.[12] Children routinely died during infancy. Periodic food shortages were expected. Catastrophic diseases were an ever-present danger, such as the Black Death that wiped out as many as one hundred million people—roughly half of Europe's population—between 1347 and 1353.[13]

Young men could be immediately conscripted for skirmishes between the hundreds of towns, "free imperial cities" (ruled directly by the emperor), principalities, and territories that dotted the vast land of the Holy Roman Empire, stretching from modern Denmark and Poland in the north to include parts of Italy and Croatia in the south. From west to east, the empire included lands from modern France and Belgium to the Czech Republic and Austria.[14] In the years leading up to Luther, the Holy Roman Empire was an unstable place politically. "Between 1350 and 1500 scarcely any city escaped uprisings and violent struggles over control of the municipal government." Civil insurrections occurred with regularity. Peasants revolted. Unemployed mercenaries "roamed the countryside terrorizing the population" with raids.[15]

Then, as now, this huge tract of land was dominated by the German nation, a land of about nine million people during Luther's lifetime. "Thus the population of Luther's Germany was about equal to the number of residents estimated to live in New York City in 2013."[16] While the borders were always changing, a fair estimate for a geographical center to this huge territory would be the modern city of Nuremburg—often referred to as the unofficial capital of the Holy Roman Empire.

Luther's world was an agricultural one, teeming with animals. As an example, one extremely productive hunter—while visiting Frederick the Wise at his favorite retreat—bagged "208 bears, 200 lynxes, and even larger numbers of wolves, boar, deer, and fowl . . . during one autumnal hunting season."[17] Four out of five people lived on farms or in rural villages. Most of these villages were controlled by a ruler who could survey his entire domain from his castle. Others, however, were rather large expanses led by princes and "highly developed central administrations."[18] Some were ruled by bishops. Each little fiefdom was ruled in a different way, and political arrangements often were changed. For example, a town could grow in clout to the point that it might declare itself a "free" city ruled directly by the emperor without any middleman.[19]

Whatever the case, there were few property rights, and rural people worked hard, all the while providing their landowners with "a secure income." Hereditary serfdom often developed. Serfdom differed from slavery in one critical sense. While slaves typically had no rootedness or connection to any particular piece of land (they could be bought and sold at will), a serf at least had the security of farming one piece of land throughout his or her lifetime. Essentially, until the nineteenth century, most peasants lived in "oppressive conditions of servitude that left them with virtually no rights at all."[20]

A Time of Change for Church and State

Before and during Luther's lifetime, two critical developments were happening within the church and the state. First of all, the Roman Catholic Church was struggling to rebound after its worst crisis since becoming a state church in the 300s. That crisis had two phases: the Avignon Papacy (1309–1377) and the Great Western Schism (1378–1417). What happened during that 108-year period is extremely complex, but essentially it was an intensely political battle for authority between Rome, France, and the Holy Roman Empire, which was primarily under German influence. For nearly seven decades, the Roman Catholic Church was based in the city of Avignon, today a city in France but then, crucially, part of the Holy Roman Empire. Historically, Avignon was a French-speaking region, however, and thus a lively three-way battle was going on for control of the papacy, with all its wealth and power and influence over the hearts and souls of the people.

Eventually, the papacy was moved back to Rome, but severe damage had been inflicted on the reputation and credibility of the institution of the church. The power of the clergy had been deeply undermined by these events. Indeed, for a time, three different individuals claimed to be pope! Who was the "real" one? It depended on who you asked.

Today, Luther is often depicted as uniquely critical of the Roman Church at a time when it was at the height of its power, but the peak of the Catholic Church's power had passed, probably reaching its zenith during the Crusades in the twelfth century. The office of the papacy had been under trenchant critique for over two centuries. As the Crusades dragged into the fourteenth century, the Avignon Crisis and Great Western Schism cast doubts upon the institution of the church as never before. Luther's critiques of the church certainly were not abnormal; rather, due to unique historical circumstances that will be explored later, they were extremely effective.

The second critical development during Luther's lifetime had to do with the situation of the state. Due to the loss of credibility and power of the church, it was increasingly unclear who ruled whom. This vacuum of leadership gave rise to national consciousness across the European landscape. The power of the church in different regions of Europe was declining. For example, as early as the fifteenth century, "we may already speak of territorial churches" in England and in France.[21] In the year 1512, the Holy Roman Empire began to rebrand itself as "the Holy Roman Empire of the German Nation." Thus, it became "more and more natural to fall back on the words 'German Nation' as the operative part of the empire's full name."[22]

Luther was able to tap into this shift in consciousness. Indeed, one of Luther's earliest works, *To the Christian Nobility of the German Nation* (1520), was—significantly—written in German, not in Latin. In that work, he introduced the concept of the "priesthood of all believers," wherein he advocated a shift in power away from the priests and toward the common man. These were brilliant moves that not only endeared him to the regular people, but also demonstrated that Luther—a Catholic monk—was looking more to his own *German* nobles for approval than south toward Rome. It would be a vast understatement to say that Luther's world was a changing world.

The sophisticated empires in southern Europe were expanding profoundly and becoming rich in the process. The Portuguese Empire was probably the first empire in history that could claim the sun never set on it. Indeed, southern Europe in general was expanding magnificently, and their cultural icons were powerful displays of their power and prestige. The construction of the largest church in Christendom—Saint Peter's Basilica—began in Rome in 1506, demonstrating the power and might of the Roman Catholic Church. The seemingly indomitable Turks—fresh off their conquest of the Eastern Roman Empire—were knocking on the doors of Vienna. But for the first time in a long time, western Europe was proving itself capable of handling the Ottoman threat. Furthermore, western European culture was reaching its zenith in terms of cultural sophistication. The mighty Renaissance was at full tilt during Luther's life. Powerful and new ideas, trendsetting art, unbelievably ambitious building projects, and a new humanism were causing many to question the old order of things.

The University of Wittenberg, up in the rural farmlands of Germany, founded only in 1502, was the last place anyone expected something truly epochal to rise and take center stage in modern Western history. And it could be said that the most important person to arise out of this storied context of great and heroic men would be an agitated German monk writing from his humble context of an upstart college in northern Europe, far away from the grandeur and splendor of Rome, the eternal city.

Notes

[1]See Diarmaid MacCulloch, *Christianity: The First Three Thousand Years* (New York: Penguin, 2009), 586. Notably, historians believe Torquemada himself was a descendant of *converso* families.

[2]See Dale Irvin and Scott Sunquist, *History of the World Christian Movement*, vol. II (Maryknoll, NY: Orbis, 2012), 37.

[3]Irvin and Sunquist, 38.

[4]Jacques Blocher and Jacques Blandenier, trans. by Michael Parker, *The Evangelization of the World* (Pasadena, CA: William Carey Library, 2013), 139.

[5]Irvin and Sunquist, 39.

[6]Irvin and Sunquist, 39.

[7]Scott Hendrix, *Martin Luther: Visionary Reformer* (New Haven: Yale University Press, 2015), 9–10.

[8]MacCulloch, 494.

[9]Mark Edwards, Jr., "Luther's Polemical Controversies," in *The Cambridge Companion to Martin Luther*, ed. Donald McKim (Cambridge: Cambridge University Press, 2003), 202.

[10]See, for example, Hendrix, 8–9.

[11] Ian Siggins, *Luther* (New York: Barnes and Noble Books, 1972), 1.

[12] Hendrix, 9.

[13] Wim Blockmans and Peter Hoppenbrouwers, *Introduction to Medieval Europe, 300–1500* (London: Routledge, 2014), 331.

[14] For the complicated borders of the Holy Roman Empire, see Hagen Schulze, trans. by Deborah Lucas Schneider, *Germany: A New History* (Cambridge, MA: Harvard University Press, 1998), 31.

[15] Ibid., 41–42.

[16] Hendrix, 9.

[17] Steven Ozment, *A Mighty Fortress: A New History of the German People* (New York: HarperCollins, 2004), 70.

[18] Schulze, 36–37.

[19] Ibid., 39.

[20] Ibid., 38.

[21] Bernard Lohse, *Martin Luther* (Philadelphia, PA: Fortress Press, 1986), 6–7.

[22] Schulze, 44.

3

THE BOY MARTIN

MARTIN LUTHER WAS BORN TO HANS AND MARGARET (MAIDEN NAME Lindemann) on November 10, 1483.[1] At least, that's what most of the history books say. However, the year of his birth is uncertain. People debated it during Luther's life, and those debates have been passed down to the historians.

Even Luther debated with his friends about what year he was born.[2] He once claimed he was born "for certain" in the year 1484, in the town of Mansfeld. However, occasionally, he would argue that he was born in 1482. His more detail-conscious colleague, Philip Melanchthon, wrote a biography shortly after Luther's death. In it, he placed Luther's birth in 1483, and that is the year that has stuck ever since.

The story is complicated, however. Melanchthon and Luther were close friends and would argue sometimes about this little fact. Melanchthon claimed Luther's brother Jacob told him the family had agreed that Luther's birth year was 1483. However, Luther's own mother placed the birth of the reformer in 1484. Melanchthon approached an Italian astrologer for help and, using a horoscope, the astrologer claimed the birth year must be 1484. The story gets even more convoluted after Luther's death. The grave marker—at the Castle Church in Wittenberg—puts the great reformer's death in December (not November, as almost unanimously believed) 1482![3]

Some debate also continues over whether Luther was born in the town of Mansfeld or in Eisleben. Despite Luther's claim that he might have been born in Mansfeld, historians are rather certain that the town of his birth was Eisleben, in Mansfeld County, in the Electorate of Saxony, in territory that belonged to the Holy Roman Empire. He was baptized at the Church of Saints Peter and Paul on November 11, and was named Martin due to the feast day belonging to Saint Martin of Tours.[4] Whether Luther was his parents' firstborn is not clear, since he claimed his parents lost a child at a very young age before he was born. The possibility of the Luthers losing a child is entirely reasonable. The infant mortality rate was around 60 percent, or even higher.[5] This high mortality was also incentive for Hans and Margaret to baptize young Martin as quickly as possible. Thus, while Luther was born about an hour before midnight, his parents were at the church building just hours later guaranteeing their son's salvation through holy christening—an act that washed away the stain of original sin and protected the child from the devil.[6]

Eisleben was a town of about four thousand souls when Luther was born.[7] Its location is about seventy miles southwest of Wittenberg, where Luther launched the Reformation, and about sixty miles northeast of Erfurt, where Luther attended university. The family remained in Eisleben only a few months. About all we know about those months is that Hans gained a little experience in mining there.[8] We also know that things were not good enough for them to stay put. The Luther family promptly relocated to the town of Mansfeld, about ten miles northwest of Eisleben, in 1484.[9] Mansfeld was good to Hans. There, he found stable work in the copper mines, and over time he worked his way up the ladder to attain some measure of success in life.[10]

Luther the Peasant

Martin Luther understood himself to be the descendant of peasants. It was a point of pride for him that he had come from humble roots. "I am the son of a peasant," he boasted. "My great-grandfather, my grandfather, and my father were real peasants. . . . Peasants have become kings and emperors."[11] Indeed, Luther thought his Saxon sturdiness to be a virtue, serving him well in his life's difficult work. A sensitive aristocrat might not have been able to weather all that Luther did in his turbulent and stressful life.

Martin's father, Hans, was "a serious-minded, severe, and industrious man." He could become jovial occasionally, especially when drinking beer, but he was by nature a hard man, blessed with a strong work ethic and "endowed with a robust, solid body."[12] His determination, combined with his good fortune of marrying up (to Margaret Lindemann), helped him move out of the struggling peasant class fairly soon. He was a self-made man; in his region (Thuringia) the family inheritance—most notably the land—passed to the youngest son, named Heinz. Inheritance laws stipulated that since the eldest children were probably stronger and more experienced, they could more easily move off the farm into one of the trades. The youngest son, therefore, inherited the land.[13] As the eldest of four sons, Hans had to forge his way alone, without access to the family farm he knew so well.[14] This would have been a difficult path for a young man who was probably illiterate since his hometown (Möhra) "had neither a parsonage nor a school."[15] Thus, when Hans's father died, his choice was simple: he could either stay put while working for his young brother, or he could branch out to a neighboring town and find something else to do.[16]

Hans Luther's father was named Heine Luther. Heine and his family lived in Möhra, "a small village of sixty families" located in the Thuringian Forest about a hundred miles southwest of Eisleben, the town where Martin Luther would be born. Heine's family lived modestly. They were not the poorest of families, since they owned a farm and raised pigs, sheep, and cows. They probably were not part of the highest classes either, since they possessed no servants or horses. In their little corner of the world, however, in the village of Möhra, they lived respectably and comfortably.[17]

So what do we make of Luther's repeated claims that he came from peasants, which had the connotation of landless laborers? Part of it was Luther's way with words. He used hyperbole often to emphasize whatever he needed to make his point. However, Luther was no liar. A thread of truth validates his claims that he had come from peasant ancestry, but Luther's own father would be better described as a man of industry, with a fairly successful career in mining. And, "in those days the German mining industry was the most important in Europe." It should be remembered, however, that it was Luther's father Hans who made the jump from the farm to the industrial class. Hans's parents, although far from destitute, were people of the land. They were peasants indeed, although "very far from being oppressed and serf-like peasants; they were relatively well placed and free proprietors, paying only a modest quit-rent [similar to a land tax] to their overlord, the elector of Saxony."[18]

Martin Luther's Mother

Perhaps the most baffling mystery surrounding Luther's ancestry is the background of his mother, Margaret.[19] Those who knew her well called her Hanna.[20] Little information about her can be found in the historical record. For nearly five hundred years, her maiden name has been in question. Suffice it to say that the current consensus of scholarship is that she was a Lindemann, but in every generation, some have claimed that she might have been a Ziegler.

Margaret was certainly not a whore who had intercourse with Satan himself in a bathhouse in Eisleben, thus producing Martin Luther—a species half-demon and half-bastard. As crazy as it sounds, this was a theory proposed by one of Luther's detractors, Johannes Cochlaeus, in a tract published in 1533. This idea gained much traction and did not fully subside until "the nineteenth century, when waning belief in the Devil robbed the legend of its impact and credibility." One high-ranking Roman Catholic clergyman named Pietro Paolo Vergerio came to the same conclusion after meeting with Luther in Wittenberg in 1535. He concluded, "On the basis of what I have found out about his birth, I am quite inclined to assume that he is possessed by a demon." Luther was able to turn attacks of this nature to his advantage, using them to fuel vitriol of his own directed at the Roman hierarchy, his despised enemy. To be sure, he was fully capable of trading punches as low or lower than even this. Historically, this widespread accusation gives us a valuable glimpse into the late-medieval world of Luther's time. Claims such as these are laughable in our day, but Luther felt the need to defend the name and honor of his "beloved mother" even into his twilight years.[21]

Martin Luther's mother, Margaret (or Hanna) Lindemann, was not from the aristocracy, but she was most certainly not near the bottom of the social ladder, either. Indeed, it is difficult to call her a peasant once the historical evidence is surveyed. Her family was from the town of Neustadt on the Saale River, about 135 miles southwest of Eisleben.[22] A branch of the Lindemann family moved to Eisenach, where Margaret was probably born. The family did well for themselves. One of her cousins, Caspar, became a professor of medicine in Leipzig and eventually was recruited by the electors of Saxony to be a personal physician. Caspar even advanced through the ranks to become rector of the University of Wittenberg for a time.[23] Martin Luther knew these people. As relatives, he played with their children and maintained good relations throughout his life. No doubt this high-class family would have inspired young Luther professionally, perhaps even encouraging him to attain a faculty position at the University of Wittenberg one day.

Why all the fuss about whether Margaret was a Lindemann or a Ziegler? The main issue here is whether Luther was as much a peasant as he claimed. If his mother was a Ziegler, then she came from a "relatively prosperous peasant" family. However, if she was a Lindemann—which in all likelihood she was—then she was from a "well-established and respected family of Eisenach burghers," with relatives who graduated from university, became doctors, priests, lawyers, professors, city councilors, and three of them even served as mayors of towns. Indeed, "the Lindemanns were a highly distinguished family."[24]

How did Hans—from a much lower social class—get in with the Lindemann clan? Various possibilities exist. The simplest explanation is that he was a quite resourceful person, driven and ambitious. The more complicated explanation has to do with the declining economic fortunes of the region, particularly in Eisenach, the place Margaret called home. When economies dive, social classes level off, and as a result, "there was probably no great barrier to social mobility." Many have commented on the fact that Hans was from a much lower class than his bride. Make no mistake, Luther's colleague Melanchthon affirmed, "Hans Luther had married above his rank."[25]

The Luthers' Upward Mobility

We can see why Martin Luther considered himself as coming from peasant stock, yet at the same time he was able to study for a living and move through the social ranks quite fluidly. The boy Martin would have had the doors of opportunity opened for him, since the Lindemanns were people with good connections in high places, including to the elector of Saxony. We find that later on Luther managed to connect himself with the elector of Saxony—Frederick the Wise—a connection that saved Luther's life on several occasions. Had a true peasant attempted to excoriate the pope in Rome with vulgar insults, as Luther did, he would have been promptly burned at the stake, or otherwise disposed of with relative ease.

Once Hans—Martin Luther's father—was able to marry a high-class woman of some means and with valuable connections, he made his way to Eisleben to try to break into the mining industry. Instead of groveling in the soot, he set his sights on a managerial position worthy of his new-found status in life. Margaret's eldest brother, Antonius, a burgher (a citizen and member of the upper class) in Eisleben, promptly offered a hand to his younger sister and her new husband once they moved there.[26] Indeed, Antonius "was a prosperous smelter-master in Eisleben and was able to advise Hans how best to obtain his own smelting franchise."[27]

Hans and Margaret did not stay in Eisleben very long, but they did stay long enough to welcome Martin Luther into the world, probably in 1483. Margaret "was in her early twenties when Martin was born."[28] For unknown reasons, when young Martin was about one year old, Hans decided to relocate his family to the nearby mining town of Mansfeld, "the center of a flourishing [copper] mining industry."[29] Hans borrowed money and started his own business in Mansfeld, and in a short time his small business was flourishing. He moved up the social ladder quickly and joined a respectable group of four men who represented the townspeople in meetings. He gave liberally to the church, got elected to the town council, bought property, and raised their children in a "comfortable, stable, and religious" setting.[30]

Hans worked hard and acquired much. At one point, he held investments in eight separate mines and three factories. Running these operations took large amounts of money, however, and Hans had to borrow more capital, thus frequently putting himself in debt to meet production costs. One historian writes, "It was in mining that capitalism began to flower." Martin Luther's parents had managed to lift themselves into the "bourgeois entrepreneur" class through hard work and thrift, although at great risk to their own financial stability.[31] Hans Luther lived with this kind of financial pressure for virtually all his professional life, and he "remained in debt until one year before his death." Nonetheless, when he died in 1530, he left a large sum of money to his survivors, "more than ten times the salary earned at that time by an average professor at the University of Wittenberg."[32]

Luther's Adolescent Years

Martin Luther's education was financed by his hardworking father. Higher learning probably was expected of him, largely because his mother's family produced so many extremely capable and learned children. Initially, young Martin decided he should become a lawyer. No doubt the idea here was that Luther would assist his father in the sprawling business he was building. The Lindemanns had produced lawyers before, and Luther could draw from the collective wisdom of his mother's side of the family.

Martin Luther was well-prepared for a life of study. His father was a disciplinarian, sometimes exacting in his supervision. The family had to be frugal in their spending because of their heavy financial commitments, which led to great strain on the parents. As Kittelson notes, "children were taught that everything the family did was to be both honorable and productive."[33] It was a tightly controlled childhood for young Martin, but certainly not uncharacteristic for his day and age.

Much has been made of the corporal punishment Luther experienced, but it was altogether common for a boy in the late Middle Ages to be punished physically when out of line. When Luther later recalled instances of harsh discipline at home, we can be pretty sure that his penchant for hyperbole was at work. He recalled an occasion where his father punished him so severely that he withdrew from his father for some time.[34] But this was not shocking during the late 1400s. Luther could tell a big fish story with the best of them, and it is likely that his fish got bigger and bigger every time he reminisced about the discipline he experienced in his childhood.

There is no doubt that Luther's parents were strict. The question is whether they were stricter than other parents in that day, and the answer is that they probably were not. Luther's love for his parents was deep and sincere. He remembered his father fondly and attributed his own success to the example his parents handed him.[35] When Hans died in 1530, Martin "genuinely mourned."[36] Similarly, Martin loved his mother deeply, wrote letters to her, and gave her gifts. She sang songs with him, and he remembered her working hard around the house, particularly bringing wood home from the forest, carrying it on her back.[37] Most importantly, she instilled a deep religiosity in her children. Luther once recalled how his mother was convinced that their neighbor was a witch who could cast spells on people who fell out of favor with her. Throughout his adult life, Luther was convinced that his own illnesses were bewitchments from those who wished him harm.[38]

Whatever dysfunction there may have been in the Luther family was not unusual for the time and place. Certainly, stress was high on account of Hans's running several businesses, and caring for a household of eight or nine children would have taxed Margaret to the point of exasperation on occasion.[39] But this was not abuse, and certainly not worth psychoanalyzing several centuries later as if it was something unique.[40]

While talking round the dinner table, Luther was recorded as saying the following on the topic of parental discipline:

> My parents kept me under very strict discipline, even to the point of making me timid. For the sake of a mere nut my mother beat me until the blood flowed. By such strict discipline they finally forced me into the monastery; though they meant it heartily well, I was only made timid by it. They weren't able to keep a right balance between temperament and punishment. One must punish in such a way that the rod is accompanied by the apple. It's a bad thing if children and pupils lose their spirit on account of their parents and teachers.[41]

Luther specialist Scott Hendrix countered this charge with the following: "The adult Luther rarely, if ever, showed signs of timidity.[42] Even still, some historians have made much of the strictness of Martin Luther's parents, judging them as altogether 'too rigorous.'"[43]

Most of the information about Martin Luther's siblings is lost to history. He may have had an older brother who died very young. He had a brother, Jakob, who will be discussed below. He lost two brothers to the plague around the year 1507. One sister died in 1520. Three other sisters married and had families of their own. Surely there were other siblings who died in infancy, a common occurrence in those days.[44]

Martin Luther's closest companion during childhood was his beloved brother Jakob, "the only sibling of whom we know much." The two of them were extremely close as boys, almost inseparable. Their love was "true and heartfelt." By all accounts, Jakob was a good and decent person. He looked after parents Hans and Margaret in Mansfeld during their last years.[45]

Luther, Schoolboy and Scholar

Luther first went off to school in the town of Mansfeld at the age of seven.[46] As a young lad, he was sometimes carried to school on the back of his future brother-in-law, Nicholas Oemer, who was older.[47] Three subjects were taught: Latin grammar, logic, and rhetoric. The Latin grammar books were written by Aelius Donatus, the same person who taught the famous Bible translator Saint Jerome in the fourth century. Medieval students also studied the moral precepts of Cato, a Latin moralist who also lived in the fourth century.[48] The curriculum contained nothing about local history or anything that might praise German culture. Rather, they were immersed in a biblical and Greco-Roman worldview. Most teaching was by rote methods, designed to train the memory.[49] They were also trained in the arts; for example, the children were taught how to sing so they could complement the music in the church.[50] Luther's school stood next to the Church of Saint George, so church and school were enmeshed.[51] Luther was most fond of the music he learned during his school days, considering it his "favorite subject."[52]

Luther attended Latin grammar school for nine years in Mansfeld, and his overall assessment was that they were hellish years for him.[53] His perspective was that in school he and his peers were "tormented."

> [We] learned less than nothing despite all the flogging, trembling, anguish, and misery. . . . How I regret now that I did not read more poets and historians, and that no one taught me them! Instead, I was obliged to read at great cost, toil, and detriment to myself, that devil's dung, the philosophers and sophists, from which I have [done] all I can do to purge myself.[54]

Luther held particular disdain for "the wolf," a classmate who was designated to tattle on students should they misbehave and thus become subject to corporal punishment.[55] The punishment could be severe, according to Luther. He was once struck fifteen times with a cane because he was unable to decline a particular noun. Students could be punished for using German instead of Latin. One historian explains such madness:

> Whipping was part of the pedagogical system. . . . There was a two-fold rationale behind the cruel pedagogy of the sixteenth century: to hammer Latin into the heads of the young pupils, whatever the cost, and to have the pupils become accustomed to informing and to being betrayed. Thus it was a primitive but effective method of training pupils to be submissive.[56]

Luther once recalled a wooden jackass sign hung around the neck of a student who was failing to keep pace with the rest of the class. The student could then pass the sign to someone else who made the mistake of speaking in German rather than Latin.[57] Luther could become caustic in his assessment of his childhood teachers and their methods, but it is obvious that they got through to him and shaped him.

It was not all bad, however, as in the case of *Aesop's Fables*. Luther read them in Mansfeld and "retained a lifelong interest in them," eventually even publishing an edition of his own. He wrote, "In short, next to the Bible, the writings of Cato and Aesop are in my opinion the best, better than the mangled utterances of all the philosophers and jurists, just as Donatus is the best grammarian."[58]

Quite obviously, Luther benefited tremendously from his education. He became a master at Latin, achieved great proficiency in music, single-handedly changed the German language, and developed a voracious appetite for reading and writing. Few people in the annals of human history shared his level of rhetorical prowess. Nevertheless, for all his excellence in language, Luther never excelled in mathematics.[59]

Around the age of thirteen, and for unknown reasons, Luther was sent to a school in the large city of Magdeburg, accompanied by his friend from Mansfeld, Hans Reinicke. It was a short chapter in Luther's life, however, as he was there only one year. He studied with a religious order called the Brethren of the Common Life. Today, we don't know whether the order took responsibility for teaching Luther, but he did live with them and was deeply influenced by them. During this year, he witnessed a Franciscan monk named Wilhelm of Anhalt who was terribly emaciated because of his frequent fasts. Luther was moved by this and considered the man's life exemplary.[60] Luther and the Brethren earned their bread by going door to door begging and sometimes singing, a practice that was not at all considered shameful in that era. Indeed, it was expected, and it provided benefactors the opportunity to fulfill their Christian duty of giving alms to the poor.[61]

At the end of that year in Magdeburg, Luther was sent to the "beloved town of Eisenach" to attend school in Saint George's parish.[62] Luther was now in the land of his mother's relatives, the Lindemanns, and he studied there for four years. Luther's close colleague, Philip Melanchthon, later opined that Luther's teacher in Eisenach—a man named Wigand Güldenapf—was stellar. Luther had nothing but good things to say about this man, and they remained close friends long after Luther's schooling.[63]

Eisenach was an exceedingly religious town of around four thousand inhabitants; there was "one priest or monk for every ten residents." It was home to three parishes and at least three monasteries: the Dominicans, Franciscans, and Carthusians. As in Magdeburg, Luther at first sang and begged for his food, although he did not have to since he had connections there. Later, he moved in with a schoolmate's family—the Schalbes—who were prominent in Eisenach at that time.[64]

Luther's schooling in Eisenach was the traditional trivium: grammar, rhetoric, and logic. As in his previous education, he was strongly attracted to whatever music was being taught. He developed his tenor voice and studied music theory. This all paid off nicely with Luther's prolific hymn-writing later in his career.[65]

In Eisenach, Luther cultivated a deep and abiding friendship with the priest of Saint Mary's Church, a kind, pastoral man named John Braun. Luther spent countless hours at this man's home with other students, singing and having discussions. Luther's 1507 letter to Braun is "the oldest authentic letter from Luther's hand." That letter shows a deep bond between the men, although Luther was much younger than Braun. Luther maintained a close connection with Braun long after his Eisenach years, and he was sure to invite Braun to his first Mass when he became a priest some years later.[66]

After four happy, quality years of study at Saint George's Latin School, Luther headed to the University of Erfurt, having every intention of becoming a lawyer. However, a conflict was going on inside of him. In a letter to his former, beloved priest, John Braun, Luther showed signs of a career struggle. Should he become a secular man of the world? Or should he give his life to Christ and to the church? This internal battle "may have taken root in Eisenach."[67] One thing was for certain, Luther's years as a student in Eisenach prepared him for either career. Clearly, his father wanted his bright and talented son to go to law school. But to the end of his days, Luther had a mind of his own.

Notes

[1]I have opted not to discuss the variants of Luther's name such as Luder, Lothar, Luothar, Ludher, Lueder, Lotter, Eleutheros, Eleutherius, etc. Particularly in the case of Luther's father, Hans, historians are prone to discuss him as Hans Luder. I have herein tried to take the route of clarity. Similarly, there is much controversy surrounding Margaret's maiden name. That debate is outlined later in the chapter.

[2]James Kittelson, *Luther the Reformer* (Minneapolis: Fortress Press, 1986), 31.

[3]See Scott Hendrix, *Martin Luther: Visionary Reformer* (New Haven: Yale University Press, 2015), 17.

[4]Martin Brecht, *Martin Luther: His Road to Reformation, 1483–1521*, trans. by James Schaaf (Philadelphia: Fortress Press, 1985), 1–2.

[5]Kittelson, 32.

[6]See Martin Marty, *Martin Luther* (New York: Viking, 2004), 2.

[7]Heiko Oberman, *Luther: Man between God and the Devil*, trans. by Eileen Walliser-Schwarzbart (New Haven: Yale University Press, 1989), 82.

[8]Hartmann Grisar, *Martin Luther: His Life and Work* (Westminster: The Newman Press, 1950), 4.

[9]Gerhard Brendler, *Martin Luther: Theology and Revolution*, trans. by Claude Foster (Oxford: Oxford University Press, 1991), 22.

[10]See Kittelson, 32.

[11]Grisar, 2.

[12]Ibid., 3.

[13]See Brendler, 21.

[14]See Kittelson, 31, and Brecht, 2. See also Richard Friedenthal, *Luther*, trans. by John Nowell (London: Weidenfeld and Nicolson, 1967), 8. Friedenthal wrote, "Luther's father was the eldest of four sons" (8). The four boys were named Hans the elder, Hans the younger, Veit, and Heinz. For these names see Brendler, 22.

[15]Oberman, 85.

[16]Kittelson, 32.

[17]Brecht, 2. See also Ian Siggins, *Luther and His Mother* (Minneapolis: Fortress Press, 1981), 45.

[18]See Friedenthal, 8.

[19]For the best discussion of this debate, see Siggins, 20–31.

[20]Oberman, 87.

[21]Ibid., 88.

[22]The town is called Bad Neustadt an der Saale.

[23]Hendrix, 18.

[24]Siggins, 45–46.

[25]Ibid., 46–47.

[26]Oberman, 90. On Antonius being a burgher in Eisleben, see Siggins, 47.

[27]Hendrix, 19.

[28]Ibid., 18.
[29]Grisar, 4.
[30]Hendrix, 19–20.
[31]Brendler, 22–24. Quotation is from 23.
[32]Oberman, 85.
[33]Kittelson, 33.
[34]Brecht, 6–7.
[35]Ibid., 7.
[36]Ibid., 8.
[37]Brendler, 24.
[38]Siggins, 13.
[39]Brecht, 7–8.
[40]Erik Erikson famously psychoanalyzed Luther in his wildly popular, but roundly discredited, *Young Man Luther* (New York: W. W. Norton, 1958).
[41]*Luther's Works* (Philadelphia: Fortress Press, 1967), vol. 54, 234 (#3566A).
[42]Hendrix, 18.
[43]See Grisar, 7.
[44]See Siggins, 14.
[45]Ibid., 14.
[46]Some scholars such as Brendler (24) think Luther may have started school as early as four and a half. However, Brecht—generally considered authoritative—believes Luther started school on March 12, 1491, at the age of seven (see 12).
[47]Brendler, 25.
[48]Hendrix, 21.
[49]Brendler, 25.
[50]Ibid., 24–25.
[51]Hendrix, 21.
[52]Brendler, 26.
[53]Ibid., 25.
[54]*Luther's Works* (Philadelphia: Muhlenberg Press, 1962), vol. 45, 369–70. This quotation is from Luther's 1524 work: *To the Councilmen of all Cities in Germany That They Establish and Maintain Christian Schools.*
[55]Marty, 3.
[56]Brendler, 25.
[57]Brecht, 13.
[58]*Luther's Works*, vol. 54, 211 (#3490).
[59]Brendler, 26.
[60]See Brecht, 15–17.
[61]See Brendler, 28.
[62]Hendrix, 23–24.
[63]Ibid., 24.
[64]Brecht, 18–19. The quotation comes from Hendrix, 24.
[65]Hendrix, 24.
[66]Ibid., 24–25.
[67]Ibid., 25.

4

The University Years

Martin Luther's father, Hans, had paid his dues in life. He had worked hard to get what he had. And he was "intent on advancing the education of his eldest son, and saving every penny to do so."[1]

Historians point out that Hans was a hard and demanding person, but one thing is undeniable: this man was firmly committed to educating his gifted son, Martin, even at great expense. The widely held assumption that Hans *pressured* Luther is true, but something can be said for the dogged commitment of this father who did everything in his power to guarantee his son's success. Luther's mother, Margaret, was equally motivated to see her son get the best education the family could afford. No doubt much of the pressure to bequeath a great education to Martin came from her. Higher education was common in the Lindemann family, and it can be safely assumed that young Martin was expected to do what so many of the males in her family had already done: achieve a high social status with real influence in the world.

Some have argued that Hans's success in business had everything to do with the connections and influence of his wife and her family. Margaret's family was, in all likelihood, responsible for the "inexplicable line of credit . . . astonishingly high credit" that enabled Hans to rise through the ranks in the copper industry. Indeed, Luther's father's "rapid rise from miner to lessee of a mine becomes more understandable" when we realize that Margaret came from very well-to-do people.[2] Margaret Lindemann Luther was not about to see her son dwell in the mines for the rest of his life without an education.

Martin seemed headed at first toward the practice of law. The Lindemanns had produced lawyers before, so it was entirely within the realm of possibility. It has been theorized that Hans needed a lawyer and thus took the necessary steps to raise one from his own house in order to benefit his own copper mining business. This could explain the disappointment Hans felt when Martin opted for another course, but it is also just as likely that Hans and Margaret were troubled and even shocked by the seeming rashness of Martin's decision to forego a lucrative career in law in order to become a monk, possibly even a begging monk. What a shock for them to see their son take such a sudden and drastic turn in his promising academic career. But before we try to comprehend why Luther made this sudden change in his career path, let us explore the context of Erfurt, the university town that was Martin Luther's home for several years.

Luther's years as a student

Town	Age at enrollment	Year	Subjects studied
Mansfeld	between 5–7	1489–97	Latin and trivium
Magdeburg	13 or 14	1497–98	Latin and trivium
Eisenach	15	1498–01	Latin, trivium, music
Erfurt	17	1501–05	University—Study of Law

Entering Erfurt

Universities were still relatively new in Luther's day. The oldest university in central Europe was the University of Prague, which had been founded in 1348. Nevertheless, universities were prestigious places already. This is where the elite sent their children. Compared to working the fields or digging in mines, the life of study and reflection was highly desirable, a rare opportunity in the late-medieval world. Only those located somewhere well above the middle of the social ladder could even dream of the kind of lifestyle a university offered.

Martin Luther entered Erfurt University in May 1501. He was about seventeen years old. He remained there until 1505. Luther's name (Martinus Luder, from Mansfeld) was written in the university ledger three times during those years. These three entries are important, as they are the earliest surviving documentary evidences of Luther. In 1501, he was recorded as having been enrolled after paying his tuition in full. In 1502, he was listed as having completed the bachelor of arts degree. And in 1505, records indicate that he had passed the exams for the master of arts degree.[3]

Erfurt was one of the three or four largest German cities in Luther's day, with around twenty thousand inhabitants. Eighty-nine villages fell under its jurisdiction. It was quite prosperous due to its being located at the intersection of major trade routes.[4] In 1392, Erfurt established its university, the oldest public university within Germany's borders today.[5]

Luther would have taken two days to walk the thirty-five miles from Eisenach to Erfurt, which he probably did in April 1501. His new home was nicknamed "the Rome of the North" because it hosted eighty religious institutions.[6]

In Luther's time, Erfurt was considered a cutting-edge, modern university. Unlike the upstart Wittenberg that would be the university town made famous by Luther, Erfurt already enjoyed a sterling reputation. Solidly established, it was considered "the finest university in Germany" at the time.[7] Erfurt was a university town with prestige, with students from many different countries with competing philosophical outlooks and with academic verve. Student protests were common and could even become violent. This is the university that almost immediately rallied behind Luther after 1517, and it continued to support his revolution with great fervor.[8]

Erfurt University was divided into four faculties. First, the college of liberal arts, where students could earn bachelor's and master's degrees. Then, three professional schools: law, medicine, and theology. The professional schools were taught by doctors, highly educated men who had attained the terminal degree in their discipline.[9]

Living the Bursa Life

When students matriculated at the University of Erfurt in Luther's time, they typically moved into a residential hostel known as a bursa. The term *bursa* is Latin and simply means "bag," "pouch," or "purse." It referred to the price of room and board. The bursa was the equivalent of today's student residential halls, but in Luther's time they were far stricter, even monastic in their organization. When a young man joined a bursa, he had immediate access to an intimate community, with its camaraderie and social clout.

However, in joining a bursa, students were far from being footloose and fancy-free. Life there was acutely supervised. Students dressed in uniform. They were required to get permission for the slightest requests. Even to attend a lecture outside one's compulsory course of study required permission from a rector. Students were not allowed to read freely, but only what had been selected for them. Even their sleep was carefully regulated, as in a monastery. They "rose with the bell at four o'clock each morning and went to bed, in obedience to the rules, at eight o'clock at night."[10] And there were consequences for those who broke the rules. Discipline was doled out frequently by a headmaster or by the student censor, who was "really an internal spy."[11]

Luther's first bursa probably was the one called *Porta Coeli*, Latin for "Heaven's Gate."[12] Evidence suggests that he later transferred to the Saint George bursa. Each bursa had about 150 students.[13] Students rose at 4:00 A.M., held their devotions, began academic study at 6:00 A.M., took a mid-morning meal, spent time in the library in early afternoon, had their afternoon meal, and at 8:00 P.M. the gates were shut. Students were able to go off campus and into the town once in a while, and when they did, they lived it up, at least according to Luther. With his typical crassness, Luther described Erfurt as a "whorehouse and a beer house."[14]

When a student entered a bursa, some minor hazing always came with it. It was called a "deposition." Rookies had to don an animal mask with horns, donkey ears, and pig teeth, admitting that they were uneducated brutes. Then, they were doused with water, symbolizing their being baptized into the more civilized, educated form of existence. The rookie student had to pay for everyone to get loaded on beer. It was a little humiliating, but everyone went through it. This rite of passage marked the new student as being now, officially, part of the group. Luther himself took part in these welcoming celebrations when he became a professor at Wittenberg some years later.[15]

Luther's life in the bursa was regimented, studious, and quite religious, as most of the students were training for the priesthood. They were certainly far from perfect, not only in their carousing around town, but with so many young men crammed into small quarters, there was no shortage of testosterone. Beer flowed in the bursa; indeed, beer consumption was "very copious" since it was what they drank with their meals. Luther's hostel was known as the *Bierstache* (the beer pot). No doubt as a result of the combination of these factors, "brawls were frequent." Students were allowed to carry a dagger with them, and things could turn violent in short order. Indeed, Luther's closest friend was killed in a fight. The death of that friend was quite possibly a key reason that Luther joined the monastery.[16]

The Bachelor of Arts

Luther was a fairly pious and somewhat studious young man during his years at Erfurt. It was at Erfurt, we are told, that he held a Bible in his hands for the first time, indicating just how uncommon it was—before Luther—for schoolboys and laypeople to handle the Holy Scriptures. Luther's first biographer—a former student of his named Mathesius—would have us believe that Luther was prayerful, faithfully attended Mass daily, remained alert in his classes, was timely in his assignments, and frequented his tutors in order to attain more than just what the books and lectures offered. According to Mathesius, Luther spent his free time in the university library.[17]

While this certainly is an idealized picture of Luther, there is probably some truth in the idea that Luther was no troublemaker, slacker, or rebel between the ages of seventeen and twenty-two. We do know that he finished his bachelor's degree in the shortest amount of time allowable—one year. He ranked in the middle of the pack, placing number thirty out of fifty-seven candidates. Immediately upon completing his bachelor's degree, he began his master of arts program. It took him two years to complete that degree, and he placed number two out of seventeen. His father was elated and presented Luther with a generous gift: a complete edition of the *Corpus juris*. Clearly, Hans believed his accomplished son was going into law as a career.[18]

What do these rankings of Luther's university performance reveal? First, we know from Luther's career that he was no academic slouch. However, we also know that he was no perfectionist either. That he placed middle of the pack for his BA may have something to do with the fact that he rushed through the program instead of taking his sweet time in order to prepare more rigorously. What is also revealing is that he improved so much during his MA program, which was considered far more demanding than the BA. Luther's brilliance was finally beginning to show. These rankings provide evidence that what Mathesius wrote was probably more or less correct. Here was a young man who studied hard, got through his programs earlier than those around him, and—based on his decision to join the monastery—was likely cultivating himself into a serious Christian.

Luther's bachelor's degree was anchored in the liberal arts. What that meant was that he studied the *trivium* (grammar, rhetoric, and logic) and the *quadrivium* (arithmetic, geometry, astronomy, and music). Logic (also called *dialectic*) reigned supreme in those days, and Aristotle (fourth century BC)—essentially the father of knowledge in their view—was the guide. "His books on logic . . . were the principal sources for teaching students how to think."[19]

At times, it appears that during his studies Luther developed a "love-hate" relationship with Aristotle. He thought the famed Greek sage was useful for helping us to gain insight into the natural world and on earthly subjects, but Aristotle offered next to nothing when it came to knowing God. Luther believed his professors made a huge mistake. Using Aristotle to understand the God revealed in the Bible, Luther believed, was at best "unsatisfying" and at worst "deceptive." Only divine revelation could shed light on the one true God.[20]

Frequently, professors asked students to debate each other on some topic that was relevant at the time. Students were expected to think logically and to offer arguments that made sense. They were also expected to critique their opponent. It was "the intellectuals' equivalent of a medieval tournament, but one fought with words rather than lances." Luther excelled in this environment and was nicknamed "the Philosopher" by his peers.[21] His ability to effectively critique the argument of his interlocutor was something that stayed with him to the end of his life. When Luther set his sights on someone, his opponent had little chance to achieve any kind of victory. Luther was the ultimate debater: tough, unflinching, and nimble. When it came time for him to critique someone, he was brutal. When Luther decided to debate, he argued as if his life depended on it. Later in his career, this was one area where even his closest allies thought him to be overly zealous and often cruel.

A New Way of Thinking

While at Erfurt, Luther would have been exposed to sweeping changes occurring in the intellectual climate of the European universities. Scholasticism was losing ground to the new approach to learning known as humanism. Scholasticism was the old way, the medieval way, the way of the church, the orthodox way epitomized by the work of Saint Thomas Aquinas (1225–1274).

Aquinas represents the high point of medieval learning. His approach to knowledge—known as "Thomism"—is essentially a blending of Aristotle with Christian theology. Aquinas drank deeply from the wells of Greek philosophy and Christian Scripture, deriving his understanding of human reason from these sources. Masterful in his theological speculations, his teachings are still revered by Christian theologians. They represent an earlier turning point in the history of Western knowledge.

Humanism, however, was a rising force in the intellectual universe of western Europe at the time. Humanism placed more focus on human beings. God was not discarded—not at all. But human dignity, human capabilities, and human rationality all were given emphasis they had not enjoyed prior to this time. This movement typically is taught as being rooted in the Renaissance. Humanism was a complex notion, and it certainly was not distinct from scholasticism. What was different was the emphasis.

One of the results of humanism being taught in the university was an awareness of the importance of primary sources: in art, in theology, and in reason. This new way of thinking impacted Luther dramatically. For example, in his theology, Luther was keen to go back to the sources of Christian theology as opposed to blindly accepting the dictates of the church. This is largely what was involved with his principle of *sola Scriptura*, "Scripture alone." Also, humanism emphasized original languages such as Greek and Hebrew. Here again, Luther took his humanistic training seriously—so seriously that he believed the only way to get people to understand the mind of God was to access it through the Scriptures. Luther believed strongly that he should translate the original languages of the Bible into German, a task he in fact completed during his career. Rather than using Latin as the primary source for "Luther's Bible," he believed strongly he should translate from the original languages. This was a natural consequence of his training as a humanist.

Luther was influenced by both of the intellectual leviathans of his day: scholasticism and humanism. His schooling, his thinking, and his career show abundant evidence that he bought into both of these ways of thinking and not just one. This is what is at the root of the important question asked by generations of Luther scholars to the present day: Was he more of a medieval (scholasticism) man or a modern (humanism) man? The answer is that Luther was both. He employed whichever system he needed, depending on what he was trying to do. It was natural for Luther to pick from both systems, since he had professors on both sides of the changing currents. It is crucial to reiterate, however, that nobody was either/or. Everybody had been deeply influenced by scholastic thought, but the new humanism was coming on strong, influencing virtually everybody who came through the university. Both intellectual systems were impossible to miss in the early 1500s.

Learning to Argue

One crucial discipline in Luther's university training was rhetoric, the art of public speaking. The key was persuasion. Students were expected to learn how to convince an audience that what they were saying was more accurate than what their debater was saying. This was at the heart of university education in Luther's time. It was also called dialectic. Two opposing viewpoints had to be resolved through reason, with one of two possible outcomes: either one view was more correct than the other, or a synthesis of the two views was to take place that would show the truth of both perspectives. Only through rhetoric could this process take place. Rhetoric was the medium by which a speaker could demonstrate to an audience that his view should be taken seriously. Such a skill was critical to the law profession—the direction Luther seemed to be headed.

Luther's education was completely bathed in these ideas and this approach to learning. They had to argue. They had to defend a thesis, employing careful logic. They had to persuade their classmates and professors of their intellectual positions. "Every day featured disputations in which teachers assigned students a thesis or a set of theses which they were required to defend according to the strict rules of logic."[22] Professors made themselves available for students to come test their oratorical prowess on all manner of subjects. These intellectual battles were ubiquitous at Erfurt

University during Luther's time, and they shaped him greatly. His entire career was one rhetorical struggle after another—both in speech and in writing. It was as if he never left the university. The daily battles and intellectual clashes continued for Luther. The Reformation movement he founded was his lifelong disputation against those who might disagree with him. And he heartily defended his stances. To the very end of his life, Luther seemed to be most comfortable when arguing a thesis and dismantling any who might summon the courage to challenge him. He came by it honestly, because this is precisely what he was trained to do.

Professor Trutfetter and Professor Usingen

During his university years, Luther was deeply impressed by two professors in particular: Jodokus Trutfetter and Bartholomaus Arnoldi von Usingen. Trutfetter had come through Erfurt as a student, beginning in 1476. He received his master's degree in 1484 and completed his doctor of theology at a riper age than most in 1504.

Trutfetter had a distinguished career in academics. He was elected rector of the Erfurt philosophy faculty in 1501, the year Martin Luther enrolled. From 1506 to 1510, he served as a theology professor at the new University of Wittenberg. He was a prolific author, producing numerous works on logic and natural philosophy. Where Trutfetter impacted Luther was in his insistence that the notion of belief is to be extended to the biblical books alone, and that all other forms of knowledge are to be scrutinized and questioned. This is why Luther was so cautious in accepting the arguments of others but placed great faith in the veracity of the Scriptures, even when it came to miracles. Scripture was authoritative; it made no sense to deny anything in it. This outlook he inherited from Professor Trutfetter.[23]

Professor Usingen was the other educator who influenced Luther a great deal. He, too, was an alumnus of Erfurt. He became a master in 1491 and earned a doctor of theology in 1514. Due partly to Luther's influence, Usingen became an Augustinian monk in 1512. During his student days, Luther probably was closer to Usingen than to any other professor. In his own right, Usingen was an accomplished author who published works on logic, grammar, natural philosophy, and Aristotle. He influenced Luther most profoundly in his interpretation of the Bible: "Undoubtedly he gave the student Luther the restrictive advice to read the Bible exclusively according to the exegesis of the church fathers." Despite all their shared interests and close relationship, however, Usingen ultimately opposed Luther's ideas. When the Reformation came to Erfurt, Usingen denounced it strongly.[24]

What Luther inherited from his teachers was this: "Test theory by experience."[25] They instilled in Luther a passion to question non-biblical sources. He tested the ideas of his teachers. He tested the teachings of the church. He adopted a hermeneutic of suspicion. Luther never abandoned this approach. Throughout his career, he constantly questioned the sources of authority around him. Luther was exacting in his interrogation of the ideas of others, especially those who claimed to be in a position of authority. In Luther's understanding, no one was exempt from critique, especially when it came to truth claims. The Scriptures, however, were immune from this line of questioning. They were from God. Luther had a respect for the Bible that he was never able to extend to human beings. For him, Scripture was "decisive."[26] It was the only source of truth. Within Scripture was philosophical certainty.

Master's Program

When Luther finished his BA, he was entitled to teach at the university, conducting courses in grammar, rhetoric, and logic. His teaching load was rather small. His main focus was on earning his master's, and he dived headlong into the writings of Aristotle. Luther attended three lectures per day and had to participate in dozens of disputations, since—it was believed—this was where real learning took place. He spent six months studying Euclid, a Greek mathematician who lived around the same time as Aristotle. He was required to study the planets, as well as some musical theory.[27]

In 1505, when he was probably twenty-two years old, he completed his master's degree. He was given the teacher's biretta and the master's ring, both signs of authority and achievement. He was also obligated to teach in the philosophy faculty for two years, and he was given approval to continue his studies in one of the professional programs if he wished. He was expected to give an inaugural address to showcase his learning, which he did. His father was so proud that he began to address him with the formal German *Ihr* (you) as opposed to the more informal—and less respectful—*du*.[28]

Music and Melancholy

During his Erfurt years, Luther became a good musician, notably in his ability to play the lute—a guitar-like stringed instrument very popular in the late-medieval world. In addition to his nickname "the Philosopher," now he was also known around campus as "the Musician." Luther always loved music, as is evident in his hymn-writing, including the still-classic piece "A Mighty Fortress Is Our God."

Biographers mention that Luther used music to overcome his frequent bouts with depression.

> Even in Luther's younger days his friends would bring him his lute when he was in the grip of one of his frequent severe attacks of melancholy. Once they found him stretched out almost lifeless on the floor; when they handed him his instrument, he ran his fingers over the strings and, on hearing the music, stood up. Gaiety and gloom were inseparable companions in Luther's life.

Luther relied on music to snatch him away from the clutches of Satan. In Luther's view, Satan was the father of gloom, and music was a source of joy. Therefore, Satan fled at the sound of music.[29]

One interesting incident occurred in 1503 or 1504 when Luther, accompanied by a friend, was traveling home to Mansfeld for the Easter holiday. For some unknown reason, Luther either slipped or fell, causing his sword to thrust deep into his leg, severing a major artery. It nearly killed him. Placing his fingertips on the severed artery, he was able to control the bleeding somewhat, but he continued to bleed throughout the night. His friend ran to the nearest town to fetch a surgeon. Luther lay there alone in a field with his thoughts, petitioning the Virgin Mary to save him. His legged swelled during the night, and Luther was genuinely afraid for his life until help finally arrived. He convalesced by playing the lute and copying music for himself.

Many of Luther's contemporaries note that he was filled with joy when playing music. But it was also becoming clear that his "fits of depression," "somber moods," and "fierce attacks of doubt" were becoming increasingly common.[30]

Law School Cut Short

In the summer of 1505, after celebrating his successful completion of the MA degree, Luther directed himself toward the study of law. After only a few weeks, though, he abruptly quit law school, sold the law books his father had given him, and joined a monastery. Why?

Luther was extremely unsatisfied by what he thought to be profound uncertainty endemic in the study of law. The conclusions of lawyers are always "uncertain and coincidental. . . . the decisions it renders may possibly be fallible. . . . In contrast to theologians, lawyers have nothing to do with certainty."[31] Luther was craving eternal answers rather than solutions merely for temporal situations. The law was ever-changing with the circumstances of the cases involved. Luther was searching for answers—permanent answers—to help him understand the human condition and humanity's relationship with the divine. Law had little to say to these vexing problems. The law was written by humans, from the mind of humans, for humans.

Luther may also have been angered by the attitude the law professors had toward theologians. He viewed them as arrogant men. They constantly referred to the theologians—men Luther admired—as asses.[32] Luther took issue with this and held a vendetta against lawyers to the end of his life. In his *Table Talks*, Luther is recorded as having said the following:

> Godliness befits theologians, not lawyers. . . . Lawyers are against God in fact. . . . No lawyers magnify the Word of God. . . . Lawyers don't give anything to God, but only to themselves.
>
> Then Luther admonished his son who had talked about possibly becoming a lawyer: The doctor took his child [Martin, Jr.] in his hands and said, "If you should become a lawyer, I'd hang you on the gallows. You must be a preacher and must baptize, preach, administer the sacrament, visit the sick, and comfort the sorrowful."[33]

By now, Luther was focusing his attention on seeking God. And the study of law did not answer the big questions for him. Only a life of study and reflection would provide Luther with the tools to search in the divine direction. Rather than spend two or three years studying something completely unsatisfying to him, he decided to quit law school. Instead, he directed himself toward the monastery, where he thought he could find relief.

Luther's father was incensed by all of this pious drama. Hans Luther was from a family of farmers, and as mentioned earlier, he would have been quite familiar with inheritance laws which specified that the *youngest* son would inherit the land. "The other children either had to marry into another family or try to earn a living in other trades."[34] Thus, it was entirely reasonable for Hans to pour his wealth into his eldest son. And in this case, the eldest son, Martin, was deserving of his father's investment because of his high intellectual capabilities. Thus, it must have been terribly unnerving when it looked as if Martin might be rolling the dice with all of that high-powered education in Latin schools and in the university. It was certainly possible that Martin could rise through the ranks of the clergy and make something of himself. One could find many examples of successful clergymen in the early sixteenth century. But another possibility loomed: this son might cloister himself in a monastery, perhaps copying manuscripts or devoting himself to holy silence.

One biographer of Luther put it more crassly when he said of Martin's father: "It was one of the bitterest disappointments of his life that his talented eldest son wanted to enter this calling of chanters and bigots instead of becoming a skilled lawyer, and thus raising the Luther family to the highest status open to it, that of advisers to princes and city councils."[35] This is probably too harsh. But whatever the reasons, the hopes that the Luthers had placed in their son were dashed when he chose the monastery. But the monastery was precisely the direction that Luther's talented life would take. Scholars remain fascinated by the suddenness of that decision, and it has gone down in history as, perhaps, *the* turning point in Luther's life. Like Paul after his Damascus-road experience, Luther changed. And he never looked back.

In the next chapter we will explore what happened on that fateful night when Luther, nearly struck by lightning, pledged his life to Saint Anne and to the Christian religion. Luther was terrorized by the storm, yet he interpreted it theologically. In his mind, the power of God was seizing him, calling him to change his ways and redirecting the course of his life. Whatever happened, Luther interpreted it as an intervention from Almighty God. And it proved to be one of the defining moments in the history of Western civilization.

Notes

[1]Richard Friedenthal, trans. from the German by John Nowell, *Luther* (London: Weidenfeld and Nicolson, 1967), 12.

[2]Heiko Oberman, *Luther: Man Between God and the Devil* (New Haven: Yale University Press, 1989), 91.

[3]Scott Hendrix, *Martin Luther: Visionary Reformer* (New Haven: Yale University Press, 2015), 28.

[4]Martin Brecht, *Martin Luther: His Road to Reformation, 1483–1521* (Vol. 1), trans. by James Schaaf (Philadelphia: Fortress Press, 1985), 23.

[5]Hendrix, 28.

[6]Ibid., 27–28.

[7]Larry Mansch and Curtis Peters, *Martin Luther* (Jefferson, NC: McFarland, 2016), 18.

[8]Friedenthal, 18.

[9]Mansch and Peters, 18.

[10]Friedenthal, 19.

[11]James Kittelson, *Luther the Reformer* (Minneapolis: Fortress, 1986), 44.

[12]Heaven's Gate was also known as Amplonian College. See Hendrix, 28.

[13]Hendrix estimates there were less than one thousand students at the University of Erfurt in Luther's time, and they were divided into five or six bursas. This is where the 150 estimate comes from. See Hendrix, 28.

[14]Hendrix, 29.

[15]Brecht, vol. 1, 31.

[16]Friedenthal, 19.

[17]Ibid., 15.

[18]See Brecht, vol. 1, 33–34; and Friedenthal, 15.

[19]Kittelson, 46.

[20]Martin Marty, *Martin Luther* (New York: Viking, 2004), 6.

[21]Kittelson, 46.

[22]Ibid.

[23]Brecht, vol. 1, 34–36.

[24]Ibid., 36.

[25]Marty, 6.

[26]Ibid.

[27]Brecht, vol. 1, 33.

[28]Ibid., 34.

[29]Friedenthal, 24–26.

[30]Robert Fife, *The Revolt of Martin Luther* (New York: Columbia University Press, 1957), 72–73. See also Brecht, vol. 1, 46–47.

[31]Brecht, vol. 1, 45.

[32]Ibid., 46.

[33]See *Luther's Works* (Philadelphia: Fortress Press, 1967), vol. 54, 150–151 (#1421 and 1422).

[34]Oberman, 85.

[35]Friedenthal, 10–11.

5

A Very Good Monk

The turning point in Martin Luther's life occurred like this: It was in the summer of 1505—Wednesday, July 2, to be exact.[1] Luther was returning to Erfurt after a brief trip home to visit his parents in Mansfeld. He was passing through a forest outside the village of Stotternheim when a sudden storm came upon him. A powerful bolt of lightning struck nearby, and he was seized with fear. He threw himself to the ground and prayed to Saint Anne, "Help me, St. Anne; I will become a monk!"[2]

Luther was raised in the mining industry, and as the son of a miner, he would have been well acquainted with Saint Anne, who was the patron saint of miners. As the supposed mother of the Virgin Mary, and thus the grandmother of Christ, Saint Anne happened to be enjoying a rising tide of prestige in the early years of the sixteenth century. "The great flowering of Anne's cult among the laity occurred between 1300 and the Council of Trent in the mid-sixteenth century."[3] Luther was "enamored" with the "fashionable" Saint Anne at that time, and he once wrote, "St. Anne was my idol." However, Saint Anne also was the most logical saint for Luther to name in this instance as she "was considered, among other things, the helper in dangers from thunderstorms and from sudden death."[4]

In Luther's mind, Saint Anne saved him from death during that storm. When he returned to Erfurt, he was committed to abruptly exiting law school and joining a hardcore cadre of Augustinian monks, known for their holiness and austerity.

This episode has spurred far more questions than answers in the study of Martin Luther. What would have caused a stellar student to make this radical decision? He had come so far. Was he promised a fast track to the bishopric? By all accounts, nothing of that sort occurred. Did he get into an argument with his father during his stay in Mansfeld? Was Luther's well-known battle with depression getting the best of him, leading him to see the monastery as a way out? In fact, Luther did testify that his depression had become unbearably severe in the six months prior to entering the monastery.[5] Or, perhaps, Luther's decision was simply an example of medieval Christianity's fundamental worldview that the surest way to God was by becoming a priest and a monk. Was Luther failing in his law studies, and perhaps he saw this as a way to save face? Certainly not. By this time, Luther's academic gifts were on full display. It was obvious that he was bright and capable, quite up to the task to take on law school. Was Luther's disdain for lawyers becoming unbearable?

Or was this case much simpler than all of that? Here was a religiously committed young man who thought he was going to die, made a rash bargain with Saint Anne, and thus felt obligated to make good on the deal. Can it be explained in such obvious terms? With all of his brilliance and promise, would Martin Luther truly have thrown his life into an entirely new direction because he was afraid of lightning and thunder?

As we discussed earlier, Luther was a medieval man in the sense that religion permeated everything he felt, saw, and believed. A twenty-first century person in the Western world can scarcely imagine the religious world of the sixteenth century. There was no scientific worldview to speak of. Illnesses and diseases were not linked to bacteria or DNA predispositions. People were more likely to think in terms of God's wrath. Storms were not understood as moisture accumulating over mountains and getting pushed with the jet stream; rather, they were acts of God. Everything—weather, accidents, coincidental experiences, emotions—all these were linked to the divine realm. Thus, it would have been perfectly normal to think that perhaps Martin Luther's life nearly had come to an end due to the wrath of

God being unleashed in a violent storm. If Luther could just throw himself at the feet of Saint Anne and bend her ear enough, then she might rescue him. And he was sure she did. So, as a man of integrity, he needed to do the honorable thing and live up to his promise. This may have been all there was to it, at least in Luther's head.

Historians have helped us to complexify the story of Luther's lightning bolt experience. Luther scholar Scott Hendrix doubts that "the storm alone" convinced him to join a monastery. It is clear that many other factors could have "precipitated Luther's decision to alter not only his field of study but his entire life." He points out that while the general story was recounted repeatedly by Luther and those around him, Saint Anne does not appear in a written version of the event until thirty-four years after the fact. Hendrix also brings up the idea that Luther's Reformation right then needed "quasi-divine sanction for resisting Rome." Thus, a Pauline story would have met that need, and the incorporation of Saint Anne into the story would have benefits as well, particularly in making Luther appear to be a man of his word.[6]

Both Hendrix and German historian Richard Friedenthal see the storm story as a way for Luther to "justify himself to his father" about his abrupt career change. It is clear that Luther loved and respected, yet feared, his father. After all, his father had footed the bill for what was, undoubtedly, a very expensive education. "No expense was too great for the father when it came to realizing his life's dream to see his son take his place among the newly rising class of lawyers." That his eloquent son had switched the distinguished halls of governance and politics for the lowly cell of a monk would have been horrifying news for Hans Luther to hear. Perhaps piety, commitment to faith, and a divine call straight from God might make the news more palatable.[7] German historian Martin Brecht theorized that perhaps Luther joined the monastery because he did not want to get married, as would have been expected of him at this time in his life. The monastery was therefore an escape.[8]

But let's not miss the forest for the trees. For all the theorizing about why Luther changed course, one thing is abundantly clear. Luther was interested in Christian theology, not in the study of law. And he was willing, perhaps for the first time in his life, to oppose his father in order to chase his dream. This would not have been easy for Luther—a twenty-two year old who owed his father everything. But for reasons we probably never will fully understand, in this instance, he made the bold decision to go his own way, despite the huge amount of pressure on him to do otherwise.

Becoming an Augustinian Monk

To get oriented, let us briefly sketch the significant dates in Luther's life between the path-changing storm and his permanent move to Wittenberg.

- July 2, 1505—Luther has his lightning bolt experience.
- July 17, 1505—Luther enters the monastery of the Hermits of Saint Augustine at Erfurt.
- April 3, 1507—Luther is ordained to the priesthood.
- May 2, 1507—Luther presides at his first Mass.
- Fall 1508—Luther is sent to Wittenberg to serve as a visiting professor.
- October 1509—Luther returns to Erfurt and lectures on the *Sentences* of twelfth-century medieval philosopher Peter Lombard.
- November 1510—Luther is sent to Rome by the Augustinians.
- April 1511—Luther returns from Rome and is transferred to Wittenberg.
- October 1512—Luther is promoted to doctor of theology at the University of Wittenberg.

Martin Luther joined the monastery chiefly for religious reasons, albeit reasons that could be described as selfish. First and foremost, he wanted to "earn the gratitude of God" through the intensity and pious service found only in monastic withdrawal from the normal luxuries of life.[9] Like most medieval Christians, Luther feared the Almighty's punishment in purgatory or hell, and he wanted to gain favor with God. In a word, he longed for salvation. The monastery promised the quickest and surest route to God: praying, fasting, and self-denial. Monasticism was martyrdom in the truest sense. It was a dying to self. It was how a medieval person—a person who lived and died before Martin Luther's revolutionary ways of thinking—bore witness to Jesus Christ as savior and judge. Monasticism, everyone knew, was the institution you turned to if you were serious about your faith. But you had to be disciplined enough to handle it. Luther was going to *earn* his salvation, and God was sure to be pleased.

It was commonly held in Luther's time that "the taking of the cowl"—donning the loose hood that was part of the monk's habit—was something like a "second baptism." Even the great theologian Thomas Aquinas declared this idea. When a person made their monastic vows, it was held that their sins were washed away and they enjoyed a new state of innocence. This was highly attractive to medieval Christians who saw their lives as an expanding list of sinful acts. The church, however, came to the rescue and offered remediation in the form of Masses, indulgences, relics, and holy orders (such as monasticism). *Ordinary* Christians could participate in frequent Communions, visit sacred reliquaries, take pilgrimages, recite particularly holy prayers, and practice frequent confession in order to reduce their guilt, thereby reducing the time spent in purgatory once this life was finished. *Extraordinary* people, presumably Luther in this case, would deny themselves the pleasures of life—most notably marriage and the concupiscence that came with it—and expedite their journey through the purification process in purgatory that virtually all Christians had to undergo after death.

History shows that Martin Luther was an obstinate person. As soon as he returned to Erfurt, he let his friends know that he was ending his stint in law school and was headed to seclusion. For two weeks, they begged him not to enter the monastery, but he persisted, with a little drama. Luther was nothing if not dramatic. He threw a big farewell party, where he fed his guests sumptuously and performed music for them.[10] Then, on July 17, 1505, his startling decision became final. One historian describes the scene very well.

> Modest and virtuous maidens and married women were present, for this was to be Martin's last opportunity for association with the other sex except in the confessional for many years to come. The next day friends marched with him to the gate of the Augustinian cloister and with tearful faces watched the heavy gates close behind him.[11]

Another scholar described the scene as overly hyped, since the friars in the monastery "were not strictly cloistered."[12] Luther's parting words were perhaps intentionally crafted to create something of the finality that he might have been feeling: "Today you see me, but never again!"[13] At that moment, he entered the gate of the high walls of the monastic compound.

The city of Erfurt—nicknamed "city of spires" and "little Rome"—was full of monasteries and religious houses. "Without walking an extra pace from his lodgings, he could have become a Benedictine, Dominican, Franciscan, or a member of one of a number of other orders. But he chose the way of the Observant Augustinians."[14]

Many theories have been posited as to why Luther chose the Augustinians, but the most obvious might be the truest: he lived so close to them. There are other possibilities, however. Luther may have wanted the strictest one he could find, which seems to match his personality. He was always up for a challenge. It is also quite possible that he chose them because they were closely linked to the university, where the Augustinian brothers taught theological courses. Another reason might have something to do with Saint Augustine, the namesake of the order, who was easily Luther's favorite theologian in church history, other than Jesus and Paul.

Whatever the case, Luther knocked on the door and "took leave of the distraught friends who accompanied him." He surrendered everything he had, even his beloved lute.[15] He was led to the chapter room—the main gathering area—and knelt in prayer before the prior, who was head of the house. When Luther's intentions were revealed, he was given a guest room in the building. That building, acquired by the Augustinian order in 1277, remains the oldest building in Erfurt to this day.[16]

Luther had now become a *supplicant* (one who formally requests to join), but his immediate goal was to gain admission and be declared a *novitiate* (a novice in the order who undergoes a probationary term of, typically, one year). So there was a short waiting period wherein Luther came to know the other fifty-one monks who formed his religious community.[17]

Once he had undergone an "exhaustive" period of confession, he went through a solemn service in the chapter room where he lay prostrate on the tile floor and committed himself to absolute obedience. Next, while Luther's head was being shaved in the tonsure style (only a circle of hair on top), the monks sang a hymn in honor of Saint Augustine. Luther's outfit—the habit—was then handed to him. It consisted of an undershirt made of wool, leggings, a woolen shirt, a cowl (a gown topped by a hood), leather straps that served as a belt, and a scapula (a huge white collar with an opening for the head to go through).[18] Luther was then admonished by the prior with the words: "Not he that hath begun but he that endureth to the end shall be saved."[19] Once approved by the prior, Luther became, officially, a novitiate.

The Path to Holiness

Monastic life in the sixteenth century could be uncomfortable and difficult. The common vows of a monk, then as now, were obedience, poverty, and chastity. If we take Luther at his word, his life as a monk was sheer agony. Perhaps most fundamentally, Luther's primary goal of achieving union with God eluded him. This was a rather common experience for monks. They had a name for it: *desertio gratiae*, "the abandonment of grace." It has been described as a feeling deep within the soul where "man feels exactly as if God had forsaken him . . . and wanted nothing more to do with him."[20]

The monastic life was also extremely regulated, organized around the Divine Office—the canonical hours, a collection of prayers and Scriptures that are recited and/or sung throughout the day. The Liturgy of the Hours is the backbone of monastic life, and it consists of prayers at Matins (night), Lauds (dawn), Prime (early morning), Terce (mid-morning), Sext (mid-day), None (mid-afternoon), Vespers (evening), and Compline (before bed). A central part of the Hours is the Psalms, which Luther's order would chant in full in Latin—all 150 of them—each week. Mass was celebrated daily, two meals were taken, and to round out their time, they would have to complete various chores, study, honor the obligatory periods of absolute silence, and listen regularly to instruction from more senior brothers.[21]

Brothers were expected to cultivate an acute consciousness of their own sinfulness and carefully analyze their own motives. They were also to be on the lookout for another brother who might wander from the straight and narrow. "Once a week the friars disclosed to the prior how they had broken the Augustinian rule or noticed another brother doing the same."[22]

Luther's master during his novitiate was an elderly monk named Johann Greffenstein.[23] Luther must have developed an extremely close relationship with this man, although it would have been made clear to Luther that this was not a relationship based on equality. Since this was an order, Greffenstein watched Luther closely, mentoring him, and providing insight to the other friars about whether Luther had progressed enough to be fully admitted. Apparently, Luther passed the test. After a year, he was accepted permanently into the order and was given his own habit to wear. A three-by-seven-foot windowed cell was made available for him, where he could study and pray. It was now late summer 1506, and Luther was fully and completely an Augustinian monk.[24]

The Augustinian brothers in Erfurt had a reputation not only for true piety, but also for being rather interested in the study of theology. Being located near a sterling university no doubt enlivened their scholarly sensibilities. Certainly not all monasteries were like this. But Erfurt was a university town, and a good relationship had grown up between the Augustinians and the university faculties. Luther's community was full of bookish, theologically astute men, many of whom had either taught theology or were being trained in theology.

Nevertheless, in spite of an academic ethos, these monks did not enter the monastery chiefly to study. Obviously, one did not have to join a monastery to become part of the university. The primary motive of a monk was to achieve holiness through extreme discipline. Luther once said, "In the monastery I did not think about women, money or possessions, but my heart trembled and pounded at the thought of God's mercy to me." True sacrifice was involved: self-mortification, frequent and painful fasts, and absolute submission to those in charge. And there was no freedom in the monastery, other than freedom from the pleasures of the world. Monks were cogs in the wheel of the Roman Catholic Church, and they were trained to know their place. It is no surprise to learn that some of the brothers went mad during their monastic years. Luther commented later that it took him "a long time before I could bring myself to disregard the pope's order. . . . Heavens! What I went through before I summoned up courage to defy the laws of the Church."[25]

Before too long, Luther would have learned about the split that existed among the Augustinians. As in most orders, there was a conservative wing and a reforming wing. "The orders not only fought each other, they engaged in the most bitter internal feuds."[26]

There was also the matter of monastic wealth. Throughout the Middle Ages, monasteries evolved dramatically. In the early years—the fourth century—the monastic communities were poor and dependent on almsgiving. In time, however, they rose to become great administrators of land.

Abbots of the more influential monastic institutions became known as "empire builders."[27] Monasteries were crucial to medieval economies, due mainly to their control of huge amounts of fertile farmland. They also were involved in banking, exempted from local taxes, and typically owed their loyalty exclusively to the pope (and not the local rulers). Abbots—the monastic chiefs—often lived like princes. Instead of remote enclaves of spirituality, many monasteries served their communities in palpable ways: caring for the sick, loaning money, preserving manuscripts and art, developing farmland, and extending hospitality to travelers. Monasteries were a crucial, stabilizing force for medieval Europe. All of this would not have been lost on Luther. He would have been quick to notice that a life in the monastery was not, in the truest sense, a withdrawal from society. It had a role both inside and outside mundane society. It must have been a relief to Luther that his future was not expected to be lived in absolute isolation. His gregarious nature would not have allowed him to live that way for long.

Life in the monastery had its perks. The fellowship of the brothers could be great. Food was never lacking. It provided ample time for Luther to reflect, grow spiritually, and study the things of God. But it was not easy. Monks had to dress a certain way. Their lives were strictly regulated. They were punished for deviating from the righteous path. "If a sin of the flesh was actually committed, the punishment was prison, with the feet manacled and a diet of bread and water."[28] The endless cycles of prayers and Scripture readings were what sustained and organized the life of monks, beginning at 2:00 A.M. for the first worship service of the day. Bells were rung, beckoning the monks to gather. They were required to be fully dressed in their habits any time they left their cells—that tiny slice of privacy that they were afforded.[29]

An Academic in the Making

For Luther, his monastic years were also a continuation of his studies. Almost immediately upon full acceptance into the monastery, he began studying for the priesthood, which meant he would enter the *professional* study of theology. Luther's professors were highly capable academicians who both taught inside the order and held a position on the university faculty. Luther's primary professor during this stage was John Nathin, an Augustinian monk who also held the doctorate degree in theology. Nathin was impressed by Luther, partly because Luther had a running start; he had already completed a master's degree in theology.

Luther's studies included "a smorgasbord of medieval sources and prominent theologians: Augustine, Bernard of Clairvaux, Thomas Aquinas, Duns Scotus, Bonaventure, William Ockham, and Jean Gerson." Luther also had to acquaint himself with commentaries on the Catholic Mass, most importantly the insights of medieval theologian Gabriel Biel (1420–1495). Nathin likely had heard some of the lectures of Biel while both men were at the University of Tübingen, in southwestern Germany. Luther also would have stepped back into the classrooms of his philosophy professors Usingen and Trutfetter, with all their Aristotelian bias.[30] We know he was also immersed in the study of Peter Lombard's work the *Sentences*, "the standard medieval compendium of doctrine."[31] Luther became something of an expert on Lombard, delivering lectures on the famous twelfth-century scholastic theologian a few years later while teaching at Erfurt University.

Luther grounded himself in Greek and Hebrew. This was to be fortuitous, for without a mastery of the biblical languages, Luther never would have been able to accomplish that great undertaking that made him a national hero among his people: translating the Bible into German. He immersed himself in the study of Augustine, patron of his monastic order and the most important theologian in Western church history. Luther studied church history, devoting himself to the church fathers and how they managed to keep the Christian faith alive while their precious Roman Empire was being sacked by Vandals and Visigoths.[32]

Luther also received basic practical training in how to be an effective pastor. He learned how to handle the confessional, what to assign when people were struck with guilt, and how to help people feel absolved for their sins. For penance, most medieval people were given a steady diet of "almsgiving, fasting, saying the rosary, making pilgrimage," and similar solutions. It was "a mechanical system that did not encourage people to change their behavior or give them genuine assurance."[33] It will become obvious later that Luther the priest dealt with the same dilemma as those people who confessed their sins to him.

Success after success continued to come Luther's way. In April 1507, he was ordained to the priesthood inside the stunningly beautiful Erfurt cathedral, which still towers over the city in spectacular fashion. He presided over his first Mass on May 2 in the chapel where he routinely worshiped. After that Mass, one of the defining moments of Luther's life occurred. His father, who was in the audience, approached him and expressed his disappointment, saying, "Let us hope that your vow was not an illusion. Have you not heard that parents are to be obeyed?"[34] Hans still very much regretted that his brilliant and talented eldest son had chosen a life in the monastery rather than in more lucrative pursuits.

For Hans, it was a bitter pill to swallow, to sit there and watch his son publicly declare himself a member of the clergy. There was no turning back now. The little hope he had that Martin might return to his senses and get back on track was finally crushed. When Hans chastised Martin for not listening to his parents, he was making it clear: this was Martin's choice. All the money spent to educate young Martin was supposed to provide a return on the investment. This choice to become immersed in the world of religion was a terrible disappointment to the family. Young Martin was crushed, and never—to the end of his days—did he forget that momentous encounter with his father after presiding over his first Mass. This was the person from whom he craved affirmation and in that moment all he received was disapproval.

It is interesting that May 2 was selected by the monastery as the appropriate day for Martin's first Mass in order to suit the convenience of Hans's travel.[35] Many of Luther's friends came from various places in order to celebrate the event. Hans, however, was the person in the room who commanded attention, not only from Martin, but from everyone else. By that point, Hans had become a wealthy and influential man. He traveled from Mansfeld, and he paid for twenty companions on horseback to accompany him on the trip.[36] He also made an extremely generous donation to the monastery in honor of his son's accomplishment, a gift that "only princes or the very wealthy could have afforded." Thus, it is clear he was not *ashamed* of Martin. He simply felt that Martin had made the wrong choice. At the banquet following the Mass, a person chatting with Hans said he heard that Martin was called to the priesthood in a heavenly vision. Hans replied, "I hope it was no illusion and trick of the devil!"[37]

In the end, as we now know, Luther conceded that his father had been right all along. In one of his works entitled *On the Monk's Vows*—essentially a scathing attack on the institution of monasticism written while Luther was in the Wartburg Castle—he wrote a dedication to his father. In that dedication, Luther recalled Hans openly questioning his entry into monasticism and into the priesthood. Luther remembered, fondly, "It drove roots into my heart, as though God were speaking through your mouth."[38]

To say that Martin Luther was an obstinate person is a gross understatement. But his allegiance to his father was unwavering. One person in the world could disarm Martin, steer him, even break him. It was Hans. And even though Hans's stern and humiliating admonition to Luther might have taken more than a decade to achieve its aim, no doubt those words anchored themselves in the very soul of the future reformer, setting the stage for a furious rebellion against the institution of "monkery," as he called it.

During his monastic years, however, Martin Luther proved to be an exceptionally good monk. He was true to his vows, and he took pride in that fact: "If ever a monk got to heaven by his monkery, it was I. All my brothers in the monastery who knew me will bear me out. If I had kept on any longer, I should have killed myself."[39] What was lurking in the back of Luther's mind, however, was the profound sense of dissatisfaction that he could never be quite good enough for God. He recounts going to confession daily in order to feel some sense of absolution, but it never came. In the Augustinian order, rigorous examinations were meant to uncover sinful motives, even if no outward sins had occurred. The result was a deep sense of guilt, even if one lived a perfectly obedient life. There was always a sneaking suspicion that even if someone could avoid outward sin, their heart and soul nevertheless were corrupted. It was painful and excruciating for Luther. He felt he was constantly under scrutiny by God, destined to receive the divine wrath. It was a life of profound fear—fear of failure and fear of God. Luther was tortured constantly by his own guilt, and it drove him to deepest despair.[40]

Luther took his roles as monk and priest extremely seriously. When celebrating his first Mass, for example, he "was so terrified at speaking directly to God without a mediator that, if the prior had not admonished him, he would have fled from the altar." Another witness claimed that Luther was struck with sheer terror when he was about to consecrate the Host with the holy and powerful words that literally changed bread and wine into flesh and blood: *hoc est corpus meum* (this is my body); *hoc poculum est novum testamentum sanguinis mei* (this cup is the new testament of my blood).[41] Luther had become an intermediary between God and man.

When he held the elements in his hands, he believed he was holding the power of salvation for all who partook.

While Luther must have been a conscientious priest, it was becoming increasingly clear that he was a man cut out for a life in academia. In 1508, Luther was sent to Wittenberg to fill in for a faculty member who had to take a leave of absence to finish a doctorate in theology. The universities of Erfurt and Wittenberg had numerous connections, and it made perfect sense for Wittenberg to turn to the Erfurt faculty to find a temporary replacement. Luther served as a visiting professor in Wittenberg for a year, unaware that in a few years it would become his home and that it would to the present day be a city that could scarcely be mentioned without also mentioning his name.[42] Teaching in Wittenberg gave renewed direction to Luther's career.

Critical to his year as a visiting professor in Wittenberg was Luther's association with a professor named Johann von Staupitz, the dean of theology and also an Augustinian monk like Luther. Staupitz mentored Luther, increasingly cognizant of Luther's great talent that was becoming more and more obvious to people. While under Staupitz's guidance, Luther lectured extensively on Aristotle, although his real passion was expositing the Bible. Luther also studied under the supervision of Staupitz. After about a year, Luther was summoned back to Erfurt by his monastery.[43]

In 1509, Luther was there, lecturing on Peter Lombard. He was also slogging away at his own theological studies, advancing "more rapidly than was usual in Erfurt."[44] However, he was also a tortured soul at this stage in his life. That is why when he was given the opportunity to go to Rome in November 1510, he gladly took it. He was asked by his monastery to help sort out some problems in the Augustinian order. This would provide Luther the opportunity to achieve relief for his troubled soul. By visiting Rome, with all its relics and holy sites, he could dip into the treasury of merit found only in the church, and he hoped to experience freedom from the heavy burden of guilt that often accompanies the drive toward monastic perfection.

Notes

[1]For the exact date, see Martin Brecht, *Martin Luther: His Road to Reformation, 1483–1521*, vol. 1 (Philadelphia: Fortress Press, 1985), 48.

[2]See Graham Tomlin, *Luther and His World* (Downers Grove: IVP, 2002), 18–19.

[3]Sherry Reames, ed., *Middle English Legends of Women Saints* (Kalamazoo, MI: Medieval Institute Publications, 2003), chapter IV, "Legends of St. Anne, Mother of the

Virgin Mary," located online at: http://d.lib.rochester.edu/teams/publication/reames-middle-english-legends-of-women-saints.

[4]Brecht, vol. 1, 49.

[5]Roland Bainton, *Here I Stand* (New York: Meridian, 1950), 20.

[6]Scott Hendrix, *Martin Luther: Visionary Reformer* (New Haven: Yale University Press, 2015), 33.

[7]Richard Friedenthal, *Luther* (London: Weidenfeld and Nicolson, 1967), 26–27.

[8]Brecht, vol. 1, 48.

[9]Robert Fife, *The Revolt of Martin Luther* (New York: Columbia University Press, 1957), 72.

[10]Friedenthal, 29.

[11]Fife, 75.

[12]Hendrix, 34.

[13]Brecht, vol. 1, 50.

[14]James Kittelson, *Luther the Reformer* (Minneapolis: Fortress Press, 1986), 51–52.

[15]Ibid., 51.

[16]Hendrix, 35.

[17]Brecht, vol. 1, 57.

[18]Hendrix, 35.

[19]Bainton, 27.

[20]Friedenthal, 30.

[21]Hendrix, 35.

[22]Ibid.

[23]Brecht, vol. 1, 57.

[24]For the 1506 date, see Fife, 89.

[25]Friedenthal, 30.

[26]Ibid., 37.

[27]Ibid., 38.

[28]Ibid., 33.

[29]Bainton, 27.

[30]Hendrix, 37.

[31]Ian Siggins, *Luther* (New York: Barnes and Noble, 1972), 41.

[32]Gerhard Brendler, *Martin Luther: Theology and Revolution*, trans. by Claude Foster, Jr. (Oxford: Oxford University Press, 1991), 47.

[33]Hendrix, 37.

[34]Ibid., 38. One contemporary described this conversation as taking place between Hans and the monks, not necessarily with Martin. See Fife, 102.

[35]Fife, 99–100.

[36]Bainton, 30.

[37]Kittelson, 54.

[38]Fife, 102–103.

[39]Bainton, 34.

[40]Kittelson, 55–56.

[41]Fife, 100, and Kittelson, 53.

[42]Brecht, vol. 1, 92.

[43]Ibid.

[44]Ibid., 93.

6

The Pilgrimage to Rome

In 1510, Martin Luther was twenty-seven years old. He was a conscientious monk, an ordained priest, and a very promising graduate student who was gaining the confidence of people around him as a good candidate for the professoriate. However, even with all the accolades he was receiving, he was still unsatisfied. He wanted a closer union with the divine and could not seem to attain it. He studied some of the great mystics in church history such as Saint Bridget of Sweden, Saint Bonaventure, and Pseudo-Dionysius. But they, too, left him with "none of the ecstasy which the books said would be there." His experiences with mysticism were quite impressive. He once stated that he was "taken up to the third heaven," although he questioned the experience. He also claimed to have spent time with angels, but "later he said he would rather have been among the devils." Luther wanted "complete identity and harmony with God," but it remained elusive. Unfortunately, "Luther was not born to be a mystic and had only limited gifts in this area."[1]

Luther took his "monkery" seriously. He was a spiritual man, and he wanted to achieve the union with God that he thought might avail itself to one wholly committed to the religious cause. Thus, when in 1510 an opportunity came up for Luther to take a business trip to Rome, he jumped at it.

Here was his chance to sink himself wholly into the wisdom of the Roman Catholic Church at ground zero.

Staupitz: the Vicar General

At this point in his life, Luther had come under the mentorship of the highly influential Johann von Staupitz, the vicar general for the Augustinian order in Germany. He was also dean of the theology faculty in Wittenberg and was the person largely responsible for Luther's steady rise, as he gave Luther several key opportunities for career advancement, both monastically and academically.

Staupitz had first noticed Luther back when Luther was a novitiate in the monastery, undergoing his year of probation. As with all novices, Luther was tasked almost exclusively with menial work: cleaning floors, doing dishes, sweeping. Staupitz befriended Luther and at some point tasked him with committing large amounts of Scripture to memory. Luther obliged, and "Doctor Staupitz was very much impressed, and kept a special eye on him above all others." In a short time, Staupitz had become the "paternal friend" Luther probably needed at that time in his life.[2]

Staupitz was a Saxon nobleman. As vicar general of the Augustinians, he oversaw multiple monasteries, including the one at Erfurt. When Staupitz took over the leadership of the order, a divisive and complicated conflict was rumbling among the Augustinian monasteries. Several issues such as leadership, papal privileges, and regional jealousies—in this case Munich in Germany versus Lombardy in Italy—were involved. There was also the age-old monastic conflict between traditionalists and progressives: how strict should the order be when it comes to following the prescriptions of the past, practices that inevitably changed and evolved over time.[3] Finally, and perhaps most important in this case, a philosophical argument was stewing over whether the Augustinian monks should focus on isolationism or mission. The minority group—consisting of seven monasteries—argued that the job of a monk was to strive for perfection in an increasingly sinful world. The majority group—nineteen monasteries—thought the best approach was to reform the outside world by interacting more deliberately with it. With support from Rome, Staupitz planned to achieve some measure of unity between the two factions by placing them all "under one central administration"—to be overseen by him.[4] Many monks fought against his efforts to unify the polarized parties. The monasteries became the battlegrounds where competing visions of the order struggled for control.

In a short while, it became clear that Staupitz had the confidence of most religious houses, but "seven monasteries, including the two most important ones in the congregation—Nuremburg and Erfurt"—believed Staupitz was taking their order in an undesirable direction.[5] They thought that when monks got too intimate with the masses, the monastic calling got watered down. In other words, the world *needs* monks who keep their distance from the pervasiveness of sin so endemic to life outside the monastery walls. However, the disagreement was likely more about leadership and organizational autonomy than anything else.

The seven cloisters who opposed union with the others continued to make noise. They reached a gridlock with Staupitz. In the fall of 1510, they appealed to the Vatican and agreed to send two of their fellow monks to represent their views. Martin Luther, who must have shown his rhetorical prowess during this complex episode, was chosen to go. This was an interesting choice. Martin had the confidence of Staupitz, but he was tasked with representing "the other side" on the issue—which meant he was chosen to oppose his mentor. Luther's Erfurt monastery was one of the strictest. They "took the rule and the constitutions of the order very seriously and followed them obediently." The choice to send Luther to Rome to try to solve this problem spoke volumes about his competency and character. He had managed to gain friends on both sides of these complicated monastic issues and was trusted by all to argue fairly and reasonably. Surprisingly, historians do not know who traveled with Luther.[6]

The Journey to Rome

Going to Rome would have been a dream come true for the zealously pious Luther. Pilgrimage was an arduous discipline of the church, but the benefits were great. Rome held great curiosity for medieval Europeans. It was the epicenter of their faith, the heart of the old empire, and the resting place of the great apostles Peter and Paul. For western Europeans, nowhere else in the world promised more in the way of relics, religious art, ecclesial pomp, and spiritual sustenance. It was the trip of a lifetime. Rome was "the goal of every devout pilgrim. To go there guaranteed a large indulgence."[7] Luther would have been most honored to be chosen. Furthermore, he would have been given good insight into other Augustinian monasteries along the way as well as in Rome, as that is where he and his companion lodged.

Martin Luther's journey to Rome was by far the longest trip he ever took. It is about 825 miles from Erfurt to Rome. Thus, this journey—on foot—would have been a walk of at least 1,650 miles. It is difficult to construct his precise path, but likely he took one route going and a different one coming.[8] They set out from Erfurt in November and headed due south to Nuremberg. They continued southwest to Ulm, and on to Memmingen, both in Germany. From there, they must have passed through the Rhine Valley to Chur in modern Switzerland, and on to Chiavenna, Italy. The next major stop would have been Milan, where Luther was unable to perform the Mass because of their population's use of the unusual Ambrosian (or Milanese) rite in church services. Next was the Po Valley, where they caught a nasty fever that Luther claimed they defeated by eating pomegranates. After that, they traveled to Bologna, Florence, Siena, and then on to Rome. Luther spoke quite highly of the hospital in Florence. He was extremely impressed by their professionalism, cleanliness, food, and high quality of care.[9]

Throughout the journey, the weather was frightful. Winter was upon them; they should have taken this trip three or four months earlier (or later), but the urgency of the fractious situation of the monasteries must have overruled their reason. We are told that they encountered snow in Bologna.[10] One can only imagine how bad, even dangerous, the conditions would have been in the Alps at that time of year.

When Luther entered the Italian lands, he was a bit handicapped because he did not understand Italian. When he tried to speak Latin with them, he was surprised to learn that "the Italian priests at that time were not usually able to talk Latin." He was impressed by their sense of fashion as well as their "urbane manners." For example, the Italians showed remarkable self-restraint in their drinking habits, in contrast to the Germans who overindulged in alcoholic beverages with regularity.[11] He noted that Italians spoke with great vivacity when they communicated with one another. But Italian society had its share of vices. They exhibited the horrid habit of relieving themselves on buildings, a custom Luther described as being similar to dogs. Their attendance at Mass was pitiful in his view, leading to what he felt was a corrupt society, full of "lying, unbelief, frivolous blasphemy, treachery, and unnatural sins."[12]

Rome—the Eternal City

When Luther first saw the great city, he fell prostrate, and with great emotion he exclaimed, "Be greeted, thou holy Rome, truly holy because of the holy martyrs, dripping with their blood."[13] He was in utter awe of the Eternal City—at first. The longer he was there, however, the more his naïve idealism began to show signs of cracking. He was in Rome for a total of four weeks. It is not known where he resided, but in all likelihood he stayed with fellow Augustinian brothers.[14]

Rome was not dominated by Saint Peter's at that time. Luther would have seen the foundations, which had been recently laid, in 1506. Funding for that magnificent building project would spark the ire of Luther a little later with the indulgences controversy. Luther, however, did see huge castles owned by aristocrats and important cardinals of the church. Most impressive would have been the immensely fortified walls of the Vatican, built to protect the Castle of Saint Angelo, Rome's tallest building at the time. Luther would have marveled at the ruins of the Colosseum, the vaulted arches of the Roman baths, and the Pantheon. Indeed, the Pantheon made a striking impression on Luther, and he recalled it in sermons for the rest of his life.[15] But Rome was no longer the city it used to be. In ancient times, it might have held a million people. In Luther's time, Rome had shrunk to sixty thousand people—about the size of the city of Nuremberg that he had just passed through.[16] It must be kept in mind, too, that Rome's great art collections would not have been on public display. "A poor, insignificant German monk had no chance whatsoever of gaining admission to one of the palaces where the collections were housed."[17] There is a slight chance, however, that Luther might have seen or even met Michelangelo. They were roughly the same age when Michelangelo was under the commission of the papacy to create some of the greatest artistic treasures in Western history.

Pilgrims to Rome often took the time to visit the seven great basilicas scattered around the city: San Paolo fuori le Mura, San Sebastiano, Lateran (the old papal residence), Santa Croce, San Lorenzo, Santa Maria Maggiore, and the old Saint Peter's. They descended into the catacombs, where thousands of Christians had been buried through the ages. Pilgrims could hear regular Masses at all times of the day and night. They could visit endless reliquaries and pay fees to see the remains of saints.

Looking back, Luther felt he had been hoodwinked by being so naïve as to think that visiting these places could somehow bolster his spiritual state: "I ran through all the churches and crypts and believed every dirty lie that was told." At the time, he even regretted that his parents were still living! Were they dead, he could have secured a large indulgence for them by visiting relics and praying for their souls from within the holy city—a most effective way to help them lessen their time in purgatory.[18]

Luther tells us that he crawled on his knees up the Scala Sancta, a staircase in Rome that was purportedly the stairs Jesus took on his way to trial during the Passion. Luther said the "Our Father" prayer on every step in hopes of redeeming his grandfather from purgatory. Those stairs were supposedly transported from Jerusalem to Rome by angels. By climbing the twenty-eight steps while on one's knees, a person could eradicate nine years of purgatory—per step—for a total of 252 years of indulgence. The step on which Christ stumbled, however, was worth double the years, so another nine years were deducted for the sincere penitent. By the time Luther got to the top of the steps, however, he began to have doubts: "Who knows if it is true?" Later, Luther mocked what he encountered in Rome, disgusted by his own holy gullibility: "I believed everything!"[19]

Years later, in 1582, Luther's son Paul reflected on his father's experience on the Scala Santa stairs. He claimed it was a turning point in his father's theology. As Luther was ascending the steps on his knees, he remembered the apostle Paul's words, "The just shall live by *faith*." Those words reflected a change of the heart in the young German monk, and eventually they became a concise summary of Luther's entire theological system.[20]

Later in life, Luther reflected on his Roman journey. His thoughts were recorded in his *Table Talks*.

> I had not been in Rome very long before I had myself held many Masses and seen much that made me shudder when I thought about it. There I heard, over at the table of some papal courtiers, among some other crude jokes, laughing . . . as some held Mass and pronounced over the bread and wine: "Bread you are and bread you shall remain" as they raised it up. . . . It disturbed me greatly.[21]

On one occasion, Luther was celebrating Mass when another priest, who was scheduled to follow him, became impatient and shouted: "Enough, enough, get through it and get out of there."[22]

In another instance when reflecting on his time in Rome, Luther was caustic in his criticism of a place he ultimately considered to be "godless."

> So great and shameless is the godlessness and evil there that neither God nor man, neither sin nor shame are given any notice. This has been witnessed by all the faithful who have been there, and all the godless who have been there come back from Italy worse than they were before. The main purpose of my trip to Rome was that I wanted to do a complete confession of all my sins from my youth on and become completely pious. . . . But in Rome, I encountered nothing but completely uneducated men.[23]

It is hard to know how much of an outspoken critic of Rome Luther became during his journey. His deeply critical reflections occurred years later, well after he had openly opposed the church and its hierarchy. There can be no doubt, however, that seeds of contempt were sown during that trip. Luther left Rome feeling "deeply depressed by what he saw of the decline of morality in Rome, including the higher and the lower clergy."[24] And not only did Luther's expectations for a holy pilgrimage become shattered once he was there, but his mission on behalf of the Augustinian order was also a failure.

To Luther's great disappointment, "his mission . . . proved futile." He was informed that he needed a letter from the vicar general—Staupitz—in order to get an audience with the papal curia. Luther had no such letter. The Roman church was a titanic bureaucracy; signatures were required in order to move an issue up the food chain. Luther, a lowly monk from Germany, was low on the chain indeed. So he was unable to gain anything like a fair hearing. All doors were shut to him. Coming to Rome thinking he might resolve a major dispute in one of the great orders of the church was delusional. He had violated church protocol by advocating a position different from his superior, Staupitz.[25] Besides this, according to church law, "the Germans are forbidden to appeal."[26] If Luther and his companion thought they were going to march into Rome and outflank the authority of the Augustinian order, they had miscalculated badly.

All was not lost, however. Luther managed to gain two things that would help him years later in his cause of reform. First, he gained ammunition that would serve him well once he came into conflict with the church. While in Rome, he heard many anecdotes about the papacy—stories he would hyperbolize in coming years. He saw the wealth, pomp, and extravagance of Rome—sights that would lead to his opposition to indulgence-based fundraising. And he began to distrust the works-based system of salvation that was then so common in the Roman Catholic Church. Second, Luther did profit in one real, tangible way: he studied Hebrew with a German Jew while in Rome.[27] This time of study certainly was critical for Luther in later years when he took on the translation of the Old Testament into German.

Later, Luther scarcely mentioned the issues involved in the Augustinian affair. After all, he cared deeply for Staupitz, who happened to be both his monastic as well as his academic superior. Not only that, but Staupitz was also his very good friend and spiritual mentor. He was one of the few from his pre-Reformation days who were able to gain the deep and abiding respect of Luther. Besides, Luther probably was not too worried about the outcome of this episode. He had sided with his brothers in the Erfurt monastery, but it was out of loyalty to men with whom he shared the intimacy of monastic life. Luther also knew Staupitz to be a fair and reasonable man and thus trusted his leadership.

An important theory arises here—a theory that, if correct, would explain Luther's transfer to Wittenberg in ensuing years. Historian Robert Fife argues that Luther probably sided with Staupitz at some point after he returned to Erfurt. Further, it is clear that Luther developed a close personal relationship with Staupitz. Luther's melancholy continued to raise its head, and Staupitz was the one who was always there for him. Fife remarks, "It does seem probable that, in the later stages of the controversy, [Luther] went over to the side of the general vicar. If so, this may have led to a difference of opinion with the Erfurt brothers that caused Martin's final transfer to Wittenberg."[28]

In fact, Staupitz did not get his way in this series of events, either. The union of the Augustinians did not happen on his watch. The Augustinians continued the dispute, and Staupitz had the wisdom to let it alone. By intervening with too heavy a hand, he could cause even deeper division and perhaps open hostility among the order he was tasked to oversee.

Staupitz therefore was forced to concede that his plan of consolidation of the Augustinians was not going to happen, and "from 1512 on there is no further mention of a union."[29]

Rome—Unholy City

Luther's trip to Rome exposed him to the many troubling realities of the church to which he had given his life. And, over the course of his career, he never forgot his pivotal experiences there. Indeed, he developed an entire catalog of vice stemming from that brief one-month stay in what he perceived to be an unholy city, including:

- The Masses were conducted hurriedly and frivolously, sometimes two being said at the same time. Italian priests would call out to him "*passa, passa,*" meaning something like, "come on, hurry up and make way." At Saint Sebastien's Church, Luther witnessed seven priests rush through Mass within one hour! In addition, the clergy in Rome were utterly incompetent in Latin. Luther was highly trained, completely fluent in the language, and it concerned him greatly that the language of the church had fallen to such a low state in the most holy city of his Catholic faith.[30]
- The intensely political nature of Rome caught Luther's attention in a way it had not before he visited. Rome's involvement in constant warring was a reality of the times. "Italy became a battlefield." Popes "pursued one campaign after another, mostly with the object of acquiring tiny fragments of territory."[31] The city itself was a fortress equipped with cannons, defensive buildings, and a large military contingent.
- Rome appeared to Luther to be morally depraved. Homosexuality was practiced openly. Mistresses were common and assumed, even for clergy. Simony (the selling of ecclesiastical offices) was a well-established practice. Nepotism (from the Italian word for "nephew," the practice of giving lucrative positions to relatives and friends) was rampant. Pope Alexander VI (ruled 1492 to 1503), from the House of Borgia, famously fathered several children and has gone down in history as living a morally bankrupt life.[32]

Luther recalled somebody in Rome saying, "If there is a hell, then Rome stands upon it."[33] He heard this kind of invective repeatedly during his stay, and ultimately it tarnished the once-glowing view he had of the city and, eventually, of his church. Luther wrote, "I, too, was so foolish as to carry onions to Rome and bring back garlic."[34]

Nevertheless, Rome did hold great importance to Luther the monk. It was the final resting place of great saints and martyrs. It was the center of his faith, the nerve center of the Roman Catholic Church. Holy relics and monuments permeated the city, and we know Luther took full advantage of these sites. Rome was crucial to the history of Christian doctrine and practice. Luther must have left Rome with extreme ambivalence. Probably more than most, he was shocked and disturbed by what he had witnessed, and his ire was always directed precisely at the clergy, not at the city itself. In his view, the city had been hijacked by people who had forsaken the truth.

Returning to the North

Not much is known about Luther's return to Germany in 1511 other than that he set out in late January or early February and returned by means of a different route than the one that brought him to Rome, probably due to war in the region.[35] His return trip was a little more to the east, taking him through Mantua instead of Milan. He then traveled to Innsbruck in modern Austria. Then, he passed through Augsburg, where he recorded one interesting visit with an old maid named Ursula Lamenit.[36] This mystical lady claimed to nourish herself by eating and drinking the bread and wine of the Holy Sacrament, and nothing else. Luther had his doubts. She was later exposed as a fake. This sort of thing was not uncommon in the highly superstitious world of medieval Europe. During their discussions, Luther was bemused by Ursula's claim that she had no desire for the afterlife; rather, she was content with her earthly existence.[37]

Interestingly, Luther did not return to Erfurt. Instead, he was ordered to go straight to Wittenberg. We can only speculate why. In all likelihood, it was becoming clear that Luther's services were needed in upstart Wittenberg University more than in the well-established University of Erfurt. However, there are other theories. Did Luther now decidedly support Staupitz, as opposed to his brothers in Erfurt? We do know that the Augustinians of Wittenberg were on the side of Staupitz during the internecine debate. If

Luther had indeed decided—especially after striking out in Rome—that opposing Staupitz was wrongheaded, then it would have made sense for him to join up with them. Another possibility is that Staupitz simply instructed Luther to go to Wittenberg and, as an obedient monk, he did as he was told.[38] Whatever the case, "It is probable that the young teacher became a member of the Wittenberg convent and university as early as the fall of 1511."[39] Luther's move to Wittenberg ruffled the feathers of his brothers in Erfurt. We know from correspondence that "in the following years the relationship of the mother monastery in Erfurt to Luther was exceedingly tense."[40]

Thus, Luther's life became more heavily associated with the town of Wittenberg, which, of course, would become his home and ground zero to the Protestant Reformation. It was also becoming clear by then that Luther's academic gifts beckoned him forward in his studies, which he continued at the encouragement of Staupitz. Brother Luther would soon become better known as Professor Luther.

Notes

[1]Martin Brecht, *Martin Luther,* vol. 1 (Philadelphia: Fortress, 1985), 96–97.

[2]Heiko Oberman, *Luther* (New Haven: Yale University Press, 1989), 136.

[3]See Brecht, vol. 1, 98.

[4]Kittelson, 58.

[5]Oberman, 141.

[6]Brecht, vol. 1, 98–99.

[7]Richard Friedenthal, *Luther* (London: Weidenfeld and Nicolson, 1967), 77.

[8]I am using Brecht's reconstruction of the journey in vol. 1, 100–101.

[9]Friedenthal, 78.

[10]James Kittelson, *Luther the Reformer* (Minneapolis: Fortress, 1986), 58.

[11]Robert Fife, *The Revolt of Martin Luther* (New York: Columbia University Press, 1957), 167.

[12]Fife, 167.

[13]Brecht, vol. 1, 100.

[14]Ibid.

[15]Fife, 171–172.

[16]Brecht puts the population of Rome at this time at forty thousand. See vol. 1, 101.

[17]Friedenthal, 79.

[18]Roland Bainton, *Here I Stand* (New York: Meridian, 1950), 38.

[19]Fife, 172, and Friedenthal, 83.

[20]Oberman, 150.

[21]Paul Maier, trans. by Charles Daudert, *Off the Record with Martin Luther: An Original Translation of the Table Talks* (Kalamazoo, MI: Hansa-Hewlett, 2009), 73–74.

[22]Ibid., 74.

[23]Ibid., 74–75.
[24]Hartmann Grisar, trans. by Frank Eble (Westminster: Newman Press, 1950), 53.
[25]Ibid., 53.
[26]Brecht, vol. 1, 101.
[27]Grisar, 53.
[28]Fife, 178.
[29]Oberman, 142.
[30]Fife, 173.
[31]Friedenthal, 87, 89.
[32]Ibid., 86–87.
[33]Fife, 174.
[34]Oberman, 146.
[35]Grisar, 55.
[36]Fife calls her Anna Laminit. See Fife, 176.
[37]Brecht, vol. 1, 104.
[38]Grisar, 55.
[39]Fife, 178.
[40]Brecht, vol. 1, 105.

7

Professor Luther

In late March of 1511, Luther returned from Rome.[1] It was increasingly evident to him that his future was in Wittenberg, not in Erfurt. Staupitz's work as vicar general to the Augustinians had become a load too heavy to bear as a mere side job. He was forced to choose, and he became convinced that he needed to relinquish his professorship. "Who should succeed him other than Martin Luther, whom Staupitz had groomed for the job?" Back in Erfurt, this move was criticized by Luther's colleagues. "In effect, [Staupitz] robbed the Erfurt cloister . . . in order to carry out his intentions in Wittenberg."[2]

In May 1512, Luther and Staupitz attended the quadrennial convention of the Augustinians in Cologne, Germany. Luther was elevated to the position of "director of theological studies" for his order. By this time, it was crystal clear that Staupitz had marked Luther as his successor in two ways: first, Luther would replace Staupitz as professor of Bible in Wittenberg. And second, Staupitz wanted Luther to take a more conspicuous leadership role for the Augustinians.[3] In just a short time, Luther became the main preacher at the Wittenberg monastery, directed the theology program there, was granted the doctor of theology degree, and was appointed professor of Bible. It was a remarkable series of events for this rising star in the German academic landscape. Typical of Luther, however, he had more mundane memories from his Cologne trip: the stupendous cathedral with its famous relics of the three wise men, as well as the very strong wine served in that city.[4]

Wittenberg was a very different place from Erfurt. While Erfurt was comparatively metropolitan and lively, Wittenberg was tiny, only four hundred "houses" with a total population of around twenty-one hundred. "One really could not even speak of houses, but only of cabins and village cottages made of mud, roofed with hay and straw." It was a dirty and plain little village. Professors living there thought it was ugly and remote, "at the borders of civilization." The monastery where Luther would take up residence was only partially completed. The university was just a decade old and very much undeveloped.[5]

Wittenberg was the capital of Electoral Saxony, however, "one of the most powerful and significant of the German territorial states."[6] It was a town that needed development and increased profile, and the establishment of a university helped this immensely. In the decades following construction of the university in 1502, the town changed dramatically, enjoying a rising economy and a great leap in prestige. The buildings reflected the city's boom. Timber structures were replaced by brick ones. The town's main church, Saint Mary's, expanded. "The number of impressive patrician homes increased."[7]

In the early sixteenth century, Germany's intellectual class was burgeoning. It was home to sixteen universities, and Wittenberg was one of the recent ones, founded only in 1502. "New trends of thought" were proving to be a great challenge to the old order of things. "By the eve of the Reformation, these German cities were at the heart of an intellectual culture as advanced as any in Europe." The famous astronomer Nicolaus Copernicus—a contemporary of Luther—had his great paradigm shifting text *On the Revolutions of the Celestial Spheres* (1543) published in Nuremberg. Fifteenth-century Mainz, Germany, was the birthplace of the printing press, arguably the greatest invention of the millennium.[8] Germany was a cutting-edge place academically. And with Luther's arrival in 1511, Wittenberg would become one of the most important cities that would help usher in a new era, commonly referred to as the modern world.

Frederick the Wise

While Martin Luther is the person who made Wittenberg famous, it was Frederick the Wise (1463–1525) who made it great. In 1486, Frederick III (later nicknamed "the Wise") took the throne when his father Ernst died in a hunting accident.[9] As an educated man, Frederick realized more than most the importance of ideas. Although religiously quite medieval—for example, his huge collection of relics—he was aware of the new intellectual excitement brewing across Europe and wanted his university in Wittenberg to have a place at the table. He was interested in art and was willing to pay handsomely for it. He sought out the advice of the humanists, including the towering figure Erasmus of Rotterdam. Frederick was a well-traveled man, having visited the Holy Land in 1493. He was a bachelor, but he fathered three children by his mistress, Anna Weller. He became something of a political mastermind and a common presence at any gathering that mattered during his career.[10]

Politically, what made Frederick tick was his belief that the empire's power and control should be held in check. He opposed all imperial expansion, both territorially and politically. "Thus among the princes he became the leading opponent to imperial power within the empire."[11] This fiercely independent posture was crucial, because Luther in effect became Frederick's most important tool for maintaining control of Electoral Saxony. Both the empire and the Roman Catholic Church wanted a piece of the pie in Frederick's region—a region which happened to be enjoying a time of prosperity under his leadership.

Frederick the Wise is known as the political protector of Martin Luther, even though they probably never spoke personally, with the possible exception of the Diet of Worms in 1521. And while he took up residence in the castle he commissioned for himself in Wittenberg, Frederick maintained a critical distance from Luther. He was certainly open to Luther's ideas, but he did not allow himself to get too close, for several reasons—the main one being Frederick's great fascination with relics. Frederick's collection exceeded nineteen thousand pieces and featured Saint Anne's thumb, a twig from Moses's burning bush, some thorns from Christ's crown, hay from the holy manger, milk from the Virgin Mary's breast, and an entire corpse of a child (as well as many body parts from children) killed in King Herod's massacre when Jesus was born.[12] Frederick obtained papal privileges for those who visited his collection. Every person who showed devotion to the entire collection could lessen their time in purgatory by exactly 1.9 million days. This was a tremendous indulgence, and it was offered to all pious pilgrims who happened to visit Wittenberg. Obviously, Luther eventually opposed relics, indulgences, and purgatory. "Thus, this was a complicated situation. . . . It was not easy for Frederick the Wise to abandon collecting and exhibiting his relics."[13]

Luther's Rise to a Professorship at Wittenberg University

In 1502, Holy Roman Emperor Maximilian I gave Wittenberg University the right to grant degrees. Papal confirmation of the university arrived in 1507. By the time Luther began his Wittenberg professorship in 1512, approximately two hundred students enrolled each year. After Luther's *Ninety-Five Theses* were published in 1517, that number skyrocketed. Luther was valuable to Frederick the Wise. Students flocked to hear this new, reformed way of thinking, so Frederick had a vested interest in keeping his young professor in Wittenberg.[14]

Critical to the university's success was competent academic leadership, and Frederick relied on the capable Johann von Staupitz. He chose Staupitz to be dean of the theology faculty. Staupitz then recruited excellent scholars—many from Tübingen—and established a close connection between the university and the Augustinian monastery. Staupitz also served as the first professor of Bible but, as we noted earlier, he relinquished this post when his duties became too heavy. To be his successor, he handpicked his fellow Augustinian brother, Martin Luther, who took up residence in the Augustinian monastery with about forty others who were either priests or monks.[15]

Staupitz's fingerprints were all over the new University of Wittenberg. Frederick the Wise gave him nearly free reign to staff the upstart college with people he deemed worthy. And Martin Luther fit the bill. Luther had not yet received the doctorate degree, however, so Staupitz ordered him to do so immediately in the famous "pear-tree conversation" that took place between the two of them. Luther tried to deflect the task; he claimed that his health was not good. Some historians think that Luther's depressive episodes may have come back with a vengeance following the journey to Rome.

Whatever the case, Luther was not in a position to deny his boss's demands. Reluctantly, he agreed to pursue a doctorate in theology, primarily out of obedience to Staupitz. It was not so much a matter of Luther agreeing to several years of study as it would be today; rather, he had to submit himself to a complicated process wherein he would receive the title of doctor. It was expensive, public, and came with enormous obligations—chiefly that he would be expected to give the remainder of his career to training students in theology. It was, more than anything, a lifelong commitment, not unlike committing to a monastic order.

Neither Luther nor Staupitz could afford the hefty fees Luther would have to pay, but Frederick the Wise stepped in to take care of these matters, with the full expectation that Luther was to give the remainder of his life to the university. Next, the faculty had to vouch for Luther, solemnly swearing to the chancellor that Luther was indeed worthy of the honor of receiving the license to teach. Then, Luther had to swear that he would obey the Roman Catholic Church, would respect all its teachings, and would promote harmony among the other scholars. Little did Luther know he would soon violate all these things, but at the time, on October 4, 1512, he solemnly swore he would be a man of peace. The decisions to accept Luther were promptly made, and he graduated on October 19, after a two-day ceremony that culminated in the Castle Church—the very place where Luther was destined to become a resolute disturber of the peace. The speaker for the occasion was Andreas Karlstadt, who would first oppose Luther's reforms, then join with him, then finally be cast out of Wittenberg by him. Luther gained admission into the senate of the theology faculty on October 21, after having to make another series of oaths. He was given the symbols of the office: a Bible, a biretta, and a gold ring.[16] Staupitz was glad to hand the Bible and theology professorship over to someone he knew and trusted. Luther was assigned to give lectures from the Augustinian monastery rather than in the university buildings, which suited him fine since that was where he resided.[17]

Luther's sudden rise caused resentment back in Erfurt. He was accused of being Staupitz's golden child. His former colleagues also accused him of breaking a previous vow that he would take his doctorate at the University of Erfurt. It was no coincidence that none of the Erfurters bothered to come to his doctoral celebrations. This spat escalated for two years, to the point that Luther had to write a letter asking for their forgiveness. He explained that the doctorate degree was thrust onto him; he did not seek it. He also explained that he had never taken the oath to receive his doctorate at Erfurt. In his view, the Erfurters were unjustified in their assumptions on these matters. His explanation did little, however, to quell their bitterness.[18]

Professorial Responsibilities

Luther's obligations were not just his lecturing duties; he still had heavy monastic commitments. In a letter to a friend in Erfurt, he vividly described his heavy work schedule. He had to write copious amounts of letters, preach regularly at the monastery, read lessons during mealtimes, preach daily in the city church, supervise students, serve as vicar (prior) to eleven monastic cloisters, look after a fish pond, and of course, provide a steady stream of lectures for the university. Luther lamented that he had virtually no time to himself due to all these commitments, not even to nourish his soul by celebrating Mass.[19]

Luther's lectures were Bible lessons. He took great pride in being a man of Scripture. In his mind, when he received the doctorate, his most important vow was that he would preach the Word of God responsibly. He also promised to maintain the peace in his teaching—not to rock the boat—and to conduct himself in a way satisfactory to the Roman Catholic Church. However, Luther felt that his obligation to preach Scripture faithfully superseded his loyalty to the church. This would become the central issue at the Diet of Worms in 1521, where these two commitments—whether to church or to Scripture—came into conflict with one another.

Luther's academic career spanned thirty-three years, and his lectures were always focused on how to interpret the Bible. The medieval tradition "equated professors of theology with teachers of the 'sacred page.' To teach theology meant to explain the texts of scripture and to discuss theological questions and their relevance as they arose from those texts. As a result, academic lectures might sound like sermons." Luther preached through many books of the Bible during his career, beginning with the book of Psalms in the spring of 1512.[20] Luther must have been an impressive teacher of the psalms. It is likely that he had them memorized after singing and chanting them for several years already.

Just because Luther's lectures focused on the Bible, though, does not mean that he disregarded the larger intellectual world he had encountered throughout his studies. Luther was a brilliant scholar, comfortable in several languages and extremely competent in Latin, the language of all his university lectures.[21] When he interacted with the text, he integrated many commentaries as well as perspectives of various leading philosophers. For his course text, he used the *Five-Fold Psalter* by his contemporary, the French humanist Jacques Lefevre d'Etaples (1455–1536). This version of Psalms contained five parallel Latin renditions: the French, the Roman, the Hebrew, the Old Italian, and a collation of all four. Luther incorporated insights from several commentators: Victor Hugo (thirteenth century), Nicholas of Lyra (thirteenth century), the Jewish-Christian scholar Paul of Burgos (fourteenth century), and Peter Lombard (twelfth century). Importantly, Nicholas of Lyra had been a professor at the Sorbonne who "strove for a literal interpretation against the prevalent mystical flights of fancy." To help students understand the original language and context, Luther trained them in biblical Hebrew, using Reuchlin's *Rudiments of Hebrew*, published in 1506. Perhaps most of all, Luther's teachings incorporated the theological insights of Saint Augustine, by far his favorite theologian.[22]

Luther was fond of the mystical writers from the Christian tradition, such as the Dominican Johannes Tauler (fourteenth century). However, he had a certain amount of reticence when it came to the mystics. Uniting with God seemed like a noble idea, but Luther had a very Augustinian view of the depravity of man. "A holy God, he thought, could never tolerate intimacy with humans who, despite their sincere ambitions, inevitably remained unholy."[23] Despite this incompatibility, Luther believed God reached out to humans through Christ. Here we find in Luther the seeds of what later became central to his theology. Humans fool themselves if they think they can *obtain* God. God cannot be grasped. Rather, he reaches out to sin-sick humans. This is grace. Thus, the mystics were right to emphasize the aloofness and wonderment of God, but they were wrong in their idea that through meditation, study, and holiness, human efforts could lead one to grasp—or unite with—this great and high God.

Luther was one of many scholars who at the time were embracing more literal approaches to the text, as opposed to the long-favored allegorical approaches. This was due to the impact of humanism and, perhaps most of all, the return to the sources (*ad fontes*) that it advocated. Luther was caught up in this shift of thinking, and it caused him to delve deeply into the study of the biblical languages.

Luther lectured on Psalms from 1512 to 1515. He provided two hours of lecture per week. He began lecturing at six in the morning and went on for two hours. In the winter months, he began his lectures at seven in the morning. After 1516, he decided to start delivering lectures in the afternoon, beginning at one o'clock.[24]

His lecture style included frequent pauses because he wanted his students to take extensive notes in the margins of their books. He was careful to explain the meaning of individual words so that students could grasp the fullness of what they were hearing and reading. He believed in precision in words, and he encouraged students to create their own glossary of sorts.[25]

Inner Turmoil

Under intense pressure with his many teaching and pastoral duties, Luther therefore began to develop many of the health problems that plagued him for the rest of his life. He complained of insomnia and constipation chiefly, often interpreting them as attacks from the devil. His old archenemy melancholy—despair and depression—regularly haunted him. Luther also was plagued with a deep sense of doubt about his salvation, or about his goodness in the eyes of God. He experienced these troubling thoughts with frequency and great intensity. The German word Luther chose to describe these experiences is *Anfechtungen*. This word is notoriously difficult to translate into English, so many scholars of Luther simply leave it untranslated. It is a hostile term, meaning something along the lines of "assault or attack."[26] It was a terrifying feeling for Luther to imagine God opposing him, condemning him, overwhelming him. This *Anfechtungen* could best be described as a massive religious crisis out of which Luther felt there was no escape. It was a distorted view of God as hostile, condemning people without mercy. Luther's Augustinian way of thinking led him to believe that God had the right to feel this way toward humans. They had sinned, and God was disgraced and disrespected by their sin. Therefore, God was entitled to erupt in wrath and punish his people. Luther, however, applied all of this in an intensely personal way. God wanted to harm Luther—personally, he believed. And it terrified him.

It was thoughts like these that led Luther to run to the writings of Paul, especially Romans and Galatians, for refuge. He lectured carefully through these texts from 1515 to 1517, and they utterly transformed his way of thinking. It was painstaking work for him, but ultimately this study led to massive relief in his own troubled soul. He was now able to see God providing a way out of the condemned status of humans. Jesus Christ was the way out. The old law condemned people, but the new law, found in Christ, was based on grace. The sinner's *Anfechtungen* was not a permanent condition. It drove one to find grace and mercy in this severe God's eternal agent—Jesus Christ.

The medieval prescription for all of this—for Luther was certainly not the only one to have these thoughts—was penance. The sinner would go to the priest to confess sin and admit guilt. The priest would assign a set of prayers, or a series of fasts, or a pilgrimage, to help the sinner to feel absolved. But, eventually, the sinner would begin to feel the effects of guilt again and would have to go back to the priest. The priest would prescribe certain acts of contrition, and the sinner could once again feel free. For the system to work, however, the sinner had to be sincere. Luther began to question his own motives—whether he was *really* sincere, or whether he was contrite *enough*. He began to collapse beneath the weight of his own guilt. He became convinced that God could not forgive him because he was not working hard enough to be forgiven. Thus, the prescriptions assigned by his mentors would never work, because even in his motives Luther felt he was inadequate and depraved. Again, this was all very Augustinian. Luther had a bedrock conviction that humans were depraved, even from conception due to the most basic sin of all: concupiscence (lust). Humans were born into sin because they were conceived in lust. Sin raced through our very blood. What right did we, sinful creatures even from birth, have in the presence of a sinless and almighty God?

The Emergence of Luther's Criticisms

At this stage, Luther's ideas were still orthodox in the sense that nothing he was teaching opposed the general consensus of Catholic thought. He was still very much a son of the church. "His writings, in fact, contain surprisingly few references to the pope and the Roman curia. What he says explicitly about Rome is positive for the most part."[27] However, a "breakthrough" was on the horizon. A deep analysis of his lectures on Psalms provides hints of dissatisfaction toward the way some in the church hierarchy were conducting themselves. In a lecture on Psalm 38, Luther charges that "sins abound" throughout the church—sins such as "sensual pleasures and all the other wretched extravagances with which the ablest and best in the Church are involved." He speaks of scandals and "foul corruption."[28]

Another area where Luther was beginning to have misgivings was the monastic institution. In the years leading up to 1517 and the *Ninety-Five Theses*, he was not openly opposing the existence of monastic institutions; after all, he was a relatively young monk who, despite that, had many other monks under his charge. He did, however, feel mature enough to openly criticize those aspects of the institution that needed reform. Later, of course, Luther would oppose monasticism altogether. But at this phase (around 1515), he was simply doing what many Roman Catholics did—offering a healthy critique.

> These things [monastic works] are not tokens derived from the Gospel. All these performances are empty of content; there is nothing spiritual or vital about them. But because these men [the monks] love to do these things they re-establish and defend them even though the Lord disapproves of such performances. . . . They are working against the Lord. . . . This zeal of theirs is utter folly. It is a zeal to establish their own righteousness. . . . Rend your heart and not your garment. Do not show so much external penitence; show it from the heart's core. . . . No one hears God except it be given him from Christ alone. . . . In Christ a man is clearly separated from those Pharisees and literal-minded Jews, for God never heard them. God hears him [the believer in Christ] in His righteousness by giving to him righteousness. . . . But because these men [the monks] are proud, they do not do this: rather they harangue the Lord, but He does not hear them.[29]

These are scathing criticisms, but they were coming from within. This kind of literary display was nothing more than a concerned member of the clergy arguing for reform.

Luther certainly was not alone in condemning corruption in the church. During the end of the fifteenth and beginning of the sixteenth century, many others thought that the church was at it nadir. It was no secret that the church had been in a crisis since the fourteenth century, when at one point three popes claimed to be in charge. At this stage, nothing in Luther's criticisms was unique. In fact, it was not long until the Roman Church started a sweeping project of reform at the Council of Trent—a major eighteen-year church conference that began in 1545, while Luther was still living. The church had problems. Those like Luther and many others who had the courage to speak out knew it. The church knew it. That's why it took the steps it did to initiate reform. But it took someone like Luther—and the unique historical context that gave rise to his reforms—to precipitate the deep soul-searching so evident at Trent.

One of the themes Luther hits repeatedly in his lectures on the psalms is humility. He rebukes the typical medieval and monastic understanding of humility—begging, wearing the monastic garments, penance, working hard in the monastery, and obeying your superiors. However, what emerges in Luther in these early lecture notes is his big idea of "Christ alone." The humble acts of a monk do little to put one in right relationship with God. Rather, the core of the gospel is surrendering oneself completely to Christ, since Christ is the only one who can do anything about our salvation. This "Christ alone" mentality emerges as the central pillar of Luther's system. And it ultimately convinced him that monasticism was useless. If it cannot get you to heaven, why in God's name would you put yourself through all that suffering?

Only Christ could bequeath true humility to the disciple. Good works only lead to temporary relief, and they are often accompanied with pride. But Christ can offer justification to a person's soul. Therefore, the individual can *know*—not just *feel*—that he or she is justified before God. Christ was righteous. Christ was sent by God to accomplish the transaction. Now that Christ's work on the cross is complete, the individual merely has to trust in God's agent—Jesus Christ, the savior of the world. Indeed, trusting in one's own works jeopardizes one's salvation, since the trust is not placed in Christ! Thus, the true believer remained humble, knowing that he or she did not *earn* salvation.

Much of this was autobiographical; it was Luther dealing with his own baggage. He became a monk, thinking this act of humility and obedience would guarantee him a clean conscience before God. But the monastic system failed him. "He himself was crushed again and again by his inability to stand in the presence of a righteous God."[30] Therefore, he decided to branch out on his own and, using Scripture as his guide, find a way to absolve his own wretched conscience.

What Luther was getting at is this: salvation cannot be achieved by external activities. It would be overly simplistic to say that Luther was advocating a cerebral system as opposed to a physical, works-based system, but there is something to that. Luther's slavish behavior in the monastery cleaning floors and reciting hundreds of prayers by memory had little impact on the condition of his soul. His solution was found in Romans and Galatians, as well as in certain psalms: justification through Christ *alone*. Luther's early lecture notes were an inchoate rendition of what eventually would reign supreme in his thinking: justification comes through Christ alone. Luther later would connect other core tenets to this idea—especially "faith alone" and "Scripture alone"—but early on, his theological "breakthrough" was found in "Christ alone." Monkery could not get one justified, nor could the severely compromised institution of the church. But Christ could.

Luther's God

Luther's conception of God was undergoing transformation as well. Before Luther was a professor, his view of God was that he was a terrible tyrant, an irascible judge, with an all-seeing eye, watching and recording the sins of his children. This was rather normal for his context. But Luther's emphasis began to change. He began to see God as merciful. Why else would he send Jesus? We must not overstate the case that Luther's theology was still very Augustinian. He was convinced that humans were depraved and made a mess of things. However, Luther did not wish to end there. He wanted to show that God offered humans the chance to be redeemed, to be declared righteous by God and therefore saved from their sins. There was only one way for this to happen, however. The sinner had to encounter the gospel. And after encountering the gospel, the sinner had to truly believe it, to fully trust in it. Luther explained, "This [process] comes about by faith alone: by that faith with which the Word of God is believed."[31]

Luther truly believed that he was onto something new, something different than the theology being taught in his day. And he laid the blame for this misunderstanding of the gospel at the feet of the Greek philosophers—most notably Aristotle, who became Luther's whipping boy during the years leading up to 1517. The main critique he had of Aristotle was his emphasis on good works. Luther's study of Romans and Galatians convinced him that good works always left one short. Righteousness could not be attained through human behavior. He wrote: "According to Aristotle righteousness follows from, and arises from, doing good works. But according to God righteousness precedes good works and works spring from righteousness."[32]

By 1517, Luther had managed to obtain unrivalled power over the university's theological curriculum, and he had pulled off a herculean feat: he had virtually expunged Aristotle from the discipline of theology. He joyfully wrote to John Lang, his talented colleague at Erfurt, explaining that "Aristotle is gradually tottering to a fall from which he will hardly rise again."[33] In a 1517 letter to Lang, Luther let out a stream of invective on the ancient philosopher:

> . . . that ridiculous and injurious blasphemer Aristotle. His propositions are so absurd that an ass or a stone would cry out at them. . . . My soul longs for nothing so ardently as to expose and publicly shame that Greek buffoon, who like a specter has befooled the church. . . . If Aristotle had not lived in the flesh I should not hesitate to call him a devil.[34]

Luther was fashioning the curriculum in the way he wanted: heavier reliance on Augustine. He wrote, "No professor can hope for students unless he offers courses in the new theology, that is, on the Bible or St. Augustine."[35]

Augustine's extremely low view of humans was all over Luther's theology. In April 1516, he wrote the following in a letter:

> Therefore, my sweet brother, learn Christ and him crucified; despairing of yourself, learn to pray to him, saying, "You, Lord Jesus, are my righteousness, but I am your sin; you have taken on yourself what you were not and have given me what I was not." Beware of aspiring to such purity that you no longer wish to appear to yourself, or to be, a sinner.[36]

The plan of salvation was simple. Humans were incapable of doing anything to help them escape their sin. Therefore, they could not achieve justification before God. But God came to their rescue, out of sheer mercy. He sent Christ. Now humans had a way out of their depravity and eternal destruction.

By 1517, Luther was convinced that his views were right, and that the theology being taught at the time was wrong. Everything needed to change. Salvation was at stake. And when Luther heard the news that the church was traveling around selling salvation for a price through indulgence certificates, he was outraged.

That's what started the Reformation.

Notes

[1]Martin Brecht, trans. by James Schaaf, *Martin Luther: His Road to Reformation, 1483–1521*, vol. 1 (Philadelphia: Fortress, 1985), 104.

[2]Scott Hendrix, *Martin Luther* (New Haven: Yale University Press, 2015), 44.

[3]Ibid., 45.

[4]Brecht, vol. 1, 126. See also Robert Fife, *The Revolt of Martin Luther* (New York: Columbia University Press, 1957), 178.

[5]Brecht, vol. 1, 107. For the number of residents, see Brecht, vol. 1, 110.

[6]Ibid., 108.

[7]Ibid., 111.

[8]C. Scott Dixon, *The Reformation in Germany* (Oxford: Blackwell, 2002), 15–16.

[9]Sam Wellman, *Frederick the Wise* (Saint Louis, MO: Concordia, 2011), xv–xxi.

[10]Brecht, vol. 1, 111–112.

[11]Ibid., 112.

[12]Martin Marty, *Martin Luther* (New York: Viking, 2004), 18–19.

[13]Brecht, vol. 1, 117–118.

[14]Ibid., 119.

[15]Ibid., 121.

[16]Marty, 14; and Brecht, vol. 1, 126–127.

[17]Hartmann Grisar, *Martin Luther* (Westminster: Newman Press, 1950), 57.

[18]Brecht, vol. 1, 128.

[19]Hendrix, 45. It should be noted that in 1515 Luther was elected to the position of "provincial vicar" for the Augustinians in Saxony and Thuringia.

[20]It should be noted that a few scholars think Luther lectured on Genesis before he lectured on Psalms.

[21]Hendrix, 48.

[22]James Atkinson, *Martin Luther and the Birth of Protestantism* (Baltimore: Penguin, 1968), 91.

[23]Marty, 20.

[24]Brecht, vol. 1, 129.

[25]Graham Tomlin, *Luther and His World* (Downers Grove: IVP, 2002), 52.

[26]Ibid., 41.

[27]Scott Hendrix, *Luther and the Papacy* (Philadelphia: Fortress, 1981), 12.

[28]Atkinson, 92.

[29]Luther, "On Psalm 4," in Atkinson, 93.

[30]James Kittelson, *Luther the Reformer* (Minneapolis: Fortress, 1986), 90.

[31]Luther in Atkinson, 113.

[32]Ibid.

[33]Luther to John Lang at Erfurt, 18 May 1517, in Preserved Smith, *The Life and Letters of Martin Luther* (London: John Murray, 1911), 26.

[34]Luther, in Preserved Smith, 26.

[35]Ibid.

[36]Luther, in Kittelson, 95.

8

Luther the Priest and Pastor

Luther's professorial career began to soar spectacularly in the years leading up to 1517. He lectured through Psalms, Romans, Galatians, and Hebrews. Students were responding well to him. He was gaining confidence. And he was reading Paul's writings in new ways, even revolutionary ways, compared to those before him and around him. His thoughts on justification and righteousness were laying the groundwork for what would erupt into a European-wide schism—Protestant and Catholic—in the years to come.

It is perhaps easy to forget that Luther was also a priest, tasked with the caring of souls. And this vocation was important to him. Luther never relinquished his calling as a pastor. From his ordination until his death, he mentored people, gave of his time to others, conducted incalculable numbers of church services, and preached regularly to the church members under his charge. Luther's great scholarly output never supplanted his ministerial commitments. While many scholars leave the pulpit to enter the academy, Luther never made such move. The two went together for him.

Scholars have often overlooked that Luther was, most fundamentally, a priest and a pastor. Very recently, however, Mary Jane Haemig turned her attention to this vital aspect of Luther's identity and career. In a volume on Luther's pastoral writings, she explains it thus:

> Luther the pastor is often overlooked. Succeeding generations have thought of him as the great prophet, steadfast reforming figure, mover and shaker of his time, best-selling writer, brilliant theologian—even the national or denominational hero. But Luther was also a pastor who explained the basics of the Christian faith, taught people how to pray, visited and comforted the sick and dying, encouraged the doubtful, advised the prominent and the obscure, counseled the faithful, doubting, and suffering, and offered concrete help in a number of situations.

Haemig then points out an obvious fact, though often missed.

> In some sense, all of Luther's works were pastoral, driven by a deep concern not for "correct" theology but to provide consolation and hope to people suffering in body, mind, and spirit. Certainly his early questions about indulgences derived as much from a deep pastoral concern for people as from a theoretical questioning of the entire indulgence system.[1]

Indeed, Luther as priest and pastor is often the "elephant in the room." It is well known that he stood up to Rome most courageously, but his pastoral side often receives short-shrift.

When we take his entire career into consideration, we will find that Luther was perhaps more a pastor than anything else. It was the engine that drove him. His theological writings were rooted fundamentally in the notion that he was helping people understand God better than they had been taught before. He cared deeply for their souls.

Luther's preaching career was breathtaking. "It is estimated that he preached approximately four thousand sermons in his lifetime."[2] In 1528, while dealing with intense headaches and overall bad health, he preached nearly two hundred times. His productivity was "almost miraculous."[3]

But preaching was only the tip of the iceberg. Luther wrote hymns for congregations. He authored *The German Mass* in 1526, based on his 1523 Latin Mass. He wrote catechisms for the churches that came on board the

Reformation. "He shaped the new Evangelical worship, catechetical, and prayer practices. He never considered himself above the usual activities of a pastor."[4] One of Luther's greatest responsibilities was safeguarding the churches that followed his lead by encouraging the pastors, writing them letters, and helping them survive the unsettling criticism that came relentlessly from Rome.

There is a little bit of irony here, however. Perhaps we can even call it contradiction. Most readers will recognize that one of Luther's great contributions to Protestant theology was his notion of the "priesthood of all believers." This is often understood as being a license of sorts that gives the authority to preach and teach to every believing person. But this is not what Luther had in mind. Yes, he had real issues with the ordained clergy as the system existed in his time. But it would be a gross misunderstanding to hear Luther implying that each believer was as qualified as any other. Luther struggled with this tension, and he was often inconsistent. The bottom line is that Luther realized some were more qualified than others. This is precisely what the peasants got wrong when they later rose up in rebellion, resulting in their own unfortunate and needless slaughter.

Luther did challenge the Roman Catholic notion of the priesthood, but by no means did he abolish the role of a preaching and teaching class. Ordained clergy still played a major role in his concept of the church. They were trained in God's word; therefore, they had a responsibility to ensure that God's word was handled with great care. So we can say that Luther did not jettison the priesthood. Rather, he molded and shaped it into what he believed it should be.

A Passing of the Baton

By far the most important influence on Luther's spiritual life and career was Johann von Staupitz. He proved to be a trustworthy and wise friend when Luther needed one most. He was a gifted leader, and the people around him elevated him to roles of great responsibility all through his career. In 1503, Staupitz was elected vicar general of the Augustinians, and he remained in that position for seventeen years. Staupitz's position was an important one. In medieval Europe, a vicar general held real power. But from all accounts, Staupitz was a fair and reasonable man. Monasteries were not immune to corruption, but virtually everything we know about Staupitz holds him up as a man of unquestionable integrity. People disagreed with his decisions at times, but his goodness was known by all. This is the man who took Luther under his wing. This is the model Luther inherited. Luther was mentored by a sincere, pious, and faithful Christian.

Earlier, we described the fracture in the Augustinian order. The church wanted Staupitz to consolidate his leadership over all the Augustinian monasteries in Germany.[5] But several monasteries wanted to maintain their autonomy—the two most important monasteries being Nuremberg and Erfurt. Since Luther was an Erfurt monk, technically, his entire monastery was opposed to Staupitz, but no kind of acrimony developed between Luther and Staupitz over this issue. By the time Luther returned to Germany from Rome, he seems to have become a sympathizer to Staupitz's view that all the monasteries should fall under the authority of the vicar general.[6] We do not know exactly why Luther made this decision. What we do know is that their relationship became closer than ever after his return. And within a very short period of time, Luther's career was up and running again. He suffered no fallout from his "official" opposition to Staupitz. Staupitz seemed to have respected Luther for making the journey to Rome, even though the mission was a failure.

While Staupitz may have won the temporary battle, the monasteries that resisted won the war. Staupitz was unable to negotiate a union among all the monasteries, and it was not in his nature to ramrod his views down their throats. He was no tyrant. Once he realized how strongly the monks opposed him, he backed off.[7]

Luther came to rely upon Staupitz's friendship. He esteemed his mentor in the highest of terms. He once said, "If it had not been for Dr. Staupitz, I should have sunk in hell."[8] Luther seems never to have lost this great admiration for his mentor, although Staupitz never joined the Reformation. Even the year before Luther died, in 1545, he praised Staupitz for "first of all being my father in this doctrine, and having given birth [to me] in Christ."[9]

We saw earlier that Staupitz played a key role in moving Luther to Wittenberg, which would become his long-term home. At the time, the Erfurt Augustinians were resentful of Luther's move. "Luther's decision to follow his patron rather than the majority of his own house was a hard one, and it cast a shadow over relations within the cloister that never really lifted."[10] Even three years later, the relationship was "exceedingly tense," and

Luther's letters to the Erfurt brothers had "a certain acidity of tone that seems to indicate previous disagreements."[11]

Called to Preach

Luther's career benefited tremendously from his decision to cut ties with his Erfurt brethren and trust the guidance of Staupitz. As we recounted in the last chapter, Luther followed Staupitz's advice—after the pear tree conversation in 1512—and successfully pursued the doctorate in theology. Luther was thereafter an officially licensed teacher of theology, a position that brought with it great responsibility. Part of his task was to protect the church from heresy. Staupitz was sticking his neck out for this young priest who was by that point nearing the age of thirty.

Like Staupitz, however, Luther was called to live a double life: he was to serve as both pastor and professor. For a man who today is so associated with courage, Luther seems to have doubted his abilities at every turn while a younger man. We know that out of the feeling of inadequacy he resisted the advice to pursue a doctorate. Similarly, he was intimidated by his obligation to preach, to the point of great inner turmoil. Once while giving advice to other pastors in 1533, Luther told them the following:

> If I were to write about the burden and responsibilities of a preacher, as I have experienced them, I would scare everyone away from it. For a good preacher must be of such a mind that nothing is dearer to him than Christ and His life; so that when he finally has lost this life, and everything, he knows Christ will say to him: "Come here to me, my dear son." I hope that He will also speak to me with those words on Judgment Day, for here all speak to me in an unfriendly way. I have the burden of the whole world, the emperor, and the Pope. But since I have been called to this, I must stand my ground and say: "What I do is right." After I was called, the devil attacked me many times and has tormented me with this argument: "You haven't been called!" As if I had been made a doctor for nothing.[12]

This long quotation reveals the tender side of Luther: his fears, his hopes, his burdens. It also conveys a deep conviction, rooted in the belief that he was called by God (and therefore opposed by Satan). This is the unfiltered

Luther, sitting around a table with trusted friends: still strong, but quite willing to show something of his vulnerabilities.

Luther struggled over whether he should become a preacher. His young life was one of anguish. Why would Staupitz choose a young man with such a tortured soul to preach to others? Historians think Staupitz was essentially saying to Luther, "Physician, cure thyself by curing others."[13] It was clear that Luther was a man deeply embroiled in spiritual warfare within himself, but equally clear was Luther's giftedness, his sincerity, and his truly spiritual heart. Staupitz recognized in Luther a man who would serve the church extraordinarily well. Instead of doubting the young Luther for all his inner turmoil, Staupitz saw these things as valuable tools to be used in the shaping of souls. It turned out to be an extraordinary insight on the part of Staupitz.

But there is another side to these developments. Staupitz was overworked, and he knew he had to relinquish some of his responsibilities. It was in his best interest to choose someone who would support him in his role as vicar general of the Augustinians. Naturally, he would have recognized the superior talent in Luther, but self-interest was involved as well. Staupitz wanted someone who shared his outlook if he was going to place him into positions of influence. Since he returned from Rome, Luther had been faithful to Staupitz, and he was about to reap the rewards. Staupitz frequently had to be gone from Wittenberg, so he tapped Luther to fill the professorship. Luther was reluctant, but he agreed to do what Staupitz needed.

Out of the Cloister

Immediately, Luther was thrust into the local limelight. Virtually overnight, he became a key leader in the Augustinian fellowship. Perhaps more importantly, he found himself standing in the pulpits both at his monastery as well as at the church. Luther had become Wittenberg's primary preacher: "He was appointed a Prior and a District Vicar within his own order, a preacher first to his fellow monks, and then an official preacher in the parish church of Wittenberg, a popular audience which became of immense importance for him."[14] The locals, as well as the Augustinian monks, would now look to Luther for their daily spiritual sustenance. Preaching to the laity required Luther's head to come out of the clouds. His effectiveness would not be measured by the headiness of his ideas. As a preacher, his effectiveness would be measured by whether he could communicate with the ordinary members of society. This was a crucial lesson for Luther to learn. And his mastery of communicating with common people was what propelled him to international fame in just five years, when he published the *Ninety-Five Theses* in 1517.

Once Luther agreed to take up Staupitz's work in Wittenberg, his ministerial responsibilities began to pile up, even though he had been plunged into a new professorship. In May 1512, he became sub-prior of his cloister—essentially the second in command at the monastery. This was also when he began to serve as program director of theological studies at the cloister. In 1514—against his wishes—he became the priest and pastoral administrator over the parish church in Wittenberg.[15] In May 1515, he joined the "senior management" of the Augustinian order when he was elected to serve as district vicar. This meant he had to oversee eleven monasteries in Saxony and Thuringia. This position came with real influence and a fair bit of travel. Staupitz soon relocated to southern Germany, leaving Luther as the head honcho of the district. Luther now "had the power to select and remove the priors of local cloisters in their provinces."[16]

Although he was ordained a priest in 1507, Luther was a rookie when it came to preaching: he "hardly preached at all in Erfurt, since for that he would have needed permission of the vicar general, who did not assign him the task of preaching until after he moved permanently to Wittenberg."[17] After a fairly routine life as a student and an obedient monk, Luther was stepping out into new frontiers.

Luther preached regularly at the parish church, as well as at the Castle Church. Wittenberg's famous Castle Church—where the theses were famously nailed—had existed since 1346, but when Frederick the Wise turned his attention to the city in the 1490s, it was completely rebuilt. In 1503, the Castle Church became the church for the university community. The church was a pilgrimage stop because of its massive collection of 19,000 relic fragments (an impressive collection, but one that paled in comparison to the one in nearby Halle, which was twenty times as large).[18]

Luther was becoming the face of the church in Wittenberg, and he knew it. His star was rising rapidly. But it was not something he welcomed, partly because he felt it was robbing him of time he used to spend in private devotion to God. In January 1517, he wrote to a friend, "God's approval declines at the same rate that human approval increases."[19]

Man of the People

Swiftly, Luther became known as a man of the people. As lead minister of the parish church, "he became a popular preacher, especially for his ability to explain biblical stories in the simple parlance of the people."[20] Communicating with the common man and woman was the most extraordinary gift Luther possessed. He was a good scholar, a competent priest, a powerful rhetorician. What made Luther unique, however, was his ability to communicate. More than anyone in the late-medieval era, he could converse powerfully with commoners, both in speech and in writing. This was the hidden talent that came to light when Luther stepped into the pulpit of Wittenberg to communicate the word of God to the local townspeople.

This era of Luther's life also evinces a pastoral concern for others. For example, on one occasion, one of the Augustinians in Wittenberg was transferred to southern Germany. The brother left behind two books and asked Luther to sell them for him to repay a debt to Staupitz. Luther advised the monk to talk with Staupitz about it and not to worry about the payment. Luther saw himself in the young monk: overly anxious, too excruciatingly scrupulous, almost too principled in his daily life. Luther advised the fellow not to trust in his own righteousness but to rely on the righteousness of Christ alone, for "Christ dwells only in sinners. On this account he descended from heaven, where he dwelt among the righteous, to dwell among sinners. Meditate on this love of his and you will see his sweet consolation."[21] Clearly, Luther's "Christ alone" idea was beginning to cement itself into his consciousness.

Passionately Pauline

Luther had an obvious penchant for preaching from the epistles of Paul. He profoundly liked the apostle simply because Paul helped him to overcome, or at least manage, his profound anxiety over the condition of his soul, that crippling *Anfechtungen*. Luther felt that Paul understood the gospel in its fullness. Jesus died to save sinners, not saints. Besides, there was no such thing as a saint without Christ, "for all have sinned and fall short of the glory of God" (Rom. 3:23). Therefore, "If anyone is in Christ, he is a new creation. The old has passed away. Behold, the new has come" (2 Cor. 5:17). These words were at the heart of Luther's so-called breakthrough.

For the rest of his career, he eagerly directed the people under his care to the liberating teachings of Paul. It would not be an overstatement to say that Paul *saved* Luther, since Paul taught, in Luther's judgment, the true gospel. On one occasion, Luther advised a pastor: "When I am troubled by thoughts regarding political considerations or household matters, I take up a Psalm or passage from Paul, and fall asleep over it." In another instance, Luther was asked what books of the Bible should be preached the most. He responded, "The Psalms [and] the Gospel according to John and Paul."[22] On another occasion, when encouraging a pastor, Luther brought up Acts 9:15, where Paul is identified by Jesus Christ as the "chosen instrument" to preach to both Jews and Gentiles.[23]

Luther's Pauline way of thinking—that all are sinners—was at the heart of his sermons. One reason Luther held the church father Augustine in such high regard was because Augustine also homed in on this central idea in Paul's theology. Indeed, Luther's theology was "heavily colored by Augustine." Again and again, he emphasized humanity's impotence to redeem itself. He insisted, "In no way can we be saved by our righteous works, but [we] must take refuge under the wings of Christ the mother hen."[24]

Students of Luther often discuss when and where his comprehension of Paul's central ideas occurred to him. Historians have often described a "tower experience" where the new insights struck him like lightning. In a vague passage in his *Table Talks*, he describes this moment as follows:

> The words "righteous" and "the righteousness of God" worked upon my conscience like a lightning bolt; whenever I heard them I was terrified. Is God righteous? Then he must punish. But once while in this tower, reflecting on the words (Rom. 1:17) "The just shall live by faith" and on the "righteousness of God," I suddenly thought that if we because of faith become righteous and if the righteousness of God is extended to everyone who believes, then righteousness is not our own achievement, but rather is a result of God's mercy. My spirit was comforted because the righteousness of God consists in our being justified and redeemed through Christ. Now these words, "God's

> righteousness," became for me beloved words. In this tower, the Holy Spirit revealed the Scripture to me.[25]

If this incident was truly the "breakthrough" in Luther's theology, then it would be important indeed. Alas, we do not know precisely when it occurred. It must have been between 1512 and 1518, but the precise date is lost. The experience has spawned all sorts of creative interpretations as well. Taking clues from an entry in his *Table Talks*, some have claimed that Luther may have had this realization while on the toilet! Others think it must have seeped into his mind gradually in the year 1515 while preparing lectures on Romans.[26]

Whatever the case, what can be known for sure is that in the years leading up to the theses of 1517, Luther's theology was becoming overtly Christocentric. He was moving away from his training in key ways. He was rejecting Aristotle and much of the scholasticism of his university days. The church's emphasis on Latin was giving way to his own emphasis on the Hebrew and Greek Scriptures. And in his teaching he was focusing more on the practical rather than the theoretical. Luther wanted to liberate people from their guilt. And the church had created myriad mechanisms for helping people to *feel* absolved, but Luther needed more than this. He desired full justification, and he wanted it to be clear in the Bible how justification could be encountered by man. Paul—specifically Paul's letter to the Romans—achieved that purpose for Luther.

Words of Encouragement to Fellow Pastors

Luther was often hostile, even vicious, toward those he disagreed with. His published treatises rarely displayed a gentler side because of Luther's singular focus on advancing his own argument or tearing down the argument of another. In his *Table Talks*, however, Luther does show real pastoral concern. Many people were moved by his ideas, and once the Reformation got going, people came to him for advice. Then, they recorded his words with some precision. Perhaps a look at some of these off-the-cuff remarks will reveal Luther the pastor, priest, and preacher in greater vividness.

Luther knew the burdens of ministry well. On one occasion, he encouraged a fellow pastor named Viet Dietrich with these words: "It takes a strong spirit to serve the people with body and soul, and suffer in return extreme danger and great ingratitude." He then compared the preacher to a carpenter. The tools of a preacher come from God's word, he said, and the preacher must use different tools for a diverse audience, depending on the occasion. He should "comfort for a while, frighten, scold, offer reconciliation, and so on."[27]

Once, in 1532, while describing the qualities of a "good preacher," Luther provided the following outline. Good preachers should

1. Teach well and properly.
2. Have a good head.
3. Be eloquent.
4. Have a good voice.
5. Have a good memory.
6. Know when to stop.
7. Be certain and diligent in one's subject.
8. Put life and limb, possession and honor into the task of preaching.
9. Be willing to accept ridicule from anyone.

He then commented that "even though a preacher may have a hundred good qualities, he spoils it all through one mistake—that's how bad the world is."[28]

On one occasion in 1532, a fellow pastor came to Luther complaining about how difficult and unpleasant it was to preach. The man felt like he never should have become a preacher. Luther encouraged him, saying:

> Be yourself! If you can't preach for an hour long, then preach for half an hour or a quarter. And don't pattern yourself too much after another prominent preacher. You will never quite capture the style and cadence of the language of my sermon or of another. Rather, develop your own sermon; keep it simple and let God take it where it will go. Seek in all simplicity the glory of God and do not follow the examples of other men. Rather, pray that God will give you wisdom and your audience the ability to understand, and let God rule! Believe me, preaching is not a human work. Even though I am an old and experienced preacher, I worry about every sermon.

Luther then advised the pastor to keep his sermons short, saying, "I hate a long sermon." In Luther's mind, when pastors preach long sermons, they "hurt themselves" because the people's desire to listen gets destroyed.[29]

One theme that recurs in Luther's *Table Talks* is that preachers should remain humble. They should not seek affirmation from those in power, but rather should make sure their message is understood clearly even by children. On this topic, in 1537, Luther told another pastor named Bernard:

> Cursed is every preacher who seeks glory in the Church, strives for honors, and out of ambition wants to please this or that person. Whenever I preach around here I step down to the lowest level. I don't stand at the level of the doctors and the masters, of whom scarcely forty are present, but the hundred or thousand young people and children. It is to them I preach, and I adapt to them, and they deserve that too. If the others don't want to listen, well, the door is open. Therefore, my dear Bernard, take care to be simple and direct, don't concern yourself with those who claim to be learned. But be a preacher to unschooled youth and sucklings.[30]

Again, he warned:,

> A preacher must pay careful attention to children, servants, and maids, without a lot of pretense. He should look after them like a nursing mother. She babbles with the child. The nourishment from her breast is not wine nor malt beer, but the simplest and best known drink. And that is the way it should be and they should preach simply.[31]

And again:

> Don't speak to the prince, but to the simple people and the uneducated, which is the type of person the prince may well be. If I directed my sermons to Philip Melanchthon and other doctors, I would accomplish nothing good. I preach very simply to the uneducated, and everyone likes that. I can speak Greek, Hebrew, Latin, and so on, but I save that for our learned assemblies. There we cause such confusion that God is amazed.[32]

Luther was also prone to instruct other preachers to "preach slowly," for the sake of precision and clarity.[33] He added, "To preach simply is a great art. Christ Himself did it. He talked about farm work, mustard seeds, and so on, and used purely simple, farm-type parables."[34]

Luther warned his pastors to stay focused on the topic at hand when they were preaching. Otherwise, they will be like "the maidservant on the way to market. When she meets another maid, she stops to chat with her for a while. Then she meets another and talks with her. She does the same with a third and fourth, and so gets to market late."[35] Luther's advice was that they must not wander with their thoughts, and as a result the sermon would suffer from a lack of cohesion.

Some of the advice Luther gave to ministers was very specific. For example, in 1544, just a couple of years before he died, Luther was asked how to handle a parishioner who was not sure whether he or she had been baptized. What if they were already baptized? Would their soul be harmed by receiving two baptisms? This was a crucial issue at the time because Luther strongly opposed the "Anabaptist" ("baptized again") movement, which advocated believer's baptism (adult baptism). Luther determined that re-baptism would be fine in this case. "In cases where someone doubts whether a person has been baptized, he should simply baptize without any reservation or distinction, as though he had never been baptized."[36]

Not all of Luther's words of wisdom were full of grace and tact, however. In his view, a pastor had to deal severely with certain sins. For example, when Luther was asked how he would handle parishioners who never took communion, he responded, "Let them go to the devil! And when they die, bury them in the knacker's (one who disposes of dead animals) yard."[37]

In one shocking and brutal passage, Luther was asked what to do if, during confession, a woman admitted to strangling her baby. Luther was asked whether he would turn her into the authorities. He responded as follows:

> Absolutely not! For one must make a distinction between the civil government and the Church. It is not me to whom she has confessed, but to Christ; and since Christ keeps it a secret, I must also keep it secret, and simply say, "I have heard nothing!" If Christ heard the confession, He would say the same thing! But

> I would still say to her privately at that time: "You whore, don't you ever do that again!"[38]

Clearly, Luther had a temper. And no one ever accused him of tactfulness. Nevertheless, in spite of what was probably a short temper and an eagerness to express himself, Luther's primary responsibility throughout his entire ministry was to pastor his flock—a flock that was growing exponentially during his lifetime.

To close this chapter, we should highlight one of Luther's most pastoral writings, "A Sermon on Preparing to Die."[39] The sermon has twenty short points, and they are powerful for their simplicity, tenderness, and true piety. After advising the dying person to properly distribute his temporal goods, he urges the following:

> We must cheerfully and sincerely forgive, for God's sake, all those who have offended us. At the same time we must also, for God's sake, earnestly seek the forgiveness of all those whom we undoubtedly have greatly offended by setting a bad example or by bestowing too few words of the kindness demanded by the law of Christian brotherly love. . . . We must turn our eyes to God alone.[40]

> We must earnestly, diligently, and highly esteem the holy sacraments . . .[41]

> Gaze at the heavenly picture of Christ, who descended into hell [1 Peter 3:19] for your sake. . . . Seek yourself only in Christ and not in yourself and you will find yourself in him eternally.[42]

> In the hour of their death, Christians should not worry that they are alone. They can be certain, as the sacraments indicate, that a great many eyes are upon them: first, the eyes of God, and of Christ himself . . . then also the eyes of the dear angels, of the saints, and of all Christians.[43]

This document shows Luther, the priest and pastor, at his best, lovingly encouraging one whose death is near. With dignity, class, and grace, Luther the pastor was able to sit at the bedside of a dying soul, administering the sacrament, guiding the person into death and the life to come. Without doubt, this great man of unwavering conviction would have been a calming and comforting presence during one's final hour.

Notes

[1]Mary Jane Haemig, "Introduction," in *The Annotated Luther,* ed. Mary Jane Haemig, vol. 4: *Pastoral Writings* (Minneapolis: Fortress Press, 2016), 1–2.

[2]Ibid., 2.

[3]Fred Meuser, "Luther as Preacher of the Word of God," in *The Cambridge Companion to Martin Luther*, ed. Donald McKim (Cambridge: Cambridge University Press, 2003), 136.

[4]Haemig, 2.

[5]Heiko Oberman, trans. by Eileen Walliser-Schwarzbart, *Luther* (New Haven: Yale University Press, 1989), 140–141.

[6]"Luther joined a minority that supported Staupitz." See Andrew Pettegree, *Brand Luther* (New York: Penguin, 2015), 35.

[7]Ibid., 142.

[8]"From 1512 on there is no further mention of a union." Roland Bainton, *Here I Stand* (New York: Meridian, 1950), 40.

[9]Oberman, 152.

[10]Pettegree, 35.

[11]Martin Brecht, trans. by James Schaaf, *Martin Luther: His Road to Reformation, 1483–1521,* vol. 1 (Philadelphia, PA: Fortress Press, 1985), 105; and Robert Fife, *The Revolt of Martin Luther* (New York: Columbia University Press, 1957), 178.

[12]Martin Luther, early 1533. From the notebooks of Viet Dietrich. See Charles Daudert, trans., *Off the Record with Martin Luther: An Original Translation of the Table Talks* (Kalamazoo, MI: Hansa-Hewlett, 2009), 211.

[13]Bainton, 45.

[14]E. G. Rupp and Benjamin Drewery, eds., *Martin Luther* (New York: St. Martin's Press, 1970), 7.

[15]See Brecht, vol. 1, 150.

[16]Bernhard Lohse, trans. by Robert Schultz, *Martin Luther* (Philadelphia: Fortress Press, 1980), 29; and Scott Hendrix, *Martin Luther* (New Haven: Yale University Press, 2015), 45.

[17]Brecht, vol. 1, 94.

[18]Ibid., 117.

[19]Hendrix, 56.

[20]James Reston, Jr., *Luther's Fortress* (New York: Basic Books, 2015), 4.

[21]Luther to George Spenlein, in Hendrix, 47.

[22]Luther, in 1531, from the notebooks of Viet Dietrich. See Daudert, 207, 212.

[23]Ibid., 207.

[24]Brecht, vol. 1, 151.

[25]Luther, in Gerhard Brendler, trans. by Claude Foster, Jr., *Martin Luther* (Oxford: Oxford University Press, 1991), 62–63.

[26]Hendrix, 52.

[27]Luther, in 1532, from the notebooks of Viet Dietrich. See Daudert, 209.

[28]From the notebooks of Conrad Cordatus. See Daudert, 218.

[29]Luther, in 1532, from the notebooks of Conrad Cordatus. See Daudert, 218–219.
[30]Luther, in 1537, from the Lauterbach/Weller Collection. See Daudert, 223–224.
[31]Ibid., 224.
[32]Ibid., 225.
[33]Luther, in 1538, from the Notebooks of Anton Lauterbach. See Daudert, 226.
[34]Ibid., 227.
[35]Luther, in 1542, from the Notebooks of Casper Heydenreich. See Daudert, 233–234.
[36]Luther, in 1544, from the Collection of Johannes Aurifaber. See Daudert, 236.
[37]Luther, in 1540, from the Notebooks of Johann Methesius. See Daudert, 230.
[38]Ibid.
[39]Text and commentary in Haemig, 290–305.
[40]Haemig, 290.
[41]Ibid, 291.
[42]Ibid., 296.
[43]Ibid., 302.

9

THE BIG BANG (THE *NINETY-FIVE THESES*)

LUTHER'S *NINETY-FIVE THESES* DEVELOPED IN A SPECIFIC CONTEXT. Without a clear understanding of the context of Roman Catholic Christianity in 1517, and of the particular location of Wittenberg, Germany, they make little sense.

First, in Luther's day, preaching about, selling, and buying indulgences were assumed and common, a normal aspect of church life.[1] Not only did they go on routinely, but they were a fundamental part of church growth and maintenance. Many important building projects were funded by papal indulgences. For example, a bridge over the Elbe River at Torgau—where Luther's wife is buried—was built by the proceeds from an indulgence that gave permission for people to eat butter, milk, and cheese during Lent, as long as they paid the full amount.[2]

To neglect the fact that indulgences were fundraising opportunities for the church would be naïve. Equally naïve, however, would be any attempt of modern historians to rip indulgences out of context, making them appear to be—merely—a corrupt way of building up the banks of Rome and lining the pockets of church officials. There was much more to it than that.

Indulgences were perceived by sixteenth-century Christians as opportunities for them to give to a charitable cause. There was a wide-ranging spectrum here. For example, in the Crusades, plenary indulgences were offered both for those who went to fight as well as for those who supported the wars with financial contributions. Most indulgences, however, were much more modest. Typically, they were small gestures a person could do or a small amount a person could pay to reduce the time they would spend in purgatory after they died. Thus, indulgences were a "win-win." The givers helped the church by supporting it, and in return they received spiritual benefits such as absolution for sin.

Almsgiving has always been a fundamental part of religion. Adherents of all religions have to give to the religion if there is to be any growth. Religious institutions require the goodwill of donors who are willing to give freely to sustain them during the present and to endow them for the future. And while the giving of alms should be first and foremost about helping someone, some truth can be seen in the notion that by building up the institution of the church, communities will benefit collectively. Churches today depend on the free-will offerings of the faithful. Does the giver receive anything in return? Should almsgivers expect anything back? Of course. Almsgiving offers the givers many good returns: 1. Good feelings—that one has obeyed the principles of their own faith requirements. 2. Goodwill—extended to them by others who may have taken notice their good example. 3. Spiritual benefits—virtually all religions uphold the notion that by giving, the religion offers spiritual (even material) returns. 4. Institutional security—giving to one's preferred institution ensures a greater likelihood that the institution's present and future will be more secure.

The particular case of Martin Luther's *Ninety-Five Theses*, however, was not just about indulgences, or about almsgiving. Luther was reacting to the *abuse* of indulgences. The official title of his tract was *Disputation for Clarifying the Power of Indulgences*. In his opposition to the abuse of indulgences, Luther was not alone. For example, in his 1509 essay *The Praise of Folly*, Erasmus assailed the Catholic Church's claim to be able to calculate the time to be spent in purgatory "without the least mistake . . . in years and months, days and hours, minutes and seconds, as if they were in a mathematical table."[3]

Indulgences

Protestants have expunged the idea of indulgences, leaving it so far away from the doctrine and practice of today's church that it is now exceedingly difficult for them to relate to this fundamental Catholic belief. However—and perhaps a bit surprising to Luther's theological descendants—indulgences have never been blotted out by Catholics. While they may have suffered from a lack of emphasis since the reforming decade of the 1960s, they are still very much a part of the Roman Catholic Church. For example, a 2009 *New York Times* article caused a splash in the religious world by announcing that indulgences were making something of a comeback. One bishop was asked why indulgences were returning, and he replied, tersely, "Because there is sin in the world." The article went on to explain that Pope John Paul II authorized bishops to offer indulgences in the year 2000 as the church celebrated its third millennium. Under John Paul's successor—Pope Benedict XVI—the various offers of indulgences "increased markedly."[4]

The word "indulgence" comes from a Latin word meaning "kind or tender." The word evolved to mean "remission of a tax or debt." It evolved further under Roman law to mean "release from captivity or punishment." Over time, it came to signify "the kindness and mercy of God." With this background, in Roman Catholic teaching, "indulgence" came to mean "remission of the temporal punishment due to sin, the guilt of which has been forgiven."[5]

Practically speaking, however, the medieval notion of indulgence meant a person would receive "time off" in purgatory. In other words, when people die, they still have to undergo a purgation period before they are fully cleansed. They have to atone for the sins they committed while in the flesh. Christ's death provided someone the *possibility* to go to heaven, but the vast majority of people had a tremendous accumulation of sin within their soul when they died. Thus, the Roman Catholic Church taught that people would go to purgatory for a period of time known only to church authorities. In purgatory, each person would be "purged" of the sin that prevented him or her from entering God's holy and sinless presence.

The crucial factor in this system is the concept of the church's "treasury of merit." The Catholic Church developed a teaching wherein Jesus and the saints accumulate a vast amount of merit that gets deposited into a "spiritual treasury." Metaphorically, think of a bank or a treasury house. Inside this spiritual bank is a huge amount of good merit. A human being can draw upon that treasury to lessen his or her time in purgatory. The church is the administrator of those "funds." In other words:

> The grantor (pope or bishop) . . . acts in his official capacity as having jurisdiction in the Church, from whose spiritual treasury he draws the means wherewith payment is to be made. The Church herself is not the absolute owner, but simply the administratrix, of the superabundant merits which that treasury contains. In applying them, she keeps in view both the design of God's mercy and the demands of God's justice. She therefore determines the amount of each concession, as well as the conditions which the penitent must fulfill if he would gain the indulgence.[6]

What is critical here is that the church "determines the amount." The church determines the time a person will spend in purgatory and how many years can be removed by an indulgence. There are many different kinds of indulgences: universal, local, perpetual, temporary, certain days, those linked to objects (crucifix, rosary, medal), those granted to a certain class of individuals (members of a monastic order, for example), those granted on behalf of the living, those granted on behalf of the dead, and many more.

A key part of the discussion of indulgences is the important difference between plenary and partial.

> By a plenary indulgence is meant the remission of the entire temporal punishment due to sin so that no further expiation is required in Purgatory. A partial indulgence commutes only a certain portion of the penalty; and this portion is determined in accordance with the penitential discipline of the early Church.

The natural question for a person to ask, then, is, "How much time does a person have to spend in purgatory before he or she is allowed into Heaven?" And, related to that question, is this one: "How much time is remitted by doing this or that indulgence?" It can be explained this way:

> To say that an indulgence of so many days or years is granted means that it cancels an amount of purgatorial punishment equivalent to that which would have been remitted, in the sight of God, by the performance of so many days or years of the ancient canonical penance. Here, evidently, *the reckoning makes no claim to absolute exactness*; it has only a relative value. *God*

alone knows what penalty remains to be paid and what its precise amount is in severity and duration.[7]

It was difficult for medieval Christians to know how to reduce their time in purgatory. They were utterly dependent on the church: 1. Church authorities set the price, based on a "sliding scale of payment depending on one's station in life." 2. Church authorities decided the value of each indulgence. 3. Only the church could grant the remittance.[8] As a result, the individual believer was utterly at the mercy of the church and its complex calculations on these matters.

When a Christian decided to purchase an indulgence, in return he or she received a large document that served as a receipt explaining what the person had just acquired. Indulgence certificates had a space where the name of the buyer could be filled in—to show that, officially, his or her sins were forgiven and their time in purgatory would be substantially reduced, if not canceled altogether.[9] It was the sweetest deal God had ever offered to humans. These official decrees were mass-produced in the fifteenth and sixteenth centuries shortly after Gutenberg's invention of the printing press.

Indulgences are among the earliest printed documents; Gutenberg started printing them himself in 1454.[10] Ironically, Gutenberg's press, so closely associated with the printing of the Bible and the spread of Protestant ideas, was used much earlier, and more prolifically, by the Roman Catholic Church to print indulgences. And the church profited splendidly: "In Germany the indulgence business boomed. Between 1486 and 1503 three campaigns led by the papal legate Peraudi raised over half a million guilders for a crusade against the Turks."[11]

A Protestant will ask, of course, "Where in the Bible does this come from?" It is important to recognize that this is a very Protestant question. This is the kind of question Luther asked, and Protestants inherited this suspicious line of inquiry. However, a Catholic—especially a Catholic in the sixteenth century—probably would not have asked the church to prove its point by showing book, chapter, and verse in the Bible. The church had been around for a long time, and through councils, laws, theologians, teachings, and traditions, it developed its own inner logic. In other words, just because something was not *explicitly* mentioned in the Bible did not mean it should be forbidden.

However, the Roman Catholic Church does (and did) have an answer for the Protestant who wants a Bible reference. The answer is found in the papal insignia: the crossed keys. The crossed keys insignia is still the official symbol of the Roman Catholic Church, emblazoned on the national flag of the Holy See (Vatican City). Why crossed keys? The answer is found in a passage in Matthew 16:18–19, where Jesus tells Peter, "You are Peter, and on this rock I will build my church, and the gates of Hades will not overcome it. I will give you the keys of the kingdom of heaven; whatever you bind on earth will be bound in heaven, and whatever you loose on earth will be loosed in heaven." Thus, the "Power of the Keys," or the "binding and loosing" powers of the church, permit it to lengthen or reduce the amount of time a person must spend in purgatory. This entire system is also built on the assumption that popes are the successors to the apostle Peter.

Luther's Context

Beginning in 1476—just a few decades before Luther's theses—Pope Sixtus IV started something new. He began allowing indulgences to apply to souls already suffering in purgatory. In other words, when a person died, they were still part of this complex system. Their loved ones could perform prayers, make a donation, or secure the giving of Masses for their departed relatives. It was considered an act of kindness for a living person to reach out to a departed soul like this, because the departed could no longer take pilgrimages or visit relics or do whatever he or she needed to do to reduce his or her own purgatorial sentence. Luther himself had these ideas in mind when he went to Rome in 1510. He had wanted to tap into the church's great treasury of merit to reduce the time in purgatory for his grandfather.

In the centuries prior to Luther, the system of indulgences became extremely complex—and lucrative. The first known plenary indulgence occurred alongside the First Crusade in 1095 when Pope Urban II offered "the remission of all ones' temporal punishment for all sins committed up until the time the indulgence was received."[12] This move was to encourage soldiers to fight to win back the Holy Land from Muslim control. Over the centuries, the plenary indulgence became more common. While the plenary indulgence was typically associated with protecting or traveling to the holiest sites in Christendom, it eventually became standard belief that if a person financially supported a pilgrim or a soldier, then the contributor would experience the benefits of the plenary indulgence as well.

In 1506, Pope Julius II authorized the rebuilding of Saint Peter's Basilica in Rome. It was to be a most sumptuous facility—five centuries later still the largest in the world—and thus required hefty funding. To finance its construction, Julius II offered an extremely attractive indulgence: "the forgiveness of future sins and the release of loved ones from purgatory." This offer did not apply to Germans at first. But, in 1515, Pope Leo X made the extension so Germans would be able to contribute to the building fund and enjoy the benefits of such a generous indulgence.[13]

Here's where things got a little suspicious. When Leo X extended this plenary "Peter's Indulgence" to Germans, two matters needed to be addressed. First was the obvious need to fund the grandiose basilica in Rome. The German indulgence market opened up entirely new horizons for fundraising. But the second matter was perhaps a little less noble: Germany's highest-ranking clergyman was swimming in debt incurred by purchasing his position from the Roman curia—the pope's inner circle.[14] This young clergyman, in his late twenties at the time, was Archbishop Albert of Brandenburg. He had borrowed money from the Fuggers—an extremely wealthy banking family in Augsburg—and was able to use the indulgences to pay down his debt. So Albert's motives may have been mixed. A charitable perspective is that by paying back his debt to the Fuggers, he may have considered himself to be supporting the church in an indirect way.

Regardless of Albert's motives, whenever people bought indulgences, they were, in effect, accomplishing three goals at the same time: 1. They were helping their own spiritual status or that of the person they designated. 2. They were contributing to the construction of Saint Peter's Basilica. 3. They were paying down their archbishop's enormous debt. Indeed, half of their indulgence payment went to the Fuggers and half went to the church. For obvious reasons, the ordinary laypeople were not in the know about the debt owed by their archbishop. In their minds, this was simply a spiritual opportunity extended to them by the pope. In addition, it is important to point out that, initially, not even Luther knew of the agreement that half of all indulgence income was to go to the Fuggers, while only half would go to Rome. "At the time of writing the *Ninety-Five Theses*, Luther knew nothing of such backroom dealings. His concerns . . . were purely theological and pastoral."[15]

To teach about Martin Luther is almost impossible without mentioning the chief church fundraiser in Germany at the time, John Tetzel (1465–1519). Luther deeply resented this man's work. In Luther's eyes, Tetzel was opportunistic and theologically deplorable. A bit unfortunate, perhaps, is the fact that Tetzel is forever and indelibly linked to the jingle he used to raise funds for the church: "When the coin in the coffer rings, the soul from purgatory springs." Many versions of the jingle have survived, but essentially it was an invitation for people to buy their relatives, or themselves upon their own death, out of purgatory for the right price.

Due to Protestant lore, John Tetzel has come to be known chiefly for his corruption. The truth is, however, that he was doing something widely accepted in his time, and he deserves to be understood in that larger context. Tetzel was a Dominican friar from Saxony. He was also the official inquisitor for Saxony, tasked with enforcing the Roman Inquisition—the elimination of heretics and their papally damned ideas.[16] He was handpicked by Archbishop Albert to serve as the "indulgence commissioner" in the fundraising campaign. Well-educated, Tetzel became involved in the indulgence-selling business in 1508.[17] As his success and reputation grew, he put together a team of functionaries who would craft indulgence letters and travel all around Germany to sell them.[18]

Tetzel was a master salesman, and he knew how to capture the attention of the uneducated masses by appealing to their emotions. Armed with those magnificently powerful certificates of indulgence, Tetzel made preposterous claims, such as, ". . . if a person had raped the Virgin Mary, they would be assured complete remission from Purgatory."[19] His claims for the power of indulgences were hyperbolic to the point of absurdity, but he had the full backing of the church, and that was crucial to his reckless self-confidence. What was also crucial to the situation, however, was that the church had exhausted much of its wealth fighting the Turks between 1486 and 1503. Thus, the stakes were raised. The church had to make bigger and better offers in comparison with the ones given during the four centuries of crusading. Though Tetzel's promises sound fantastic and bizarre today, they were considered a bargain in 1517. To commoners who worked the fields for a living and worried about their afterlife, a plenary indulgence was worth the cost—virtually any price was a reasonable one. In modern parlance, Tetzel held all the cards.

Pomp and circumstance accompanied Tetzel as he brought these highly prized certificates into a town before the selling began. Important governors and church officials met him at the city gate. They escorted him in a procession to the town's main church. The papal coat of arms and the papal bull decreeing this indulgence were displayed prominently for all to see. The organs played music and the bells in the tower welcomed the procession, making very clear the importance of what was happening. Full attention was given to Tetzel as he laid out the offer from the church in great detail, but his message was simplified for the masses in that now-immortalized ringing coffer ditty forever linked to Tetzel's name.[20]

Important to the story is this: Frederick the Wise was also profiting handsomely from the selling of indulgences through his massive collection of relics. So he banned Tetzel from electoral Saxony. Put more crassly, "He also feared the drain of gold from his lands." In response, Tetzel set up shop just around the edges of Frederick's borders: in Eisleben (where Luther was born), Halle, Zerbst, and Jüterbog. Frederick and Luther saw this as a highly provocative act, an effrontery. Wittenbergers, however, simply wanted their time in purgatory reduced. So they made the journey—usually a day or two—to purchase the free pass to heaven for themselves or for someone they cared for. Naturally, Wittenbergers who made the purchase came back home showcasing their new certificates of indulgence.[21]

Luther heard about Tetzel's campaign in the spring of 1516 while he was traveling on business. He was visiting other Augustinian houses when he ran into his old mentor, Staupitz. Both of them were outraged, but Luther particularly so. He remarked, "I'll put a hole in that drum." Several months later, after returning to Wittenberg, Luther preached a series of sermons on true repentance, how it required a changing of the heart, not simply a monetary transaction as Tetzel was proclaiming.[22]

Throughout the spring of 1517, as the coins jingled into Tetzel's coffers, Luther continued to rail against indulgences. He also launched into a serious study of the entire concept of indulgences, using a method of research he learned in his student days: *ad fontes*—going "back to the sources." This method of research is taken for granted today in historical studies. It assumes that the earliest, most primary sources are the most reliable. Thus, after surveying church history, canon law, the church fathers, the Bible, and more, Luther concluded that "the pope had authority to grant indulgences but could offer them *only* for ecclesiastical punishment established in canon law, which had nothing to do with divine punishment."[23] The preaching of indulgences had to be stopped. Not only were the preachers mistaken in their theology, but the entire operation had become "purely a scheme for making money."[24] And Luther was willing to go to battle over this issue, even publicly if he had to.

Was It a Nail or the Mail?

Anyone who visits Wittenberg today can easily locate the place where Luther supposedly nailed the theses onto the door of the Castle Church. But church historians love to debate the details of that epochal event. Was it a nail or mail? In other words, did Luther actually nail his theses to the door? Or did he simply send letters to people, and the myth became unstoppable? Luther never mentioned nailing the theses to the door, but the evidence is strongly in favor of his having done so. Historian Scott Hendrix cites the best sources we have on the matter.

> Evidence for a posting is found on a handwritten note, which was rediscovered in 2007 and was originally written between 1541 and 1544 by Luther's secretary, George Rörer. It says outright that on October 31, 1517, Luther posted theses concerning indulgences on the doors of the churches in Wittenberg. It is also possible that a 1517 posting of the theses was witnessed by fifteen-year-old George Major, who years later became a theology professor in Wittenberg and mentioned the posting in a letter he wrote in 1553.[25]

In addition, Luther's right-hand man in Wittenberg, Philip Melanchthon, writing years later, assumed the traditional account. The only problem here is that Melanchthon did not arrive in Wittenberg until 1518, so he was not an eyewitness. What is undoubtable is that disputations were routinely posted on the Castle Church door. In fact, "records kept by the deans of the theology faculty from the university's founding in 1502" show that it was standard protocol for people to make postings in this way. Postings occurred on all the church doors of the city, which leaves little room for doubt that they would have been posted on the Castle Church doors, which "functioned as a kind of University of Wittenberg bulletin board."[26]

With accumulated evidence this compelling, little reason is left to doubt that the theses were nailed to the Castle Church doors. Even so, historians are a critical and suspicious bunch. And since the discovery of the rather convincing proof in 2007, they now like to ask whether Luther may have nailed the theses or *glued* them to the door of the church![27] In the spirit of Luther, many scholars today are ever-eager to participate in a hearty dispute.

We do know that Luther sent some letters when his theses were published. He mailed a letter to Archbishop Albert dated October 31, 1517, the day of the posting. It was a bold move for Luther to make since Albert was the one who commissioned Tetzel to do the preaching he was doing. In addition, the indulgences were issued in Albert's name; indeed, "Albertus" was the first word on the certificates! Thus, Luther's letter was a warning to the young archbishop that the unbridled and unorthodox preaching of indulgences was spiritually dangerous for his own soul as well as the souls of the people. Luther respectfully exhorted Albert to adopt "a different kind of preaching." He advised him to authorize only "the gospel that Jesus actually commanded to be preached."[28] Attached to the letter was a copy of the *Ninety-Five Theses*. That very letter, written in Luther's own hand, is preserved in the royal archives in Stockholm, Sweden.[29]

While the posting of the theses on the church doors is more celebrated, the greater impact happened through the mail. Luther's superiors took notice of this thirty-three-year-old monk who had the audacity to correct them. Luther was not at all famous at this point. He was a preacher, a bright professor, and a trusted administrator in the Augustinian order. Church leaders could never have guessed that those *Ninety-Five Theses* would shake the foundations of Western civilization, split the Roman Catholic Church, and set into motion the process of European secularization.[30]

Unmistakably, the Protestant Reformation began with this one text. In just two months, the *Ninety-Five Theses* were celebrated, defamed, and debated all over Germany. Almost immediately, it was obvious to all how high the stakes were. Historian Lyndal Roper describes it graphically.

> Luther was implicitly striking at the heart of the papal Church, and its entire financial and social edifice, which worked on a

> system of collective salvation that allowed people to pray for others and so reduce their time in Purgatory. It financed a whole clerical proletariat of priests paid to recite anniversary Masses for the souls of the deceased. It paid for pious laywomen in poorhouses who said prayers for the souls of the dead, to ease their path through Purgatory. It paid for brotherhoods that prayed for their members, said Masses, undertook processions and financed special altars. In short, the system structured the religious and social lives of most medieval Christians. At its center was the Pope who was the steward of a treasure of "merits"—grace which could be disbursed to others. Attacking indulgences, therefore, would sooner or later lead to a questioning of papal power.[31]

A lot was at stake here. If Luther succeeded in his bid to eradicate the use of indulgences as the primary means of fundraising in the church, then the entire institution of the church could collapse like a house of cards.

Luther's desired disputation took place, but not at all in the way he envisioned. He was now in the big leagues. Albert sent Luther's theses to certain theologians for their reaction. They advised that the matter should be taken up by Rome. A papal investigation was sure to arise out of this, and Luther would surely be found guilty of heresy. What might happen after that was anyone's guess. Would he burn at the stake? Would he recant? Would they imprison him? Would the inquisitors get hold of him?

The *Ninety-Five Theses*

On October 31, 1517, the eve of All Saints Day, Luther went public with his *Ninety-Five Theses*. The document was an open invitation to a disputation about indulgences. Luther began the document with the following words:

> Out of love and zeal for bringing the truth to light, what is written below will be debated in Wittenberg with the Reverend Father Martin Luther, Master of Arts of Sacred Theology . . . presiding. Therefore, he requests that those who cannot be present to discuss orally with us will in their absence do so by letter.

The formal, local debate Luther was seeking never happened, but in a very short time all of Europe was involved.

Theses 1–4. The first two theses get to the heart of Luther's intentions. He thought Christians should live an "entire life" of repentance, rather than merely going through the routine of "confession and satisfaction as administered by the clergy." These theses also transport us to the mind of a late-medieval monastic, as Luther refers to "mortifications of the flesh" and "hatred of self" in favorable terms.[32]

Theses 5–13. Here Luther begins to discuss the pope. He also draws a sharp distinction between the church's authority and God's authority. His point is that the church has authority over a Christian until a person's death, but not after. Luther's tone is quite respectful. Luther was angry at Tetzel and the abuse of indulgences. At this stage, he was not opposed to the entire concept of indulgences, nor was he opposed to the pope. He was a faithful monk, a son of the church, and a theologian. And, in his judgment, these fundraisers were preaching heresy when they offered time off in purgatory for a fee.

Theses 14–24. This section reveals Luther's then-steadfast belief in purgatory. He speculates on a variety of matters regarding purgatory. His central point here is found in thesis 21: "Those indulgence preachers err who say that through the pope's indulgences a person is released and saved from every penalty." Luther stated that the people were being "deceived" by these "indiscriminate and high-sounding" promises offered by Tetzel and his crew.

Theses 25–34. Here Luther began to show cracks in his once-high view of the papacy. These theses must be carefully considered because they show Luther was starting to doubt the papal "power of the keys." He also took a potshot at Tetzel, especially at that jingle Luther could not get out of his head. Thesis 32 is probably the strongest of the 95. Luther wrote, "Those who believe that they can be secure in their salvation through indulgence letters will be eternally damned along with their teachers." Those were strong words that would come back to haunt Luther. They were extremely self-confident words. Was Luther damning to hell the indulgence preachers and the institution of the church that approved them? A bookish monk in a remote town in Germany held no such authority.

Theses 35–47. Luther wrote that indulgences must be "preached with caution" (thesis 41), especially when they conveyed the idea that true, inner repentance was unnecessary. This went to the heart of the theses. In Luther's estimation, Tetzel was teaching that true remorse was not necessary for the indulgence transaction to work. What was most important was paying the fee and receiving the certificate. When the monetary transaction occurred, the individual—whether on Earth or in heaven—received time off in purgatory. Typical of Luther, he got blunt here, arguing that money spent on indulgences was money "squandered" (thesis 46).

Theses 48–66. Luther was no antagonist of the pope at this stage. Thesis 50 made that clear when he said that if the pope knew what was happening in Germany—that indulgences were being sold to finance the construction of Saint Peter's Basilica—he would be outraged. In thesis 53, we see evidence of Luther's emerging *sola Scriptura* teaching. He argued that when preachers spent more time on indulgences than on the word of God, they had become "enemies of Christ and the pope." In theses 56 and 57, Luther critiqued the concept of the "treasury of merit" on which the entire indulgence idea rested. In an almost jocular wording, Luther said the fundamental problem with the treasury of merit was that it did "not so much freely distribute such riches as only collect them." He continued with this sarcastic tone in thesis 66: "The treasures of indulgences are nets with which they now fish for the wealth of men."

Theses 67–80. In this section, Luther assailed the "insanity" (thesis 75) of some of Tetzel's claims. It is shocking to read some of Tetzel's promises; Luther lambasted them in theses 75–79. Tetzel preached that not even Saint Peter himself could make greater offers than Tetzel's indulgences. He preached that the papal coat-of-arms—set up prominently when Tetzel sold indulgences—was "of equal worth to the cross of Christ." Luther said in thesis 80 that someone would have to answer for these blasphemies.

Theses 81–91. In this section, Luther did something brilliant. He criticized the pope, but in an indirect way so that he could not be condemned for insubordination or worse. He began this section by saying that "the laity" might slander the pope in various ways if the pope does not put a stop to the indulgence preachers. He then offered a slew of hypothetical accusations that the laity *perhaps might* make, when all along it was precisely Luther who was making them. This shows Luther's ambivalence. As a member of the clergy, he was sworn to protect the dignity of the pope. But as a committed disciple of Jesus, he was incensed at the indulgence scandal by its offering of false hope. Here, Luther asked why the pope didn't just empty purgatory and send everybody to heaven if indeed he had power over the afterlife. He then asked why the pope didn't just build Saint Peter's with his own great wealth, rather than relying on the poor to do it for him. Luther shows a deep contempt here for how the love of money had crept into the church in such reprehensible ways.

Theses 92–95. Luther concluded in a rather surprising way. He argued that Christians must be prepared to follow Christ "through penalties, death, and hell." He then quoted Acts 14:22, "We must go through many hardships to enter the kingdom of God." In other words, Tetzel's promises were false. The only way to work one's way into heaven was to do it the old-fashioned way: die, descend into hell as Jesus did (Acts 2:31, as echoed in the Apostles' Creed), suffer through whatever penalties God deems appropriate, become purged of all unrighteousness, and finally enter heaven.

When Luther wrote the *Ninety-Five Theses* in 1517, he still believed in purgatory. His views evolved over time, however. In 1521, he wrote the following:

> The existence of a purgatory I have never denied. I still hold that it exists, as I have written and admitted many times, though I have found no way of proving it incontrovertibly from Scripture or reason. I find in Scripture that Christ, Abraham, Jacob, Moses, Job, David, Hezekiah, and some others tasted hell in this life. This I think was purgatory, and it seems not beyond belief that some of the dead suffer in like manner. . . . In short, I myself have come to the conclusion that there is a purgatory, but I cannot force anybody else to come to the same result.[33]

By 1530, however, Luther had completely and explicitly rejected purgatory. In his work *Disavowal of Purgatory* (or, *Revocation of Purgatory*), he argued that the chief passage for the doctrine of purgatory came from 2 Maccabees 12:43–46. That book is an apocryphal Old Testament work, he reasoned, and thus cannot be considered binding. Other passages frequently cited for establishing purgatory "were improperly interpreted in an allegorical fashion," which Luther rejected. In Luther's mind, "Anyone who died in the Lord was with God." His opponents charged that Luther was in the wrong, since the church fathers often taught purgatory. Luther argued the church fathers were in no way immune from error. They erred often and disagreed with each other. Luther had come to the point that he saw purgatory as aiding and abetting all sorts of atrocities in the church that were nothing but money-making schemes. These people had substituted God with mammon.[34]

Luther never intended for the *Ninety-Five Theses* to become a national, indeed a civilizational, conversation. To one of his friends, he explained that they were written for a small circle of people. But Luther's little writing on indulgences, and his reputation, would soon explode into reforms, revolts, wars, and conflict on a scale that Europe had never seen before and would not see again until the two World Wars of the twentieth century. How did "an unknown German professor in an intellectual backwater" touch such a nerve?[35]

To that story we now turn.

Notes

[1]James Kittelson, *Luther the Reformer* (Minneapolis: Fortress Press, 1986), 101.

[2]Robert Fife, *The Revolt of Martin Luther* (New York: Columbia University Press, 1957), 249–250.

[3]Scott Hendrix, *Martin Luther* (New Haven: Yale University Press, 2015), 59.

[4]Paul Vitello, "For Catholics, a Door to Absolution is Reopened," in *New York Times*, 9 February 2009, located at: http://www.nytimes.com/2009/02/10/nyregion /10indulgence.html?_r=0.

[5]W. H. Kent, "Indulgences," in *The Catholic Encyclopedia* (New York: The Encyclopedia Press, 1910), 783.

[6]Ibid. Italics mine.

[7]Ibid., 783–784. Italics mine.

[8]Timothy Wengert, ed., *The Annotated Luther*, vol. 1 (Minneapolis: Fortress Press, 2015), 18.

[9]Lyndal Roper, *Martin Luther: Renegade and Prophet* (London: Bodley Head, 2016), 4.

[10]The earliest date of issue for printed indulgences is October 22, 1454. See "The two Mainz indulgences of 1454 and 1455," The University of Manchester, The John Rylands University Library, located at: http://www.library.manchester.ac.uk/firstimpressions /assets/downloads/01-The-two-Mainz-indulgences-of-1454-and-1455.pdf.

[11]Hendrix, 57.

[12]Wengert, 16.

[13]Hendrix, 56.

[14]Ibid., 58.

[15]Wengert, 17–18. See also Hendrix, 56.

[16]Roper, 111.

[17]Ibid., 30.

[18]See Wengert, 18.

[19]Roper, 3.

[20]This account, based on "contemporary accounts and pictures," comes from Wengert, 18.

[21]Ibid., 19–20.

[22]Hendrix, 58.

[23]Wengert, 22–23. Italics are his.

[24]Martin Brecht, trans. by James Schaff, *Martin Luther*, vol. 1 (Philadelphia: Fortress Press, 1985), 188.

[25]Hendrix, 61.

[26]Wengert, 23.

[27]Roper, 1.

[28]Hendrix, 60.

[29]Wengert, 22.

[30]See Roper, 2.

[31]Ibid., 4.

[32]Wengert, 34–35. The translation Wengert uses is based on Charles Jacobs, was revised by Harold Grimm, and is found in *Luther's Works, American Edition*, vol. 31 (Philadelphia, PA: Muhlenberg Press, 1957), 17–33.

[33]Luther, "Defense and Explanation of All the Articles," in *Luther's Works, American Edition*, vol. 32, 95.

[34]See Martin Brecht, trans. by James Schaff, *Martin Luther,* vol. 2 (Minneapolis: Fortress Press, 1990), 397–398.

[35]Roper, 96.

10

A Gathering Storm

THE *NINETY-FIVE THESES* SPREAD QUICKLY. THIS SURPRISING DEVELopment was due to the advances that had been made in the six or seven decades since Gutenberg's technological breakthrough of a printing press with moveable type. It caught everyone off guard, especially Luther, although he was not fully aware of the extraordinary spread of the theses until around February 1518. Nevertheless, in just three months, the church hierarchy came to fully appreciate the threat this document posed. By the end of 1517, the theses had already been printed in Nuremberg, Leipzig, and Basel.[1] Interestingly, Luther "never received a penny of the yield."[2] No contract was involved. In this dawn of modern printing, Luther's famous publication profited presses, but not him. His interest was in bringing people to his cause.

Initial Reactions to the *Ninety-Five Theses*

Although Protestant lore allows no room for Luther's self-doubts and fears, Luther must have had misgivings about the uproar he had caused, as well as concerns about his own safety. Not only did no one come forward to accept his invitation for a debate, but his friends and colleagues either remained silent or expressed skepticism about what he had just done. Luther sent a copy to his good friend John Lang in Erfurt, from whom he sought feedback on the theses.[3] Luther's close colleague Andreas Karlstadt outright opposed the theses. A friend in Nuremberg, Christoph Scheurl, expressed regret: "I have certain doubts about them myself, and should have spoken differently and more distinctly, had I known what was going to happen."[4] Luther's own Augustinian monastery became deeply anxious about his brazen defiance of the church.[5]

Years later, Luther remarked that after posting the *Ninety-Five Theses*, he felt like he was all alone for three long years. No one came to his defense. He said he felt "abandoned." Before long, Luther became bitter, which may have served his cause by emboldening him even more. When his Augustinian prior and sub-prior expressed their concerns, Luther relied on a promise from Scripture: "If this work is not from God, it will soon come to an end. But if it is from God, you will not be able to stop it. You will only find yourselves fighting against God" (Acts 5:39).[6]

The *Ninety-Five Theses* spread quickly through the Roman Catholic food chain. Luther sent copies to his superiors, Archbishop Albert and Bishop Jerome of Brandenburg. Bishop Jerome advised Luther to let it go, since he was openly challenging the power of the church. Reflecting later, Luther surmised that the devil was speaking through the bishop. Archbishop Albert did not reply to Luther, although it was not out of neglect. He viewed the matter as extremely urgent. Immediately, he sought the opinion of advisors, theologians, and jurists. And he signaled how serious the matter was seen by reaching out directly to Pope Leo X. The pope ordered Luther's Augustinian superior, Gabriel Venetus, to quieten this troublesome monk in Germany.[7]

In 1517, grave consequences could follow when the church cast suspicion on a person's beliefs. John Tetzel knew this, and almost immediately upon learning of Luther's well-publicized views, he retorted: "In three weeks I shall have this heretic thrown to the flames." Tetzel had the strong support of the Dominican order, and this did not help Luther's cause because Dominicans and Augustinians had many years of bad blood between them. For the Dominicans, Luther's public stand against one of their own—one of their most recognized leaders—would have been offensive. Initially, some people viewed the entire affair as a "squabble between monks." The Dominicans were said to be "jumping for joy" because, potentially, the entire Augustinian order would be publicly shamed by the fiasco in Wittenberg.[8]

All the individuals who held the theses in their hands realized this was no ordinary document. So they passed them on to others, or translated them, or wrote reactions to them. One thing was certain: it could not be ignored. Written from a fiery monk in small-town Germany, the *Ninety-Five Theses* quickly ignited a wildfire; Luther even wrote that he believed God's angels were on his side "fanning the flames."[9] In another place, he said he felt "as though the angels themselves were the messengers carrying the news to all peoples."[10]

Luther's goal in writing the *Ninety-Five Theses* can easily be forgotten. Clearly, his intention was that they might lead to a public debate on the topic of indulgences, and, hopefully, arouse a conversation among his colleagues, and perhaps even among students. Public disputations were common. They were the backbone of the European university curriculum during Luther's time. They were deeply etched into the psyche of professors and students. Luther's invitation should have led to a normal, fairly predictable sequence of events: certain people would step forward in agreement or disagreement. One side would question the theological premise of the indulgences being sold in towns nearby. The other side would defend the practice as being anchored in church history as well as in the Bible. This all should have come to nothing. Two positions should have been discussed in a small university town with various people chiming in. Perhaps it would lead to another public dispute or two. Maybe some students would get worked up and make some noise in the university. Indeed, "the theses stood a good chance of being forgotten as most other such propositions for debate have been."[11]

But what happened—and the rapidity and scale at which it happened—was utterly unforeseen. Luther could not have imagined this situation exploding like it did within only a few weeks of the document being written.

By the next spring, Luther was hard at work trying to explain himself in print. What is crucial here is that now he felt the need to expand this debate to the largest possible audience. This was why he made the calculated decision to start writing for Germany's laypeople who were unacquainted with academic Latin—the original language of the *Ninety-Five Theses*. Thus, Luther wrote two important documents in 1518 to unpack his ideas for both lay and academic audiences. For the common German layperson. he wrote

Sermon on Indulgences and Grace in the local vernacular. The other work, *Explanations of the Ninety-Five Theses*, written in Latin, was meant to unveil his theological justifications for having taken such a public stance against the sale of indulgences.[12]

The work that deserves more attention here is the *Sermon on Indulgences and Grace*. It is a straightforward summary of Luther's concerns about indulgences, and it was an absolute success. The popularity of the *Sermon* "far surpassed" that of the *Ninety-Five Theses*. "This tract more than any other catapulted Luther into the public eye and made him a bestseller overnight." Luther's intentions were easily summarized in the sixteenth (out of twenty) point: "My will, desire, plea, and counsel are that no one buy an indulgence. Let the lazy and sleepy Christians buy indulgences. You run from them." Importantly, Luther did not outright condemn indulgences in this sermon. He said they were technically "permitted and allowed." However, his caution was that if people wanted to give money for the construction of Saint Peter's, they might do so, but they should not expect an indulgence for it, for God's mercy cannot be purchased with money. Luther's deep suspicion of Tetzel was on full display in this sermon: "Avoid . . . those who search for your soul in a moneybag. And when they find a penny in the purse, it is dearer to them than any soul whatsoever."[13]

While Luther claimed that he felt extremely isolated after publication of his theses, the truth is that he had defenders from early on, even well outside his sphere of influence in Wittenberg. Albrecht Dürer, perhaps Germany's greatest artist, sent wood carvings and etchings to Luther as gifts of gratitude for authoring the theses.[14] One bishop, in Merseburg, wanted Luther's *Ninety-Five Theses* to be posted everywhere. Others quietly agreed with Luther, but knew that embracing his critiques and positions too brazenly could cast suspicion on their own beliefs.

The Heidelberg Disputation

In April 1518, Luther traveled 250 miles to speak to an academic audience in the university city of Heidelberg. There were valid concerns about his safety, but Elector Frederick the Wise provided a letter guaranteeing safe passage, specifying that Luther must not be handed over to church authorities. Furthermore, Luther's old mentor—Staupitz—was the provincial vicar and would do everything in his power to protect his former protégé, even if he disagreed with Luther's outspoken approach.[15]

The immediate reason for meeting in Heidelberg was because it was the triennial gathering of the Augustinian monastic order. Luther already was slotted to speak at the convention, even before the events that had propelled him to become the most famous monk in Germany. After all, he was a high-ranking member of the order, serving as a district vicar. His lecture was to be a disputation-style defense of Saint Augustine's theology. Nobody doubted Luther's ability to provide a good lecture, especially on a topic he was so passionate about. An air of excitement lit up the venue, however, because everyone expected him to address the recent events, especially his take on the indulgence controversy that he ignited. He did not take the bait, however. Rather, he did not even mention indulgences in his twenty-eight theological and twelve philosophical theses he had prepared for the occasion. Luther saw this as a chance to win his brothers over to his very Augustinian theology rather than his specific views on indulgences. Luther chose to go deeper instead of simply reiterating his misgivings on indulgences. He wanted to undercut the entire system that gave rise to something so wrongheaded.[16]

The Heidelberg Disputation became a turning point in Luther's life, and some see it as a "paradigm shift" in the movement that would become the Protestant Reformation.[17] Many prominent people heard Luther's lecture there, and they were impressed. He was fully prepared for the occasion, wowing the audience not only by the clarity with which he presented his material, but by the content itself. Many of Luther's emerging ideas—ideas that would ultimately become key Reformation ideas—were unveiled at this gathering: his "theology of the cross," his rejection of free will, the righteousness of faith in Christ, and the impotence of human beings to achieve their own salvation. He overtly embraced Paul and Augustine and continued his fierce condemnation of Aristotle.[18] Luther's thoughts at Heidelberg were "far more accomplished" than his previous work.[19] His potential for greatness was grasped by his audience that day in a way not previously seen.

Martin Bucer, a young and talented Dominican theologian, was in the audience that day. Eventually, Bucer became one of the most important Protestant reformers, and the Heidelberg Disputation was the turning point for him. After listening intently to Luther, Bucer sent a letter to a friend. That letter sheds remarkable insight on how Luther's performance was received.

> Although our chief men refuted him with all their might, their wiles were not able to make him move an inch from his propositions. His sweetness in answering is remarkable, his patience in listening is incomparable, in his explanations you will recognize the acumen of Paul, not of Scotus; his answers, so brief, were drawn from Holy Scriptures, easily made all his hearers his admirers.[20]

Bucer also compared Luther to the famous scholar Erasmus—then in his prime—although in his estimation Luther was a much clearer thinker and communicator.[21]

Interestingly, two of Luther's former professors were in the audience that day: Bernhard von Usingen and Jodokus Trutfetter. They were unimpressed. Indeed, they were "revolted to death" by his views. Acrimony was developing between Luther and his former teachers. Luther knew they despised his ideas, but that did not hinder him from arguing with them in person and writing letters to them to try to change their minds. Luther became "ruthless" in his dealings with them after this falling out. When Trutfetter was nearing death, Luther showed no mercy on the man because of his illness; rather, he explained in a letter that not even Trutfetter's respected and authoritative status over Luther—that of a former teacher—could deter him. In one historian's view, "This was the darker side of Luther's personality."[22]

Luther's disputation at Heidelberg was a resounding success, "a triumph in nearly every imaginable way." On his way back to Wittenberg, some attendees gladly gave him a ride in their wagon, whereas Luther had walked to get there.[23] Instantly, he had become a rising star in the theological constellation. To say that the Heidelberg Disputation changed the lives of some of the people in the audience that day would be no overstatement. They would soon find themselves on Luther's side in a theological game of chess that was to last for generations.

Rising Tide of Opposition

When Luther got back to Wittenberg in late May or June of 1518, he quickly began a serious round of intellectual sparring with John Eck, one of the leading theologians in Germany.[24] Luther and Eck had been friends, but when Eck wrote a text called *Obelisks*, Luther felt betrayed. *Obelisks* was a harsh rebuttal of the *Ninety-Five Theses*. Luther was caught off guard by this work because he assumed Eck was in agreement with most of what he had been saying and writing. He could not have been more wrong. Eck's stinging critique left Luther no option but to fight back, viciously. Luther promptly accused Eck of "acting like an irritated prostitute, who 'vomits up exactly the kind of curses and oaths that you have inflicted on me.'"[25] The tension between Eck and Luther rose steadily, and they would have it out a year later during a famous debate at Leipzig.

Before long, others were joining in. Luther was now fair game for heretic hunters. "Theologians loyal to Rome were lining up against Luther and preparing an official charge." Quite predictably, the slick indulgence salesman Tetzel got in on the action. He viewed Luther as a gadfly who needed to be silenced, by any means, even by a heretic bonfire.[26] In response to the theses, Tetzel penned two "forgettable" treatises against Luther's core ideas.[27] Unbelievably, when eight hundred copies of Tetzel's counter-theses went up for sale in Wittenberg, Luther's students "ripped the theses from the book merchant, turned his cart over, and burned the books."[28] This action—unauthorized by anybody—deeply concerned Luther, making him realize, perhaps for the first time, that the entire ordeal was spiraling out of his control.

Tetzel's fury was a serious matter because of his official position as inquisitor for Saxony. Luther tried to inform the people close to him that he had nothing to do with the burning of Tetzel's works, but the rumor mushroomed: Luther and his followers were rebels. They were careless and obstinate, willing to publicly burn texts written by recognized religious officials. This was scandalous.

Luther waffled between obeisance and defiance. On one hand, Luther could write a letter to Pope Leo X stating his innocence. He was simply a theologian who wanted to debate important issues. "Prostrate at your feet, I offer you all that I am and have. Whatever you decide, I will treat your voice as the voice of Christ speaking and presiding in you."[29] On the other hand, Luther could be openly rebellious and provocative. With sarcastic humor, he dismissed his detractors as unsophisticated and amateurish, "like a sow pushes about a sack of grain."[30] With impunity, he dismissed Tetzel's critiques as "an unparalleled example of ignorance." One thing was certain: Luther's writings were being reprinted with great frequency due to popular demand. Indeed, Luther's rebuttal to Tetzel was reprinted eight times in 1518 alone. Tetzel's works, on the other hand, "failed to find an audience."[31]

Luther's written attacks could be brutal. He was a skilled communicator; no one ever doubted that. Luther could make his opponents wither. Indeed, this happened to Tetzel. Just a year after Luther's public lashing of him, he died. He was a "broken and defeated man" at that point. He had taken refuge at a Dominican monastery in Leipzig, but "the public had turned against him and his career as an indulgence salesman." He was useless to the Catholic Church, too, so they used him as a scapegoat. If they could somehow save face by demonstrating that indulgences were fine—that the problem was the abuse of indulgences by Tetzel—then maybe they still could bring in the huge amounts of cash they needed to finance Saint Peter's and pay back the Fuggers. In the end, the church hierarchy "subjected Tetzel to a calculated public humiliation." They chose to "throw him to the wolves."[32]

Pope Leo X Gets Involved

Luther was soon embroiled in written attacks coming from all sides. And then, on August 7, 1518, the hammer fell. Luther received a letter from Rome declaring the *Ninety-Five Theses* to be heretical. He was summoned to appear in Rome.[33] As a faithful Augustinian, he was fully expected to remain compliant and to make the journey. In all likelihood, this journey would end at the stake. Luther's days were numbered. Just twenty years before this, in 1498, Italy's great reformer Savonarola was burned publicly in Florence. And now, with a personality as big as Luther's involved, and with his inability to keep his thoughts to himself, who could doubt that history was about to repeat itself?

Pope Leo X was a man of privilege. His real name was Giovanni di Lorenzo de' Medici. He was from the famous Medici royal house that ruled the Republic of Florence in the first half of the fifteenth century. His father was Lorenzo the Magnificent, one of the most powerful men of the Renaissance era. Lorenzo ruled Florence for more than twenty years and is perhaps best known for bankrolling such artistic icons as Botticelli, Leonardo da Vinci, and Michelangelo.

Pope Leo X was declared a cardinal in the Catholic Church at the age of thirteen. He was elected pope at the age of thirty-seven. Upon receiving the papal keys, he reportedly declared, "God has given us the papacy; let us now enjoy it." Calling him a spendthrift would be a vast understatement. He loved the high life. For example, as pope he frequently patrolled Rome atop his pet white elephant, named Hanno, a gift from the king of Portugal. He has become famous, however, as the pope who first opposed Martin Luther. His reign as pope lasted from 1513 to 1521. The scandal caused by the *Ninety-Five Theses* unfolded on his watch, and his delayed and uncompromising reactions to the German monk only caused matters to get more out of hand. By the time of his death in December 1521, the Protestant Reformation was well under way. Luther had managed to escape capture, and public opinion was turning against the papacy in many parts of Christendom.[34]

As mentioned earlier, Luther submitted himself to the pope's authority by means of a letter forwarded to Leo in 1518. This was a tactical move that probably was given to Luther by his mentor Staupitz.[35] Leo did not take much notice. He handed the matter over to one of his Dominican henchmen, Sylvester Prierias, who studied the *Ninety-Five Theses* and immediately summoned Luther to Rome with the insult, "Just as the Devil smells of his pride in all his works, so you smell of your own malevolence."[36] Luther was under formal suspicion of heresy.

Luther, however, believed he had Scripture on his side. He also knew the politics of the church. It was an old, tried-and-true tactic of the Inquisition: if you admit heresy, then you are probably going to be punished as a heretic. If you refuse the charge of heresy, then you will probably be tortured or otherwise coerced into admitting you are a heretic. Luther was now backed into a corner. And his instincts were to fight.

The Diet of Augsburg (1518)

Of all the mistakes history attributes to Pope Leo X, his underestimation of Luther was undoubtedly the greatest. Instead of having Luther come to Rome, he bowed to various parties such as Frederick the Wise, who petitioned to hold Luther's hearing in Germany, in the city of Augsburg. "As they often did, the political stars aligned themselves in Luther's favor." Leo was focused on fighting Ottoman advances in Hungary. He felt sure that representatives in Germany could certainly handle a boisterous monk.[37]

The pope's major oversight, however, was that Luther was now publishing regularly in German, and the masses not only were aware of his reforms, they saw things his way. Luther had a magnetic way of drawing Germans to his cause: he suggested that they were being abused by the lavish-living southern Europeans who built huge cathedrals on the backs of German peasants. Luther was able to turn this fiasco into a nationalistic crisis, an outcry against economic injustice—us versus them. Let the Italians finance their own bank-busting projects; leave the Germans alone. Possibly because he wanted to advance this strategy, "for the first time, Luther presented himself as a *German* theologian." He wrote, "I thank God that I hear and find my God in the *German* tongue."[38] The embattled professor realized that if he was going to gain the support of his people—and perhaps save his own neck—he needed to write for a more popular audience. And he did just that, with astonishing success.

Once the German city of Augsburg was chosen as the trial site, Rome designated Cardinal Thomas Cajetan to take charge of the proceedings. Cajetan was a Dominican priest, an expert on Thomas Aquinas, and he was fully abreast of Martin Luther as well as his writings. The events were scheduled to take place from October 12–14, 1518. It was to be a three-hundred-mile journey for Luther, on foot.[39] He arrived on time, but in poor health. He was extremely apprehensive about the likely outcome. He was also distressed over the possibility of ruining his parents' good name. Luther began to suffer severe stomach cramps toward the end of the long, two-week journey.[40] A wagon had to give the ailing traveler a lift for the final three miles.[41]

Cajetan knew of Luther's ability to persuade a crowd. The pope had already "ordered via a papal communique" that Cajetan should avoid debating Luther. Rather, he should simply order him to recant. For some reason, Cajetan failed to take this advice and soon found himself verbally sparring with Luther.[42] Cajetan's strategy, however, was to take a "fatherly" tone with Luther. He would politely admonish him, like a child, and persuade him to admit guilt. Luther was annoyed by this cardinal who kept calling him "my dear son."[43]

For three days, Luther and Cajetan argued. The first day, the longest, was held in private. Cajetan's major indictments had to do with Luther's understanding of papal authority. Cajetan took issue with number 58 of the *Ninety-Five Theses,* wherein Luther wrote that God's grace can work in human beings "even without the pope."[44] Cajetan argued that the pope indeed had the power to forgive sins and the power to grant indulgences. He cited John 20:23, "If you forgive anyone's sins, their sins are forgiven; if you do not forgive them, they are not forgiven." He then pointed out a papal decree of Pope Clement VI—in the early fourteenth century—who claimed that popes can grant indulgences.[45]

In response, Luther argued that Scripture was more authoritative than any pope. When Cajetan insisted that a person "should never be certain of his or her standing before God," Luther countered that the promises of God should give a person great confidence in their own salvation. For Luther, God's promises in the Bible were real and could be trusted. And he insisted that no human—not even a pope—could get in the way of those promises.[46]

On the second day, Luther requested that their debate become a public event. Cajetan denied the request. Luther then asked if they could at least argue before a theological faculty so that the proper experts could evaluate their reasoning. Again, Cajetan refused. The second day was also noteworthy in that Luther unleashed one of his most striking and profound ideas: that he was compelled by his own conscience to do the right thing.[47] This was to become the quintessentially Lutheran idea.

On the third day, Luther was accompanied by two lawyers from the court of Frederick the Wise. This ploy was crucial because it demonstrated in a rather official way that Frederick was now standing firmly by the side of his increasingly famous professor. Luther, seemingly with more confidence on this third day of the debate, argued that a general council held authority over a pope. This was an important argument that had pervaded church history. In general, the Eastern Orthodox world held to this view, whereas the Catholic Church emphasized the primacy and authority of the Roman pope.

On the third day, Luther also argued his foundational idea of "justification by faith." His central point was that faith granted a person justification in God's eyes, and the church was unable to preempt that promise of God to people. This was a rehashing of Luther's key points from the first day, and Cajetan became increasingly agitated. He abruptly stopped the debate and demanded that Luther "recant or leave his presence immediately and not return." Luther left. But he did not recant.[48] Cajetan was disturbed by "this beast" with "deep-set eyes and strange ideas in his head."[49]

When Cajetan urged John Staupitz to rein in Luther, Staupitz said he would try, but that Luther's knowledge of Scripture was greater than his own. "Staupitz was effectively refusing to control or discipline his former protégé."[50] Quietly, however, Staupitz pulled Luther aside and explained that he was releasing him from his monastic vows of obedience. Not only was Staupitz protecting himself by releasing Luther, but he also was cutting Luther loose to give him a chance to escape the gathering storm.

Being freed from his monastic vows was a turning point in Luther's life. No longer was he under the authority of Staupitz. It was a carefully calculated move by Staupitz to protect his longtime friend. Staupitz urged Luther to return to Wittenberg, where he would be under the protection of Frederick the Wise, along with many other ardent supporters in the university. Luther understood Staupitz's good motives, but the release granted to him was nonetheless a formal separation. Luther was no longer under the institutional protection of the Augustinian order. He later wrote that at this moment he felt forlorn and all alone.[51]

Around the time he left Augsburg, Luther arranged for someone to post a public appeal to Pope Leo on the cathedral door. This was Luther's way of going straight to the heart of the Roman Catholic Church in a very public way. No longer could Luther mend bridges via Cajetan or any other member of the Catholic hierarchy. Luther now wanted the pope's ear, without mediators.

After posting that public appeal, Luther escaped under the cover of night, surreptitiously, by climbing the Augsburg wall. He fled on an unsaddled horse that had been provided to him. And he was in a hurry, no doubt worried about his perilous future. He arrived in Wittenberg on October 31, 1518, exactly one year since he first came onto the radar screen with his *Ninety-Five Theses*. In just a year, Martin Luther's life had changed dramatically. The formerly obedient Augustinian monk and professor was now a fugitive. The pope wanted him arrested. And popes usually got what they wanted.[52]

A month later Luther began to appeal for a church council, arguing the Eastern Orthodox idea of "conciliarism"—that a church council has more authority than any bishop, even if that bishop is based in Rome. This would have been extremely offensive, even heretical, to the Roman Catholic authorities, and especially to Pope Leo. Luther was burning bridges left and right.[53]

The Leipzig Debate (1519)

Luther became a household name shortly after the Leipzig Debate of 1519. Surprisingly, he lost this debate badly. But it motivated him. His literary output became even more prodigious after the spectacle. Now, he became a man fighting for his life, and it may have saved him. It certainly made him realize that he would have to work—much harder than he could ever imagine—if he was to reform the church with any measure of success.

Luther's opponent at Leipzig was John Eck (1486–1543). Here was a man who bettered Luther in virtually every category. He was taller and more handsome, spoke better, was a more accomplished scholar, was better with people, and had much more experience in public debates. The two men were almost contemporaries. Luther was just three years older than Eck and lived three years longer.

Like Luther, Eck was a German to the core. He was from Swabia, in the southwest of the German lands. He had studied at Heidelberg, Tübingen, Cologne, and Freiburg. He became associated, however, with the University of Ingolstadt, where he taught theology and eventually rose to become pro-chancellor. He was able to shape the university into a bastion for Roman Catholicism. Eck was one of the major players who would prevent much of southern Germany from joining the Protestant movement when most of the northern part of the country became dominated by Lutheran ideas.

Eck was clever and well informed, fluent in Latin, Greek, and Hebrew. He was a man with sophisticated interests, having published studies of the nomadic peoples of Iran as well as having a keen interest in the indigenous people of the newly discovered West Indies. He was tremendously competent on his feet. His memory was stupendous. His physicality matched his intellectual prowess. He possessed a clear and commanding voice. Eck was ambitious and sensitive to the critiques of others. He had political experience and was a good friend to the famous Fugger family—the wealthy bankers from Augsburg. He had taken their side on whether Christians could charge interest; he advocated an interest rate of 5 percent.[54]

The Leipzig Debate was supposed to be, mainly, a debate between Eck and Karlstadt, Luther's colleague at Wittenberg. Karlstadt's wagon broke down just outside the Leipzig city gates, an ominous portent for what was to come.[55] Karlstadt brought with him "a whole posse of assistants"— Luther, Melanchthon, and several others from the university, including a team of Wittenberg graduates who would help them in between the debate rounds. The contest was to last for three torturous weeks, from June 27 to July 15, 1519.[56] The audience in attendance included the duke, his court, the professors at the local university, and many scholars who had come from all over Germany to witness the battle.

The debate began with extensive formalities. Seats were assigned, protocol established, proper introductions made, notetakers appointed, and guardsmen stationed around. Two pulpits were set up to face each other. Duke George, a staunch Roman Catholic who ruled Saxony for nearly four decades, presided. The duke was chomping at the bit to host this debate, which, in his view, would silence Martin Luther once and for all. While Karlstadt and Eck had previously been embroiled in a fairly well-publicized quarrel, no doubt a public slaying of Luther would be the biggest prize of all.[57] The introductions were polite, but the tension was palpable.

Once the debate began, it was clear that Karlstadt was no match for Eck. He was verbose, uninteresting, and frequently had to refer to his notes and consult with his team. He did not have the gift of eloquence, a fact that was obvious from the start. At one point, he compared good works to menstrual blood.[58] His point was that we cannot earn God's favor; rather it comes to us by grace alone. But it just sounded horrible. Eck was a seasoned debater, and he took full advantage, mocking Karlstadt for "childishly spouting what others had written."[59]

With the debate going so badly for Karlstadt, Luther was obligated to step in and provide Eck a more worthy opponent. Besides, Luther was the real fountainhead of the ideas being analyzed. Teaming up Luther and Karlstadt against Eck turned out to be a colossal error of strategy because it made Eck look like he was strong enough to handle two men. When Luther stepped to the podium, Eck had already leveraged himself against the small-time Wittenbergers. Too much damage had already been inflicted. Luther would not prevail as he had done at Heidelberg. The battle was virtually over before he began.

Luther did not help himself. He came across as angry, sullen, and vindictive. He hinted at an idea that would later bloom more fully in his thinking: that the pope was the anti-Christ.[60] Another idea that the audience found novel and offensive was Luther's claim that the existence of purgatory could not be proven by Scripture. Naturally, this was in conjunction with Luther's condemnation of the sale of indulgences. Luther also dug in his heels on papal authority, noting that when Jesus said, "On this rock I shall build my church," he was referring to himself, not to Peter. He also insinuated that since the Eastern Orthodox Church never put itself under the authority of Rome, then others did not have to either.[61]

Where Luther put his own head into the noose, however, was when the topic of John Huss came up. Huss was a Bohemian reformer who lived about a century before Luther and Eck. He and John Wycliffe often are considered early Protestants because they embraced many of the ideas credited to Luther today. While Wycliffe lived a full life, Huss was burned at the stake as a heretic in 1415. He was a highly controversial character, particularly for his belief that the Eucharist should be distributed to the laity *in both kinds*. By that he meant that the laity should receive the wine, which they were forbidden from taking, in addition to the bread. Eck baited Luther, and Luther bit. Luther publicly admitted that Huss might have been correct on certain issues. Eck then went for the jugular, pointing out for all to see that Huss was a condemned heretic, killed for his false beliefs.

During the debate, Luther's core idea—*sola Scriptura*—was taking shape. The church had no right to condemn him because he was fully capable of searching the Scriptures himself. Luther argued that the church had built up false ideas and made empty promises that had no foundation in the biblical text. The pope was not the authority on matters of faith; indeed, the pope had proven himself to be susceptible to corruption on all levels. The true source for Christian faith can be found only in Scripture, and the pope got in the way.

Eck had little work to do once Luther condemned the papacy, disavowed papal supremacy, aligned himself with a condemned heretic, and essentially declared the Roman Catholic Church to be in error on a whole host of things. Luther had hanged himself, metaphorically. The audience knew what must eventually transpire: Luther must burn.

Even the most pro-Luther scholars agree that he was destroyed by Eck during those three long weeks in the summer of 1519. Luther came off to several in the audience as "wrathful" and "overcome by anger." On one occasion, when Eck managed to pin Luther to John Huss, Luther exploded—in German—accusing Eck of being a liar. This was bad form on two fronts. Luther clearly lost his cool. But it also was in bad taste for an academic theologian to slip into German like that during a formal proceeding.[62] Luther and Karlstadt left town with their tails between their legs.

Leipzig's Aftermath

One would think that Eck would reign triumphant in the theological universe of Germany, but surprisingly it did not work out that way. By all accounts, he won the debate, but people simply were not interested in his ideas. He represented the establishment. The fiery monk from Wittenberg got all the press. Hardly anyone bothered to purchase Eck's writings, but Luther's were selling out the moment they were printed.

People were truly hungry to read Luther, not just because of his novel ideas, brazen critiques, or crass condemnations. Luther was an extremely talented writer. Consequently, his writings surpassed all other German writers in popularity. In fact, 20 percent of all the works published by German presses were Luther's. [63] His output in this period defies belief. In the six months following the debate at Leipzig, he penned sixteen new works. They were reprinted in 150 editions in 1519 alone. Within a year, Luther had two hundred fifty thousand copies of his writings in circulation.[64] In 1520, Luther authored his three most important theological treatises: *To the Christian Nobility of the German Nation*, *The Babylonian Captivity of the Church*, and *The Freedom of a Christian*. These were the most famous, but he published many other works during this period as well.[65]

Part of the reason for Luther's sensational ability to sell books was that his theology was becoming tauntingly radical. He openly adopted the laity's taking of the Eucharist "in both kinds," he attacked the priesthood as well as the monastic orders, and he dismissed his opponents by calling them Jews. An awkward and irrational hostility against Jews began to surface, only to be escalated all through his career. More on this later.

While Luther's star was rising, things just kept getting worse for Eck. Shortly after the debate, he was accused—it was not the first time—of enjoying the "women of pleasure" while he was in Leipzig. Luther's reputation grew. Eck's name cratered in infamy. He tried to publish his work, but the printers were consistently reluctant.[66]

Eck was hailed a hero in Rome, however. When he went to the eternal city for a victory lap, he argued that a "bull of excommunication" against Luther should be published at once.[67] By this time, Cardinal Cajetan, Luther's opponent at the Diet of Augsburg, also was urging papal censure of the Wittenberg monk.[68] Finally, on June 24, 1520, Luther was officially condemned by the papal bull *Exsurge Domine*, which means "Arise, O Lord." Luther was given sixty days to either recant or receive formal excommunication by the pope.[69]

By now, Luther was throwing caution to the wind. On Monday, December 10, 1520, at nine o'clock in the morning, he marched several of his students to the Elster Gate of Wittenberg and ignited a bonfire. With outright defiance, he burned the papal bull. That was not all, however. He incinerated many papal documents, books of canon law, and scholastic theology along with it.[70] Luther was now prepared to fight.

The papacy responded by issuing a final document that declared, once and for all, that Martin Luther was a condemned heretic officially excommunicated from the Roman Catholic Church. That bull, titled *Decet Romanum Pontificem*, was published on January 3, 1521.

Luther, therefore, was now to be tried for heresy. He was summoned to appear at that now-famous imperial gathering: the Diet of Worms. He was in poor health, due likely to the stress of knowing his life was reaching its end. He blamed the illness on Satan and swore that not even the gates of hell would prevent him from attending.[71] Before he departed to go to the trial, he turned to his closest friends and advisors, including Staupitz, for encouragement. On April 16, 1521, at around ten o'clock in the morning, Luther and a few companions rolled through Saint Martin's Gate into the city of Worms.[72]

Notes

[1] Martin Brecht, trans. by James Schaaf, *Martin Luther*, vol. 1 (Philadelphia, PA: Fortress Press, 1985), 204.

[2] Martin Marty, *Martin Luther* (New York: Viking, 2004), 34.

[3]Timothy Wengert, *The Annotated Luther,* vol. 1: *The Roots of Reform* (Minneapolis: Fortress Press, 2015), 22.

[4]Gordon Rupp, *Luther's Progress to the Diet of Worms* (New York: Harper, 1964), 54.

[5]Brecht, vol. 1, 204.

[6]Ibid.

[7]Ibid., 205–206.

[8]Richard Friedenthal, trans. by John Nowell, *Luther* (New York: Harcourt Brace Jovanovich, 1970), 156–158.

[9]Gerhard Brendler, trans. by Claude Foster, Jr., *Martin Luther* (New York: Oxford University Press, 1991), 113.

[10]Brecht, vol. 1, 205.

[11]Marty, 33.

[12]See *Luther's Works*, vol. 31, 80. The longer title of this work is *Explanations of the Disputation Concerning the Value of Indulgences.*

[13]Wengert, 58–59, 64.

[14]Brendler, 113.

[15]Ibid., 122. See also Marty, 40.

[16]James Kittelson, *Luther the Reformer* (Minneapolis: Fortress Press, 1986), 110–111.

[17]For "paradigm shift" see Dennis Bielfeldt, "Heidelberg Disputation, 1518," located in Wengert, *The Annotated Luther,* vol. 1, *The Roots of Reform*, 67.

[18]Bielfeldt, in Wengert, 72.

[19]Lyndal Roper, *Martin Luther: Renegade and Prophet* (London: Bodley Head, 2016), 106.

[20]Wengert, 79.

[21]Kittelson, 112.

[22]Roper, 107–108.

[23]Kittelson, 112.

[24]For late May or June, see Scott Hendrix, *Martin Luther: Visionary Reformer* (New Haven: Yale University Press, 2015), 71.

[25]Roper, 110.

[26]Hendrix, 65.

[27]Marty, 35.

[28]Brendler, 121.

[29]Hendrix, 66.

[30]Kittelson, 115.

[31]Andrew Pettegree, *Brand Luther* (New York: Penguin, 2015), 82.

[32]Ibid.

[33]Roper, 111.

[34]Hendrix, 67.

[35]Brendler, 125.

[36]James Reston Jr., *Luther's Fortress* (New York: Basic Books, 2015), 11.

[37]Hendrix, 72.

[38]Ibid. Italics mine.

[39]Roper, 112.

[40]Brendler, 129. See also Hendrix, 73.

[41]Roper, 113.

[42]Suzanne Hequet, "The Proceedings at Augsburg, 1518," in Wengert, 124.

[43]Roper, 116.

[44]Stephen Nichols, ed., *Martin Luther's Ninety-Five Theses* (Phillipsburg, NJ: P&R Publishing, 2002), 37.

[45]Hequet, in Wengert, 124.

[46]Ibid.

[47]Roper, 116.

[48]Hequet, in Wengert, 124–125.

[49]Marty, 43.

[50]Roper, 119.

[51]Ibid., 118–119.

[52]Oberman, 197, and Kittelson, 125.

[53]Hequet, in Wengert, 125, and Roper, 120.

[54]Hartmann Grisar, *Martin Luther: His Life and Work* (Westminster: The Newman Press, 1950), 112. See also Roper, 128–130.

[55]Roper, 132.

[56]Ibid., 136–137.

[57]Brendler, 146, and Roper, 132.

[58]Roper, 135.

[59]Ibid., 133.

[60]Grisar, 113–114.

[61]Roper, 134.

[62]Ibid., 137.

[63]Ibid., 142.

[64]Hendrix, 81.

[65]See "A Chronological List of Luther's Works from the American Edition," located at: https://lutherantheology.files.wordpress.com/2010/02/luthers-work-chronological-website2.pdf.

[66]Roper, 137.

[67]Friedenthal, 240.

[68]Bernhard Lohse, trans. by Robert Schultz, *Martin Luther* (Philadelphia: Fortress Press, 1980), 48.

[69]Kittelson, 149.

[70]Lohse, 48; Hendrix, 98; and Marty, 56–57.

[71]Hendrix, 103.

[72]Brendler, 203.

11

The Diet of Worms

"Up to this point we have played around, but the matter has now become serious," Luther wrote to Staupitz in mid-January 1521. There was no telling how all this was going to pan out. Luther knew deep down it could go either way.[1]

But Luther did have some hope. He was now famous. People were reading his books and pamphlets with gusto. He knew he had the ears of thousands of people, based on his book sales alone. He was a rising star, but in no way did this exonerate him. Only two decades before, Girolamo Savonarola's reforms had drawn praise from great numbers of Christians in Italy. But crowds are fickle. In a very short time, public opinion turned against Savonarola. He was stripped, hanged, and burned to ashes. Luther was aware of that event. That famous execution took place in Florence when Luther was a teenager.

Luther's most important supporter, however, was Frederick the Wise. Although a politician who kept his cards close to the vest, Frederick was powerful. He was a significant player in the Holy Roman Empire, one of only seven who had the power to elect the Holy Roman emperor.[2] Historians struggle to explain why Frederick took to Luther as he did. Was he convinced by the monk's arguments? Was he looking out for his own interests? Was he irritated by the church's constant reaching into German affairs? Arguments can be made in all directions, but his support for Luther was unwavering. While he never made a formal conversion to Protestantism, Frederick certainly did whatever he could to protect the rogue monk.

The Diet of Worms lasted four months, from January 27 to May 25, 1521. Luther was present only for a week and a half, from April 16 to 26. Much business had to be covered, but what to do with Martin Luther and his burgeoning movement was first on everyone's mind. The many delegates present—bishops, secular authorities, the seven electors, and the Holy Roman emperor—showed extreme ambivalence about what to do. Some wanted Luther dead. Others supported him strongly. Many were undecided. One thing was realized early on: "a popular revolt would erupt if Luther were condemned without a hearing." Thus, it became clear that Luther must at least appear before the diet.[3]

Presiding over the Diet of Worms was Holy Roman Emperor Charles V (1500–1558). He was young, only twenty years old, when the diet began. However, he had ruled the Spanish Empire since he was sixteen, so he was not without experience. Charles V is famous for two things: his extremely successful expansion of the Spanish empire into Asia and the Americas, and his nearly forty-year opposition to the Protestant Reformation. When he first arrived at the Diet of Worms, however, he probably was undecided on whether to support this unbridled priest in Wittenberg. Once he had a chance to visit with the delegates, he reluctantly agreed to allow Luther to come to the diet and speak. But there was a catch. Luther's visit was to be brief. He was to show up and promptly and fully recant his writings.[4] Obviously, Charles had no idea what kind of person he was dealing with.

The decision to bring Luther to Worms was made in March. They would expect Luther to appear before them in mid-April. In the meantime, Charles declared that all Luther's books should be burned. He did not want to be portrayed as a friend to heretics. The handwriting was on the wall. In two months, Charles had turned firmly against Luther. To avoid unnecessary trouble with the powerful Pope Leo X, the emperor made the carefully calculated decision to rid the world of Luther. After all, Luther was no longer a part of the Roman Catholic Church. As of January 3, 1521, Luther had been officially condemned by the pope. What else could Charles do but get on board with the papal decision?

What Was Really Going on at Worms?

The Diet of Worms was a complicated event. The main political issue was how to deal with the expanding Ottoman Empire. A new caliph—Suleiman the Magnificent—had just taken the Ottoman reins in 1520. He would go on to rule for nearly fifty years. Suleiman (1494–1566) was ambitious and powerful. His ultimate goal was to conquer Europe and bring it into the house of Islam. In 1521, just a few months after the Diet of Worms ended, he conquered Belgrade in modern Serbia. Much of central Europe was falling to Islam right under the nose of the Roman Catholic world. His vision of a Dar-al-Islam was happening, and in a few short years he would be knocking on the door of Vienna. Charles V understood the growing reputation of his Ottoman counterpart all too well, and he knew the German nobility were aware of this. He knew he held a few choice cards because the Germans needed his military, and he needed the Germans as well.

The political dynamics involved caused the Diet of Worms to be a sophisticated chess game. First, a few years earlier, Pope Leo X had campaigned for Frederick the Wise to be the emperor. So the relationship between Pope Leo X and Charles V was a little suspicious and very coy. Second, a high level of distrust prevailed between the Holy Roman electors and Charles V, because Charles spoke no German. He was a foreigner to them, at a time when German nationalism was mushrooming. Third, Frederick the Wise had handed Charles his emperorship. Frederick had been the top man for the job, but to avoid a long conflict, he had allowed Charles V to accept the title of emperor. So Charles was obligated to Frederick. Fourth, the German people were overwhelmingly in favor of Luther. One Catholic cardinal wrote to the pope, "Nine-tenths put up the battle cry 'Luther!' and the other tenth, 'Death to the Roman curia!'"[5]

On February 19, the decision was made to summon Luther to the diet. He was not to debate with anybody. He would simply recant his writings and allow himself to be interrogated by the theological police. If Charles was going to convict Luther, he would at least need to cover his own arse by putting up the veneer that Luther had been given a fair shot at justice. What Charles never seemed to grasp, however, was how popular Luther had become.

Charles's mind was, quite justifiably, in the west (Latin America) and in the east (the Ottoman advance), rather than in the north flank of his empire. Indeed, the famous conquistador Hernan Cortes was assaulting the Aztec Empire during the Diet of Worms. The Siege of Tenochtitlan occurred in 1521, from May 26 to August 13, and resulted in Charles V not only gaining control of the New World, but also obtaining much needed gold and other resources to sustain Western Christendom against the great Muslim advance. Eastern Christendom was now in shambles as Suleiman seemed to be a juggernaut, rolling across eastern and central Europe at will, with no signs of stopping. Unfortunately for Charles, Suleiman decided in 1522 to test his military genius in the eastern Mediterranean, a goal he successfully accomplished at the Siege of Rhodes in 1522.

In other words, while he was confronting Luther's challenge, Charles V had bigger fish to fry. What was a little theological squabble in Germany in comparison with the specter of Muslim dominion all across Europe? Suleiman once referred to himself as "emperor" and to Charles as "king of Spain." To capture Charles and have his way with him would be utterly delightful for Suleiman. Charles understood the Muslim threat very well, and to meet it, he needed the Germans badly. Otherwise, he simply would have let these northerners untangle their own theological mess. But now, he was in the unfortunate position of having to arbitrate their theology squabble to gain an alliance with their military.

The Journey to Worms

By now, Luther realized the stakes. It gave him fear, but his fear was mixed with hate. He was now in the habit of referring to the pope as the antichrist. Luther knew he was asked to appear at the diet to recant everything. In typical fashion, he wrote to one of his friends: "This shall be my recantation at Worms: 'Previously I said the pope is the vicar of Christ. I recant. Now I say the pope is the adversary of Christ and the apostle of the Devil.'"[6]

While these thoughts betray a certain recklessness, they leave no doubt that Luther by now believed in his cause deeply and knew that martyrdom might await him at Worms. While Luther knew that Frederick had been his advocate in the past, Frederick was outnumbered at Worms, and more importantly, Frederick was not the emperor. And Luther had no guarantee that Frederick would remain in his corner. The Diet of Worms was a huge political gamble for everyone involved.

As a condemned heretic, Luther's trip to Worms was a perilous one. Any zealous thug would likely have received a blessing from the church had he taken justice into his own hands and attacked Luther during his journey. Luther's crime of heresy was much more serious than the crime of assaulting a condemned heretic. Luther knew this, so he must have been elated when he saw the crowds appearing alongside his wagon with cheers, often giving him "a hero's welcome" in the towns he traveled through. Indeed, when Luther stopped to preach in his former city of Erfurt, "the church was so packed that a balcony nearly collapsed under the weight of the throng."[7]

Near the city of Oppenheim, Luther and his party crossed the Rhine on a ferry and rode into Worms on the morning of April 16, 1521. It was a spectacular event. Two thousand people spilled into the streets to catch a glimpse of the man who had skyrocketed to fame in the Germanic world.[8] The imperial herald walked in front of Luther's wagon, singing a ditty, "The one we sought so long has arrived at last; we expected you even when days were at their darkest."[9]

Then, in one of the most dramatized moments in church history, as Luther cast his eyes on the steeples of the city, he is reported to have risen in his chariot and belted out these lines of the most important hymn in the history of Protestant Christianity:

> A mighty fortress is our God,
> A bulwark never failing;
> Our helper He, amid the flood
> Of mortal ills prevailing.
> For still our ancient foe
> Doth seek to work us woe;
> His craft and power are great,
> And armed with cruel hate,
> On earth is not his equal.[10]

That song, a paraphrase of Psalm 46, was destined to become an anthem for the Protestant Reformation.

The city of Worms was jam-packed. Everyone clamored to meet the man who was now the stuff of legend.[11] Indeed, one hundred nobles on horseback rode out to greet him and personally escort him into Worms, much like one would expect for royalty. Trumpets blasted, announcing that Luther had finally arrived. People strained to touch his cloak. Luther was carefully watched by all. One overwhelmed priest suddenly charged toward Luther and embraced him; it was as if the priest had touched the Lord himself.[12] One prominent historian wrote, "The entire world, old and young, boys and girls, was flocking to the monk, and no one was able to prevent this. The people appeared to be possessed by a mad passion for Luther." Worms's normal population was seven thousand, but that more than doubled during the diet. Luther had to share a room with two others.

Luther's arrival in Worms turned out to be an intoxicating experience for all who witnessed the event. Instantly, he became the center of attention. His spirits must have been greatly encouraged by the welcome he received that day. His detractors, on the other hand, were disgusted by the exuberant reception of the aberrant monk and began labeling him "the Saxon Dragon."[13]

At the Diet of Worms

Luther was given almost no time to settle in. The day after he arrived, April 17, Luther's group was led to the episcopal palace, where the emperor was staying and where the diet was held. They took side streets because the main streets were too crowded with people wanting to see or possibly meet the famous Wittenberger.

The meeting was scheduled for 4:00 P.M., but proceedings were running late. Luther and his advisors finally encountered the imperial presence around 6:00 P.M. Finally, Luther and Charles V looked into each other's eyes. Charles was seated with advisors all around him. Just twenty-one years old, Charles had a large protruding lower jaw that is obvious in every likeness of him. Luther, thirty-seven years old at the time, stood with a slightly bent knee, as etiquette required. During this first meeting, Luther awkwardly bent several times—much to the delight of his opponents. Luther was not to speak unless spoken to first.[14]

The scene in Worms that day was packed with drama. Luther, a simple monk, was standing before a ruler who possessed great power—far greater than Luther could ever imagine. Charles had more titles than all other monarchs of his time. He was a true European scion with a most impressive pedigree. Luther's dad had worked his way up in the sweaty and dangerous mines of Germany. Here was top royalty facing off with a humble, albeit brilliant, monastic priest whose greatest claim to fame lay in his insults of the Roman Catholic Church.

The master of ceremonies was John von Ecken, not to be confused with the John Eck from the Leipzig Debate in 1519. Ecken was no friend to the nascent Reformation. Previously, he had organized a book burning of Luther's works in the city of Trier.[15]

Laid out on a bench was a stack of Luther's works: twelve books in German, ten in Latin, a volume containing Luther's lectures on Psalms 1–13, various pamphlets, and some other publications. Ecken asked Luther if he wrote the books stacked there. Luther acknowledged that he was indeed the author. Then, Luther was asked whether he wanted to publicly recant his writings or uphold the contents of them. All at once, Luther lost his confidence. He "seemed ill at ease," and "unsure of himself," even despondent. Quietly, Luther asked if they could give him some time to think through the implications of the moment. Observers reported that Luther's voice could hardly be heard.[16] After conferring amongst themselves, they consented—although Ecken advised against it. In his view, this well-published theologian should have come prepared.[17] Ultimately, however, Luther was asked to come back the following day at 4:00 P.M.[18] This was by no means what people had come to expect from the fiery monk. He was cautious and reticent. One Spanish onlooker wrote that Luther conducted himself "with great trepidation and little serenity in countenance or gestures."[19]

On day two, April 18, Luther was led to a more spacious room to allow for an expanded audience. The room was stifling because it was lit by torches. It was nighttime. They had standing room only. Luther was wet with perspiration.[20] Even princes were forced to stand for the proceeding. Luther was asked the same questions as the previous day. With a firmer voice, first in Latin and then in German, Luther remarked that he was "a man accustomed not to courts but to the cells of monks."[21] This was the beginning of the speech that would alter the course of Western civilization.

Luther then addressed the emperor and the electors specifically. His books fell into three distinct groups, he told them. First, he wrote books that explained the word of God very plainly. Second, other books he wrote attacked the papacy for all the trouble it had caused. Third, he wrote books that were directed specifically to his opponents, and, although sometimes biting, these writings were necessary. Besides, Luther explained, "I do not set myself up as a saint." He asserted that the reason his writings reflect an ugly viciousness is because they are directed toward foul teachings coming out of Rome. Furthermore, Luther argued, he would not recant his writings against the pope's idolatry and tyranny because the pope deserved condemnation on these matters. Nor could he revoke his other works until someone could expose his errors using the Scriptures. If Luther's writings could be proven to contradict the prophets and evangelists, then he would be the first to cast them into the flames. However, Luther claimed, he was sure he could not be proven wrong. The word of God was finally being preached, and, as Jesus said, "I have not come to bring peace but a sword."[22] This last comment got their attention. Was Luther threatening a popular rebellion?

Ecken was visibly angered by both the content of Luther's speech and its length, since Luther had been directed to answer questions with a simple yes or no. Ecken meant to quell Luther's arguments by repeating his two questions. He tersely informed Luther that he had not answered the questions and reminded him that he and his doctrines had been condemned by the pope already. Ecken then lashed out by saying that he doubted Luther had somehow discovered something new in Christianity after fifteen centuries of history. He then reiterated his demand that Luther either recant or not so they could move on with the proceedings.[23]

At that moment, Luther intoned those famous words that echo every bit as loudly today as they did that day in Worms:

> Unless I am convicted by Scripture and plain reason—I do not accept the authority of popes and councils, for they have contradicted each other—my conscience is captive to the Word of God. I cannot and I will not recant anything, for to go against conscience is neither right nor safe. Here I stand. I cannot do otherwise. God help me. Amen.[24]

Historians differ on whether Luther actually said "Here I stand. I cannot do otherwise." The official record did not have those words, but the record published in Wittenberg—the earliest printed record of the event—did have them. Whatever the case, it certainly represented Luther's spirit that day, and it soon became famous as the most fitting end to his defiant testimony.[25]

What happened next was nothing less than pandemonium. "Great uproar and indignation" ensued. The emperor was confused since he lacked fluency in German, and he abruptly walked out during the translation of the speech into Latin. The audience began exiting the stuffy, stifling hall.[26] Spaniard onlookers jeered at Luther with derisive gestures and began shouting, "Burn him, burn him!"[27]

Luther went into celebration mode, lifting his outstretched hands into the air, exclaiming, "I have succeeded!" He then went to a nearby tavern to drink. People awaited him there, congratulating him with great merriment. But, despite their joyful abandon, "no one realized the gravity and responsibility of the situation."[28]

Worms and Its Aftermath

In the days following the Diet of Worms, a palpable sense of tension hung in the air. Some said a violent *coup d'etat* might have taken place had Luther been seized or mistreated. All over Worms, the sign of the *Bundschuh* (a peasant's boot) began to appear on the walls. Among the hardworking classes, this symbol was code language for revolution, and everyone in Worms would have understood its not-so-subtle meaning. The powerful politicians gathered for the occasion were frightened.[29] Luther was far more popular than they imagined. They no longer had the option to do whatever they wanted with him. Reports warned that six to eight thousand peasants were ready to fight on Luther's behalf.[30] More empowered now than ever, Luther mocked the diet proceedings in a letter to his good friend, the famous painter Lucas Cranach. What had his accusers been able to accomplish? "Nothing else was done there than this: Are these your books? Yes. Do you want to renounce them or not? No. Then go away." Luther lamented the fact that the Germans—his own people—were so blind to the conniving "Romanists." Importantly, Luther mentioned in the letter that he would soon "be hidden away."[31]

On May 1, two weeks after Luther's now-famous speech, an edict was written. After some back and forth debate about the document, it was prepared for the emperor's signature. The outlook for Luther was not good. The events of Worms were reviewed, and the conclusion reached was that Luther was an "obstinate, schismatic heretic," who should be apprehended and duly punished. Furthermore, his accomplices and anyone who aided him in any way were also under imperial condemnation—an obvious allusion to Elector Frederick of Saxony, who even then was giving asylum to Luther at

Wartburg. His books were not to be bought, sold, kept, or read by anyone, and all existing copies were to be burned. Any writings and drawings of others who sympathized with and supported Luther should be treated in the same manner.[32] The final document was presented to Emperor Charles V on May 12. Luther, however, was gone. He had left the city.

On May 26, the Edict of Worms was officially promulgated by Emperor Charles V. It prohibited people from receiving Luther into their houses and/or feeding him. All support or encouragement of Luther was officially forbidden. Luther was placed under "a ban and double ban." If anyone saw Luther in the street or anywhere, they were to "seize him and overpower him." They were to "capture him" and get him into the hands of the royal authorities immediately.[33] Luther's dramatic plea at Worms was an utter failure in the eyes of the Holy Roman emperor.

It is interesting that the Edict of Worms expressly forbade people from hiding Luther anywhere, because that is precisely what happened next.

The Disappearance

Luther was now an outlaw. Not that he wasn't one already, but an official document now affirmed it. The pope and the Holy Roman emperor were united against him. Very few people could escape that kind of condemnation. The two most important people in Europe wanted this man dead. Yet because of the popular support he enjoyed in Germany, they could do little to harm him.

Shortly after the conclusion of the Diet of Worms, a flurry of discussions were held, aimed at getting Luther to at least recant a few of his more aggressive charges against the church. The diet's participants thought they could save face if Luther could simply step back a bit. Perhaps by getting Luther to back down just a step or two, they could avoid the depiction of themselves as having failed in their attempts to silence the noncompliant monk. They dangled carrots before Luther, offering leniency for even a shred of regret for what he had done.[34] Luther would not budge. He kept coming back to Scripture: if someone wanted to prove him wrong, they must do it in accordance with the Bible. Luther knew they couldn't. After his speech at Worms, he became even more convinced in his thinking. He had reached the point of no return.

Emperor Charles V found himself in a quagmire. He had previously promised safe passage to Luther, both to and from the gathering at Worms. If he violated that oath to Luther, he would face consequences. First, the people of Germany would be up in arms if they learned that Luther had died unjustly after being promised safe passage. Second, Frederick the Wise would never approve of breaking that promise. In fact, he would be incensed if the emperor took that course of action. Furthermore, people in Germany had not forgotten about John Huss (1372–1415), a fifteenth-century reformer who had been promised safe passage to and from the Council of Constance but was tricked and executed. Huss's death triggered in Bohemia the Hussite Wars that lasted for a decade and a half and resulted in thousands of casualties and a church in Bohemia that officially split from the Roman Catholic Church. Based on the enormous popularity of Luther, that kind of outcome was a real possibility. As a result of this potentially incendiary outcome, Luther was given twenty days of safe passage back to Wittenberg, as long as he refrained from preaching or conversing along the way.[35]

Seemingly, Luther was in good spirits. His commitment to his cause increased in the days following the Diet of Worms. He left the city by carriage on April 26, precisely ten days after entering it.[36] Against the explicit orders of the emperor, he preached in several churches on his way home. Luther was defiant at this point, and the pressure for him to continue to grow his movement was mounting. Would he obey orders and silence himself? Or would he continue to build his momentum to win over more people? Luther took the route of "flagrant defiance."[37] By this point, it made no sense for Luther to capitulate to the emperor or to the pope. He had chosen his course and was not looking back.

On the way home, Luther stopped to preach in Hersfeld and Eisenach—where he studied as a boy.[38] He also stopped in Möhra to preach and to visit his grandmother.[39] Crowds continued to come to him wherever he went. Germany had found itself a hero in Martin Luther. If nothing else, tremendous intrigue surrounded this priest who was important enough to provoke the two most important men in Europe, the pope and the emperor.

Luther's trip back to Wittenberg was a victory lap for the young theologian. By all accounts, he seemed to be not only enjoying the aftermath of the diet, but also using it to his great advantage.

Suddenly, however, on May 4, while still en route to Wittenberg, Luther was confronted by horsemen near the fortress of Altenstein,[40] a place Luther knew. It was in the Thuringian forest, where he had run and played as a child. The horsemen blindfolded Luther and took him away.[41]

Notes

[1]Scott Hendrix, *Martin Luther: Visionary Reformer* (New Haven: Yale University Press, 2015), 99–100.

[2]Steven Ozment, *A Mighty Fortress: A New History of the Germany People* (New York: HarperCollins, 2004), 73.

[3]Hendrix, 100.

[4]Ibid., 100–101.

[5]James Kittelson, *Luther the Reformer* (Minneapolis: Fortress Press, 1986), 157–158.

[6]Roland Bainton, *Here I Stand* (New York: Meridian, 1950), 139.

[7]James Reston, Jr., *Luther's Fortress* (New York: Basic Books, 2015), 27–28.

[8]Martin Brecht, trans. by James Schaaf, *Martin Luther,* vol. 1 (Philadelphia: Fortress Press, 1985), 451.

[9]Hendrix, 103.

[10]See Reston, 29.

[11]Brecht, vol. 1, 451.

[12]Gerhard Brendler, trans. by Claude Foster, *Martin Luther* (Oxford: Oxford University Press, 1991), 203.

[13]Brecht, vol. 1, 450–451.

[14]Brendler, 204. See also Richard Friedenthal, trans. by John Nowell, *Luther* (New York: Harcourt Brace Jovanovich, 1970), 275.

[15]Hendrix, 104.

[16]Lyndal Roper, *Martin Luther: Renegade and Prophet* (London: The Bodley Head, 2016), 180.

[17]Bainton, 141.

[18]Friedenthal, 274–275. See also Brendler, 204.

[19]Hartmann Grisar, *Martin Luther* (Westminster: The Newman Press, 1950), 184.

[20]Brecht, vol. 1, 459.

[21]Roper, 181.

[22]Ibid., 182.

[23]Grisar, 185.

[24]Bainton, 144.

[25]Roper, 183.

[26]Grisar, 185.

[27]Roper, 183.

[28]Grisar, 186.

[29]Kittelson, 162.

[30]Grisar, 186.

[31]Sam Wellman, *Frederick the Wise* (Saint Louis: Concordia, 2011), 207.

[32]De Lamar Jensen, *Confrontation at Worms* (Provo, UT: Brigham Young University Press, 1973), 65–66.

[33]Heiko Oberman, *Luther* (New Haven: Yale University Press, 1989), 203.
[34]Brendler, 210.
[35]Reston, 47.
[36]Grisar, 187.
[37]Friedenthal, 285.
[38]Wellman, 208.
[39]Marty, 69.
[40]Wellman, 208.
[41]Marty, 70.

12

The Wartburg Castle

Who orchestrated the kidnapping of Martin Luther on his way home from Worms? It was none other than Frederick the Wise. However, Frederick did not want to know more about it than was necessary. Stealing Luther like that was an act of sedition, so Frederick had to cover any tracks. Once he made the initial arrangement to get Luther to a safe place, he opted to remain in the dark about the details.[1]

The decision to put Luther into Wartburg Castle was a closely guarded secret. Only a handful of Luther's friends were in the know. But Frederick the Wise—who did not have a relationship with Luther—was also in the know. And he was the person who mattered most. Frederick was a quintessential politician. He had his goals, and he knew how to accomplish them. He was an extremely patient man when it came to getting what he wanted. And, for the time being anyway, he wanted his star theologian to remain alive. According to his calculus, a time might come when the price to pay to keep Luther alive would exceed the benefit. But in the aftermath of Worms, when Frederick saw that Luther was not only Wittenberg's leading light but was possibly *Germany's* leading figure, it was worth the risk for him. It is well known that Frederick deeply wanted his university to succeed, and Luther clearly was the key to that success. Wittenberg would be unknown to outsiders had Martin Luther never moved there. As Luther's reputation increased, so did Frederick's university, and so did Frederick's clout in the political constellation.

Now, Frederick was truly in a dilemma. He supported Luther, but by no means did that convey that he was an enemy to the Catholic Church. In 1519, he had received from Pope Leo X the Golden Rose, an ornately crafted floral arrangement covered in gold leaf honoring his exceptional service to the church.[2] No small honor, this award was meant to "sweeten the deal" to get Luther sent to Rome. Frederick, however, was quite deft and managed to keep Luther on German soil. Frederick had history with Rome, and he knew he needed the church if he was going to accomplish anything significant in his realm. By all accounts, Frederick was a devoted Catholic. While he did indeed protect Luther, he never officially renounced his Catholicism. And he never publicly declared his approval of Luther's writings, either.

The consummate politician, Frederick neither approved nor disapproved of Luther's performance in Worms. On the night of Luther's famous defense, Frederick summoned his secretary, George Spalatin, and told him that while Luther spoke well, he "was too audacious."[3] Incidentally, Spalatin was one of Luther's closest friends, and they were in close contact. Thus, Luther would have been aware of Frederick's every word.

Wartburg Castle

The castle is a medieval fortress in the Thuringian Forest that sits about 1,350 feet above the town of Eisenach. The word Wartburg can be translated into "watchtower fortress." Constructed in the eleventh and twelfth centuries, it had served as a defense position for ruling families and their guests.

When Luther was kidnapped on May 4, 1521, he knew something like this was going to happen.[4] The two captors who intercepted him were the governor of Wartburg Castle and a lord who lived nearby. They were close friends to Frederick the Wise.[5] One of Luther's companions who had been kept in the dark about the plan bolted when he saw weapons. Whether these interceptors were for or against Luther would not have been immediately clear. Luther's carriage driver was asked sternly if he had Luther, and he responded yes.[6] Luther was placed on a horse. After only a few minutes, he would have realized that he was now in the hands of people he could trust.

Their journey was only fifteen miles through the forest. They arrived to the castle at midnight.[7] This was to be Luther's home for the next ten months.

The key to the plan's success was that everything remained secret. Luther was to stay hidden in the castle. He was given a spacious room near the front of the fortress. He had a spectacular view that is still today enjoyed by thousands of visitors each year. He was given a table and a fireplace. He had access to the castle chapel just downstairs from his room. Food was prepared daily for him, and he was well cared for. Famously, Luther grew his hair out, donned a beard, and referred to himself as "Junker Jörg" (Knight George) to those few he happened to meet.

The person who was paid to watch Luther and ensure his safety was Hans von Berlepsch, the captain of the castle. He was tasked with keeping this entire episode totally quiet, so he introduced Luther to the people in the compound as a "knight of the lower nobility." Luther's monastic garb, for the first time in sixteen years, was discarded in favor of a knightly uniform.[8] Luther's friend Lucas Cranach made a famous painting of him as Junker Jörg. No longer did Luther have the monastic tonsure; in a short time, he had the appearance of a common man.

Almost immediately, Luther got to work. He visited the Franciscans in the town and borrowed books from them. He wrote and received hundreds of letters, as well as treatises that would get whisked away to Wittenberg for publication. He spent some time riding horses. He was tutored in how to act like a knight—stroking his beard and grasping his sword with confidence and poise.[9]

"Wild rumors" abounded regarding Luther's whereabouts.[10] Had he been quietly murdered and his body disposed of so as not to provoke his thousands of followers? Had he escaped on his ride back to Wittenberg to avoid eventual punishment from Rome? Had he been poisoned? Some, however, surmised correctly that Luther was in friendly hands. The outstanding question, then, was who exactly had mustered the courage to defy the emperor and pope so openly? Of course, everything was conjecture.

Solitary Confinement . . . and Its Discontents

At first, this was no prison for Luther; rather, he quite enjoyed himself: reading, reflecting, and writing. His life had been extremely hectic for the last three or four years—ever since he posted those fateful theses on the church door in Wittenberg. Luther's constant companion while at Wartburg was his Bible in the original languages.

In a short time, however, Luther's restlessness began to surface. He started sending meditations on the psalms to his parishioners in Wittenberg. He completed some projects started before the Worms interruption—for example, the translation of the *Magnificat* into German. He wrote many sermons that are considered some of his best. But Luther's naturally social nature was causing him to feel claustrophobic and isolated. He compared his time in Wartburg to Saint John's exile to Patmos.[11]

Historians have made much of Luther's depression and erratic behavior during those ten months. For example, legends abound regarding Luther struggling with Satan during the confinement. He purportedly threw an inkpot at the devil at one point. On one occasion, he was brought a sack of walnuts to eat and then later in the night began hearing noises, like that of someone cracking nuts outside his window. That same night, he felt his bed shaking and became convinced that Satan was making loud noises outside his room. Luther took refuge in Jesus Christ during these moments, as his understanding of Satan as a real and physical being was vivid and intense.[12] To Luther, Satan was not merely restricted to the realm of the spiritual. Rather, he was alive and physically present in the very rooms where Luther lived. He lurked around, causing trouble.

Luther's letters during this time reveal that he was often sick, especially with constipation. He would go days without a bowel movement. He wrote, "Now I sit in pain like a woman in childbirth, ripped up, bloody, and I will have little rest tonight."[13] The physical ailments were overshadowed by the loneliness. He slept poorly and often complained of his rear end being sore. He eventually requested the assistance of a physician, but he had to settle for friends bringing medicine to him.[14]

Over time, Luther began to feel extremely constrained. Not just because of the separation from his friends, colleagues, monastic brothers, and students, but he also began to starve for sexual companionship. This may or may not have had something to do with Luther's complaint that he was "drowning in sins."[15] He wrote to his good friend Philip Melanchthon that his "unruly flesh burns so fiercely." He confessed that his thoughts were constantly on "the flesh" rather than on the realm of the Spirit. He asked for prayers for his slippage into vice.[16]

Undoubtedly, part of Luther's predicament was that he had created a religious movement, and he was not around to nurture it. He was the point person in the massive reforms taking place, and he wanted to shape the new developments. And this brings us to Luther's Achilles' heel. He struggled to let others have a say in what he deemed to be "his" Reformation. For the rest of his life, he would battle with those who might disagree with him on even the finest points of theology. Like a hound, he would sniff out where a fellow reformer might disagree with him, and he would either persuade them to conform to his ideas for reform, or he would reject them in the strongest of terms.

During his Wartburg days, Luther knew what was happening in Wittenberg due to his frequent correspondence with friends, which began after only eight days at the castle.[17] Melanchthon, Spalatin, and Nicolaus von Amsdorf all worked to keep Luther abreast of developments. He was always particularly eager to have Spalatin tell him what was happening in Elector Frederick's mind. From Melanchthon, Luther learned that Wittenberg's curriculum was being changed in the direction that Luther wanted.[18] Their exchanges were quite personal and pastoral. Luther was a big brother figure to Melanchthon, and all signs pointed to Melanchthon's desperate hope that Luther would return and take back the leadership of the movement that he had rightly earned. Others had stepped up into positions of leadership, and Melanchthon was not always sure if Luther would want things to go in the direction they were going. Melanchthon was steadfast and loyal to Luther, even if their communication was limited to the post. Melanchthon was insecure and unsure of himself without Luther's confident presence.[19]

Luther published many writings while in Wartburg. He took a keen interest in his publications, the price of his books, how large the books would be, and how his works were being received. Luther had a short fuse about how his publications were being managed. One gets the sense that this is one area Luther struggled with because he was confined. He had become a legend in his own time through the careful control of his writings, but now he was unable to have the influence over them that he did when the press was located a few steps from his home. Frequently, he lashed out at the publishers, calling their work "dirty, slovenly, muddled printing! Bad type, different kinds of paper! Hack work from beginning to end!" Luther's relationship with one press "came close to total collapse."[20]

While at Wartburg, Luther was like a horse chomping at the bit. He wanted more control but could not have it. At least, not until he decided to take a perilous chance and head back to Wittenberg in disguise, which he did on horseback in early December 1521. Surprisingly, his plan worked. He avoided his brothers in the monastery by staying in Melanchthon's home. He stayed there only about a week, and even the artist Lucas Cranach failed to notice Luther when some friends played a joke and asked Luther to sit for a portrait, under the guise of a visiting knight. "Even Cranach, with the eyes of an artist, did not recognize him."[21]

Ratcheting Up Reform in Wittenberg

Luther was quite pleased with the progress of reform he observed during his incognito visit to Wittenberg, but he was outraged by the incompetence of the publishers.[22] They were late in publishing several tracts Luther cared about immensely, they printed some of Luther's works in formats that were too large, and in Luther's mind, their quality was lousy. Luther was a slave-driver when it came to dealing with presses. He knew as well as they did that he was their golden child, so he held all the cards in that relationship. They would lose most of their business if they lost Luther.

One matter arose from his brief trip to Wittenberg that caused Luther some serious concern, and that was the Reformation's leadership there. It was not a major concern immediately, but after Luther returned to Wartburg, he began to ask more detailed questions via mail correspondence. Luther learned that the person at the helm of the reform movement in Wittenberg was his friend and colleague Karlstadt, as well as an Augustinian monk named Gabriel Zwilling. They were introducing reforms Luther had not authorized.

The first reform that alarmed Luther was Karlstadt's introduction of the practice of eating the communion bread with one's hands rather than passively allowing the priest to put the bread on the tongue. Karlstadt was also directing people to drink the Eucharistic wine straight from the chalice. This was all new for the parishioners. In medieval times, it was uncommon for laity to receive the communion wine at all; only the clergy were considered worthy to drink it.[23]

Another strange development was Karlstadt's insistence that he should be called "brother Andrew," which was striking in its informality. Further,

Karlstadt decided to marry a fifteen-year-old girl named Anna Mochau. Luther approved of the marriage, but after all, Karlstadt was the first reformer to marry and thus an important line had been crossed. Luther spoke about the dignity of marriage, and he had questioned the Roman requirement of priestly celibacy, but Karlstadt had the audacity to dive in.

Further, Karlstadt began to question infant baptism because it was not authorized in the Bible. He concluded that a child's baptism was questionable because the child had no voice in the matter. It seemed contradictory to the plain teaching of Scripture that when a person comes to Christ they should be baptized for the remission of their sins. Infants were pure and did not need the purifying water of baptism yet.

Perhaps the reform that incensed Luther the most was Karlstadt's decision to remove all the paintings, icons, statues, crucifixes, and other religious artifacts from the church walls and dispose of them. Karlstadt's reasoning was that venerating all these images amounted to idolatry. And worship should not include music, either, he had decided. Karlstadt wanted to focus on the Scriptures alone, and all this art and accoutrement got in the way of the precious Word of God. He declared that Christians should "relegate organs, trumpets, and flutes to the theater" and not to the worship of God.[24]

Luther was enraged. In his mind, this was iconoclasm. Luther saw no need to remove the religious art and, since music was so important to Luther, he certainly had no sympathy with the evisceration of music in worship. And Luther's strong Augustinian understanding of original sin—that babies were born with it—caused him to be outraged that Karlstadt would contradict something so central to Christian theology. As a classic Augustinian theologian, Luther believed fundamentally that babies should be baptized to remove the stain of sin.

Gabriel Zwilling seemed to emerge as the great preacher in and around Wittenberg without Luther around. His fiery sermons attracted the people and even received the enthusiastic approval of Melanchthon.[25] Zwilling's preaching caused many Augustinians to leave the cloister. He shook the foundations of the ancient faith by refusing to celebrate the Mass in the Augustinian chapel until the reforms he had in mind were instituted. "He would rather have no Mass than to have it mutilated." He and others came to the determination that private Masses—a staple practice in the church for centuries—were completely useless. Consequently, in October of 1521,the Wittenberg Augustinians simply stopped having Mass.[26]

Riots by Enraged Riff-Raff

Luther had started all of this, but he was unable to control it from his seclusion in Wartburg Castle. Reports began to spill in that violence was erupting. Statues and icons were being pulled down. The Augustinians feared for their own safety, especially after an attack on priests in early December. Anger against indulgences raged. Even Frederick the Wise was hearing about the chaos and became alarmed by the reports he was receiving.[27] Luther did his part to quell the rising vehemence against the church by writing a pamphlet entitled *Sincere Exhortation to Beware of Revolt and Insurrection*. The title is revealing, shedding light on Luther's worst fears.[28] It was Luther's attempt to urge patience, with the understanding that reformation would come, but it must come within the parameters of a civil society and according to the rule of law.

Change was happening. This was necessary and expected. But Luther did not anticipate violence or disruption on this scale. Nor did he expect the suddenness of the changes. Luther blamed Karlstadt for the senseless turmoil.

Just after Christmas in 1521, another incident occurred that was truly disconcerting. Two simple cloth-weavers named Nicholas Storch and Thomas Drechsel visited Melanchthon in Wittenberg. They were accompanied by a former Wittenberg student named Mark Stübner, the son of a bathkeeper. The people began to call these three men "the prophets of Zwickau," since they were from a nearby town of that name. They claimed that God was speaking through them. They advocated violence against clergymen, against authority, and against what they deemed to be "godless people." They fiercely rejected infant baptism and thus were known as "Anabaptists" (meaning "baptized again"). They argued for a radical interpretation of Scripture, particularly when it came to authority. In their view, "God's authority was being poured out onto laypeople to preach and prophesy."[29]

The incident involving the Zwickau prophets was a shining example of the worst possible scenario—that Luther's reforms would get into the hands of the uneducated and would lead to catastrophic social upheaval. Many people followed this path, however. In Erfurt, forty clerical houses were destroyed. Libraries were ransacked. One person was killed during the melee. Riots broke out in Memmingen, Nuremburg, Eilenburg, and many other places.[30] Mayhem ruled the day, overrunning villages and communities across Germany, and Luther could do little to rein it in.

Luther wrote a letter to his parishioners in Wittenberg, urging them to rethink the radical steps they had taken recently.

> You have gone about the business in a way of which I cannot approve . . . using your fists, and if this happens again I shall not take your part. You began without me, so carry it on without me. What you have done is wrong, no matter how many Karlstadts approve of it. . . . Believe me, I know the devil well, and he is at the root of all this and has led you to attack the sacrament, etc., so that he might injure God's Word, and meantime faith and love are forgotten.[31]

Luther had no other means by which he could try to fix the problems. His only available resource at the time was his pen.

Luther's Great Achievement at Wartburg

Luther's literary output was breathtaking and magnificent while he resided in Wartburg in 1521 and early 1522. He wrote several books and pamphlets during that period of only ten months. He made a tender translation of the *Magnificat*—the song of Mary in Luke 1—which he dedicated to the heir of the Saxon throne. While Luther later in life denied Mary's intercessory role between humans and God, his devotion to her saintliness and perpetual purity is striking in this text.[32]

In November 1521, Luther completed *On Monastic Vows*, an important text in his corpus because it shows his changing views on monasticism, an institution to which he had given nearly two decades of his life. The work is a hypothetical letter to Luther's father, although it was written in Latin, a language his father could not read. He apologizes to his father in the text, pointing out that Hans was correct to try to keep Luther out of the monastery. Luther wrote that his famous vision in the storm—when he called upon Saint Anne—so many years prior had not been from God. However, he said, God had used Luther's insolent attitude toward his father for good anyway, by giving Luther an inside perspective on the monastery and the corruptions in the church. For that vital perspective, Luther was thankful. In the work, Luther asked his father, "What do you think now? Will you still take me out of the monastery? . . . God, who has taken me out of the monastery, has an authority over me that is greater than yours." Luther was clearly working out some intensely personal issues in this text. Perhaps more than anything, he was trying to make sense of his struggle against authority: against his father and against the pope. Christian "liberty" is a theme Luther struggled with in that work. The Christian enjoys tremendous freedom, he taught, but it is a freedom that comes from living in absolute obedience to God.[33]

Luther's leviathan accomplishment during his Wartburg stay, however, was his translation of the New Testament into German, "a deeply personal translation that seems to have been written in a single breath."[34] Luther did not have his library, which may have been a key reason he managed to complete the work in a mere eleven weeks.[35] Without the sophisticated literary tools necessary to check and recheck his translations, he was freer to proceed. He worked as one possessed during that winter. He was on a mission, and there can be little doubt that he knew what he was up to: he was getting the Bible into the hands of the common people. Many other attempts had been made to translate the Scriptures into German.[36] However, none of them rivalled Luther's. Luther knew his mushrooming band of followers would soon encounter the word of God in the German tongue for the first time, and he wanted to be their guide.

Luther's translation of the New Testament into German is puzzling because it is a work of "undeniable excellence . . . truly monumental," yet it was completed with such breakneck speed.[37] Here we see Luther's gifts on display perhaps more than anywhere else. He understood the German mind. He was a Bible scholar, competent in Greek. But that was not his uniqueness. What was different about Luther was his gift of expression. He was able to communicate the power of the gospel in ways that had not been accomplished before. Luther's goal was nothing less than winning a war for the hearts of his beloved Germans. To accomplish that goal, he would have to usher their minds out of Rome and the world of the Latin Vulgate and into their mother tongue, into the language of the heart: German.

Luther's translation of the New Testament into German would be unbelievable were it not for the evidence. Melanchthon wrote a letter dated

March 6 wherein he mentioned that Luther had returned from Wartburg with a complete translation of all twenty-seven books of the New Testament. As his source, he had used Erasmus of Rotterdam's second edition (1519) of the Greek New Testament.[38]

Luther's theology surfaces in his German translation of the New Testament. He frequently emphasizes faith *alone*, as well as the righteousness *of God*—the twin engines of his great theological breakthrough. He wanted the Bible to speak directly to people, and his translation captures that directness. Luther "conceived of the gospel more as an oral message than as a literary text, and this was why his translation took on a spoken character that is picked up by the ear." He chose "forceful words, succinct expressions, and simple declarative sentences." Extensive marginal notes elucidate what Luther thought the text was saying to people. At times, he took "astonishing liberties" with the text, but he did not have a stifling rhetorical principle to smother his creative genius. In a word, Luther's translation is *memorable*. He employed an effective use of cadence—the "rhythm of the sentence."[39] It was a marvelous feat, and it seemed to come so naturally for Luther, a man uniquely gifted with a sense of how to express himself with power, concision, and effectiveness.

As was common with Luther's publications, he included many pictures. The book of Revelation alone contained twenty-one woodcuts by Cranach to convince the reader that Rome was Babylon and the pope was its whore.[40]

Luther's translation of the New Testament is described by German scholars with the rarest heights of praise.

> Today there is agreement that Luther, in his translation of the Bible, was not the first nor the only person to develop High German as a literary language, although his Bible translation was one of High German's most significant and widely distributed documents, through which he became quite the "most influential author in the German tongue."[41]

Another scholar declares:

> Luther's Bible translation gave the evangelical movement an inexhaustible source for its proclamation and provided the German people with an overflowing well for nourishing its new

> language. . . . It was from Luther's Bible that the German people learned to speak the language they were to have in common.[42]

Without a doubt, the German people loved Luther's translation. Its sales were unprecedented. Luther's understanding of the gospel was extremely influential almost overnight. People began to cite his version immediately upon its publication on September 25, 1522. Quite naturally—due to the crass and horrible depictions of the papacy—it was banned by the Catholic Church as heretical and dangerous. Rome knew that the cat was out of the bag, however. They even made the surprising offer to refund anyone their money if they would only return their copy of Luther's New Testament.[43]

Luther's name was not listed as the translator, but everyone knew it was him.[44] Three thousand copies of the first edition sold out immediately. Within twelve years, two hundred thousand copies had been published. This was to be added to Luther's other publications, estimated to be around three hundred thousand copies of his works in 370 editions by the time he returned from Wartburg in 1522.[45]

Luther, always the fighter, seemed to gloat in the face of his increasingly hostile detractors. He taunted his critics by boasting that while they might be able to write books, none of them could expound the psalms or the prophets the way he could. He could translate the Bible; they couldn't. Was he being arrogant? Yes. But what he said was mostly true. Indeed, Luther tapped into the zeitgeist of his German countrymen in a way no one else had before him. His German-language Bible established him as the religious folk hero of the nation. Through it, he left his indelible mark on Germans and Germany for centuries to come. He had created "the Book" that for the next two or three hundred years was to mold their language. German classical literature itself is unthinkable without Luther's German.[46]

Return to Wittenberg

Finally, on March 1, 1522, Luther left Wartburg for good. Elector Frederick the Wise wanted him to stay longer, but Luther was ready to take his place at the helm of the ship he had launched.

He had important work to do. In his opinion, the Reformation in Wittenberg had gotten out of hand. Incited by Zwilling, the people by now were destroying everything in sight: statues, altars, vessels, and all manner of sacred objects. He had persuaded the people to chop off the hands and heads of the saints since they had not brought them closer to God. Fires raged in churchyards all around Wittenberg, fueled by objects considered most holy just months before.[47] Luther was disgusted and felt that he must intervene, even at great personal risk. The door was opened for him to come home. The Wittenberg parish council invited him back as soon as possible, hoping to prevent irreparable damage to their churches, to members of their community, and to their city.[48]

Very sensitive to his protégé, Philip Melanchthon, Luther always trusted his opinions. Concerning the influence of the radicals, Melanchthon wrote to Luther, "The dam has broken, and I cannot stem the waters."[49] This cry of desperation moved Luther to immediate action.

Luther knew that Elector Frederick would not be pleased that he had returned to Wittenberg. Luther responded to him in a letter with wit and persuasion, and great verve.

> For many years your princely grace has sought to acquire relics from every possible land, but now God has answered your prayers and without your effort or expense has sent me like an entire cross with nails, spears, and whips. Fear not, but stretch out your arms on this cross and allow the nails to sink in; be thankful and joyful.[50]

In other words, Luther was returning, against the advice of the ruler who had protected him. And while Frederick continued to try to persuade Luther that his return to Wittenberg was premature, Luther continually appealed to his conscience.[51] He could do no other. He had to fight for what he believed in, no matter who got in the way.

Luther entered Wittenberg—still in disguise as Junker Jörg—on March 6, 1522. He was escorted by a group of knights. A Swiss student by the name of Kessler described the scene. He said Luther walked "erect . . . bent backward rather than forward; his head was lifted high." His "deep-set black eyes" were "twinkling like stars."[52] Luther was back in town. Change was coming

Notes

[1]Sam Wellman, *Frederick the Wise* (Saint Louis: Concordia, 2011), 207; and James Reston, Jr., *Luther's Fortress* (New York: Basic Books, 2015), 49.

[2]Scott Hendrix, *Martin Luther: Visionary Reformer* (New Haven: Yale University Press, 2015), 77.

[3]Ibid., 107.

[4]This is known from a letter written by Luther to his friend, the artist Lucas Cranach, on April 28 of 1521. See James Kittelson, *Luther the Reformer* (Minneapolis: Fortress Press, 1986), 164.

[5]Hendrix,109.

[6]Richard Friedenthal, trans. by John Nowell, *Luther* (New York: Harcourt Brace Jovanovich, 1970), 285.

[7]Hendrix, 109.

[8]Ibid., 110.

[9]Friedenthal, 297.

[10]Ibid., 287.

[11]Martin Brecht, trans. by James Schaaf, *Martin Luther,* vol. 2 (Philadelphia: Fortress Press, 1985), 2.

[12]Friedenthal, 296–297.

[13]Lyndal Roper, *Martin Luther* (London: Bodley Head, 2016), 198.

[14]Brecht, vol. 2, 2.

[15]Ibid.

[16]Friedenthal, 299.

[17]Heinrich Bornkamm, trans. by E. Theodore Bachmann, *Luther in Mid-Career, 1521–1530* (Philadelphia: Fortress Press, 1983), 2.

[18]Larry Mansch and Curtis Peters, *Martin Luther: The Life and Lessons* (Jefferson, NC: McFarland, 2016), 126.

[19]Friedenthal, 317.

[20]Ibid., 300. See also Andrew Pettegree, *Brand Luther* (New York: Penguin Press, 2015), 139–141.

[21]Kittelson, 173.

[22]See Roland Bainton, *Here I Stand* (New York: Meridian, 1950), 158. See also Brecht, vol. 2, 29.

[23]Mansch and Peters, 132.

[24]Ibid., 132–133. See also Hartmann Grisar, *Martin Luther* (Westminster: Newman Press, 1950), 208–209.

[25]Grisar, 209, 212.

[26]Bainton, 157.

[27]Ibid., and Grisar, 212.

[28]Friedenthal, 318.

[29]Roper, 228, and Grisar, 213.

[30]Mansch and Peters, 127, 131.

[31]In Mansch and Peters, 134.

[32]See Grisar, 210–211. Grisar is an important perspective here since he was a Jesuit priest. He looks carefully at Luther's Mariology in this section.

[33]See Roper, 204–206.

[34]Ibid., 209.

[35]Pettegree, 142.

[36]Friedenthal notes that more than a dozen translations into German were already published. See 305.

[37]Grisar, 211. Note: Grisar was a Roman Catholic priest.

[38]Hendrix, 126.

[39]Brecht, vol. 2, 49–50.

[40]Ibid., 53.

[41]Ibid., 48.

[42]Bornkamm, 49–50.

[43]Brecht, vol. 2, 53.

[44]Ibid.

[45]Mansch and Peters, 128.

[46]Friedenthal, 309–310.

[47]Hendrix, 127.

[48]Mansch and Peters, 136.

[49]Bainton, 163.

[50]Hendrix, 127.

[51]Ibid., 128.

[52]Grisar, 216.

13

Killing the "Thieving Hordes"

Luther's arrival back in Wittenberg on March 6, 1522, meant changes were on the horizon. He met with close friends privately over the next two days to stage a comeback that would play to his advantage. The one major obstacle to Luther having his way with Wittenbergers was Andreas Karlstadt, his one-time colleague and friend.

The Sacking of Andreas Karlstadt

Three days after he got home, Luther began preaching a series of eight sermons intended to ruin the credibility of Karlstadt.[1] He wanted to reclaim his place as the leader in Wittenberg, and Karlstadt would have to be publicly challenged and defeated if Luther was to win the hearts and minds of the townspeople. These were two alpha males, and according to nature, only one could enjoy the spoils of this intellectual war. Karlstadt had acquired the scepter of Wittenberg during Luther's absence. But like a prizefighter who has to work his way back after losing his crown, Luther was eager to get back into the ring.

Luther constantly reminded Wittenbergers that this movement was his. He had started this. Karlstadt was second. From the pulpit, Luther argued, "Dear brothers, follow me. . . . I was the first whom God placed on this arena. It was also me to whom God first revealed to preach these words." Luther began to tear into Karlstadt as a "radical," and he explained himself as someone who had fought with Satan during his confinement at Wartburg Castle. Thus, he had earned the right to be their leader. This was an odd strategy. Many of the emerging Reformation leaders claimed to have interacted with God in a special way. But Luther justified himself by emphasizing his duels with the devil![2]

While Luther was at Wartburg, he corresponded with young Philip Melanchthon, hoping he could lead the reforms. But Melanchthon was too youthful. And his disposition was not that of a valiant soul capable of winning the hearts and minds of a great majority of people. Karlstadt was able to talk big and make waves, like Luther. But Luther's leadership capabilities were of another order. Luther's rhetoric, gifts of persuasion, tireless desire to fight, and superb command of words overshadowed any and every one that might be compared to him. Luther was a leader par excellence.

Luther had distrusted Karlstadt for some time. He did not correspond with him during the Wartburg confinement. Once Luther set foot back in Wittenberg in 1522, however, he immediately put a big bullseye on Karlstadt. Luther had to sink him. So he began to methodically tear apart any semblance of authority Karlstadt had worked to acquire during the previous year. According to Karlstadt, Luther had excoriated his reputation so thoroughly that it was like he was trying to put Karlstadt's head into a noose.[3] There could be truth to that accusation.

Karlstadt was the first of many whom Luther would ruin once he sensed that they were disloyal. One historian writes, "There is something chilling about the no-holds-barred nature of Luther's hatred." He regularly associated Karlstadt with Satan.[4] Karlstadt had ruined the momentum of the Reformation in Luther's mind. Luther rightly accused Karlstadt of abandoning the notion of the "real presence" of Christ in the Eucharist. When Karlstadt began to argue that the Lord's Supper was a memorial, Luther was incensed. The actual body of Christ in the bread and the actual blood of Jesus in the wine were vital ideas to Luther. While he was averse to the term "transubstantiation," Luther never abandoned the notion that the bread "is" the body of Jesus and the wine "is" the blood. Later, as we shall see, Luther would condemn Ulrich Zwingli (1484–1531)—the leader of the Reformation in Zurich—on this same issue.

With surprisingly swift effectiveness, Luther was able to neuter any authority that Karlstadt had mustered. Karlstadt was banned from preaching in the city. The university censor prohibited him from publishing.[5] Soon, due to the force of Luther's power and popularity, Karlstadt became a social pariah. It signaled a turn in the Reformation in Wittenberg. What had once been a dynamic, collective, exhilarating movement quickly came under the direction of Martin Luther. He was in charge. The people movement that so many thought they were part of diminished quickly when Luther returned from hiding. And this is why Luther is sometimes referred to as a Protestant Pope. For the rest of his life, Luther distrusted the collective action of "the people." This all played out most conspicuously and tragically in the Peasants' War.

Why did Luther feel so threatened by Karlstadt? It seems rather obvious that Luther would never play second fiddle. However, other reasons for Luther's distrust of Karlstadt revolve around the loss of social order. Karlstadt seemed to care little about whether the governing, secular authorities could be persuaded to back the Reformation cause. He was radical in this sense. He believed the reform must take place with or without the approval of rulers and their civil magistrates. Luther picked up on this blind spot in Karlstadt's thinking. What Luther was beginning to see—especially after having his head saved at Worms by Frederick the Wise—was that he needed to proceed cautiously and carefully if he was going to truly change the society around him. Luther was convinced that change must occur at the top, and you won the larger, higher battles—the political battles—not through violence but through persuasion. Even if a small peasant band could win a few victories in the countryside, in the end they would fail due to the utter force of the leviathan—the state.

Luther would have been aware of smaller, more radical Reformations happening across Europe. The reports were shocking: routine attacks on clergy, opposition to town councils, rebellion against all manner of authority, boisterous interruptions of sermons in the middle of church services, altarpieces destroyed, icons smashed, rocks thrown through stained glass windows, overturned furniture in the churches, robbers, people urinating in chalices to draw attention to their cause, destruction of Mass books, and outright mocking and public humiliation of clergymen. Indeed, there was an overall sense that the social order was beginning to unravel.[6] This was the way of Karlstadt, not Luther. At least, this is how Luther perceived it, and there was truth to his interpretation.

Black Bear Inn

The discordant relationship between Luther and Karlstadt exploded on August 22, 1524, at the Black Bear Inn in the town of Jena, where Luther had a room. Luther had just preached a sermon in the main church. Wearing a disguise, Karlstadt had attended, and he sent a messenger to Luther after the sermon, asking him to meet and visit. They agreed to meet at Luther's hotel. Both had with them supporters who witnessed the event: the two Wittenberg stalwarts were about to either iron out their differences or dissolve any remaining alliances.

The debate was long, highly emotional, and full of personal attacks. Words were not minced. Karlstadt openly acknowledged his resentment of Luther for turning people against him to the point that he could scarcely preach or publish. Luther critiqued Karlstadt for being arrogant: "You go about in a grandiose fashion, boast grandly, and want only yourself to be exalted and noticed."[7] As the ferocious debate was winding down, Karlstadt accused Luther of muzzling him. Luther pulled out a gold coin and presented it to Karlstadt, encouraging him to publish. Karlstadt had implied to the onlookers that the only reason Luther was winning their public battle was because Luther had silenced him by persuading the presses not to publish his work. By presenting the gold coin, Luther was doing something rather common at the time. He was essentially saying, "Go ahead and publish. You have my approval. Here's payment for all to see that I will not prevent you from publishing." Karlstadt bent the coin—part of the public display that an agreement was being made—and the two men shook hands to cement the contract.

Publisher Martin Reinhard produced a pamphlet-length account of the Black Bear Inn meeting. Luther was incensed by it, thinking it was too much in favor of Karlstadt (although it was quite measured and factual). Luther used his power to drive Reinhard out of business; indeed, when he resurfaced in Nuremberg, Luther made sure he was again fired from his post and sent packing.[8] Luther ruined Reinhard. And he made sure to ruin Karlstadt even more than he already had. Luther was relentless. Those who ran afoul of him rarely rose from the ashes after he torched them.

The Peasants' War

Luther was aware of developments happening all around him. The movement he had birthed was metastasizing all over the empire. Between 1523 and 1525, a series of revolts broke out in Germany. While they certainly were fueled by the exhilaration of the Protestant Reformation, they were part of a much bigger picture that reached back decades, even centuries. Since at least 1304, "common man" rebellions had flared up against the power structures of late-medieval Europe: Italy in 1304, Flanders in 1323, France in 1356, England in 1381, Bohemia in 1419, Spain in 1437, and Hungary in 1514. Peasant rebellions in Germany had burst forth in 1476, 1493, and 1514.[9] As noted earlier, often they took a peasant shoe as their logo, which explains why these uprisings were known as the *Bundschuh* ("peasant's boot") movements in Germany and beyond. They put the peasant shoe on their flags, and they marched in protest, and often into war, fighting for their rights.

So the German Peasants' War came in a long line of protests by the common folk—peasants, minders, townspeople, workers—rooted in what can only be seen from a modern perspective as flagrant oppression. These people were politically powerless, without a vote, without agency, without a process for getting their voices heard. They were, by and large, peasants, and they were locked into a world of serfdom, a medieval form of bondage that included few freedoms.

What touched off the German Peasants' War is debated, but one small incident has received some attention as a possible beginning. When a certain countess in the city of Lütphen forced her peasants to pick strawberries for a banquet she was hostessing, these angry workers may have sparked what grew into a mighty conflagration.[10] They resisted her orders. Other peasants in nearby towns were motivated to take similar action. When more radical Protestant leaders heard about the courage of the peasants, they urged them on. Again, this was something Luther could not endorse. He sympathized with peasants and on occasion even described himself as being from peasant ancestry (not exactly true), but he could not support the sudden disruption of the social order.

Other historians point to a peasant revolt in the town of Stühlingen—in the southernmost part of Germany, not far from Zurich, Switzerland.[11] This would make sense, because in Zurich the Reformation was in full swing, led by the famous pastor Ulrich Zwingli. Zurich was one of the first cities of Europe to institute the Protestant Reformation, so it is very possible that the uprisings grew up in and around that region. In that story, the Stühlingen peasants revolted against their countess when she required her workers to gather snail shells so she could wind her yarn.[12]

Many of these early revolts had to do with the paying of grain tithes. Peasants rebelled against their overlords by burning grain openly in the fields. This act of rebellion spread and morphed into rent strikes, protests against the feudal system itself, and a robust anti-clericalism. Peasants began to refuse to pay their tithes, dues, rents, and even withheld their labor services to the landowners. They wanted a voice. Some even went so far as to demand self-government.[13]

It is important to note that many priests as well as lay preachers openly supported the peasant rebellions: Balthasar Hubmaier, Hans Müller, and Thomas Müntzer are only three of a long list of clergymen who fanned the flames of rebellion. By 1524, Germany was home to numerous peasant revolts that spread like wildfires. The term "peasants" is not entirely accurate, because often these movements for social reform included clergy, miners, more middle-class townspeople, and even some from the ranks of lower-level nobility.[14]

In a short time, the peasant revolts began to mobilize. They made their demands in writing and took on a militaristic character.[15] Some of their militias were well organized, consisting of up to fifteen thousand men.[16] They developed a rotation system so that some could return to their farms and work the land while others formed military squads able to respond quickly to an invading force from the ruling authorities of the region. These weekend warriors were at a grave disadvantage, however. They were not professionally trained; they were only part-time soldiers. They could certainly saber-rattle, and they had great moral strength in numbers, but they would prove no match for a professional military in the case of all-out war.

The peasants were chiefly concerned with what they perceived to be economic exploitation. For example, they opposed a "death tax" where the lord charged families a tax—the "best head of cattle"—when a married worker died. These death taxes could be punishing for widows and orphans especially. Peasants were outraged that their access to game and fish was being curtailed. They began to be charged for firewood, which they had previously gathered from the forests for free. They pleaded for rulers to stop creating new laws that had the effect of limiting rights they had enjoyed from time immemorial.[17]

The Twelve Articles

In 1525, a journeyman furrier (one who deals in animal skins and furs) named Sebastian Lotzer streamlined the list of peasant grievances to four core requests. This document came to be known as *The Twelve Articles of the Upper Swabian Peasants*. He was well-acquainted with and influenced by the teachings of Zwingli, the great Swiss reformer. *The Twelve Articles* became the "key manifesto" of the Peasants' War, selling twenty-five thousand copies in less than two months.[18]

The *Twelve Articles* were not just economic in nature; they contained clear religious motifs as well. Religious language pervaded them. They were not militaristic in nature at all. They supported peaceable solutions. Their requests were of a nature that we take for granted today. In Article One, they expressed the desire to be able to appoint their own pastor and to remove him if he became immoral. In Article Three, they requested the right to be considered free, as opposed to being "regarded as a lord's personal property." With great force, they argued, "Scripture establishes that we are and want to be free." They begged their overlords to "release us from serfdom, or show us from the gospel that we should be serfs."

Their attitude in this document was humble, not proud. Indeed, they were quick to point out their obedience to authority, but they simply wanted to have basic human freedoms. There was a pervasive complaint threaded throughout the document that "new laws are constantly being made," and thus their overlords were always finding fault with them for breaking these new and ever-expanding laws. Often, the peasants were unaware of the new laws being made. Thus, they felt it was unjust to accuse them of breaking laws of which they had no prior knowledge.[19]

The Peasants' Leader

In time, the Peasants' Revolt found its great leader in the person of Thomas Müntzer (1489–1525), one of Luther's earliest followers. Müntzer has come to be known as the epitome of a *radical* reformer. He had a way of attracting ire everywhere he went, but he also had some obvious gifts for leadership; he was never at a loss for followers.

By 1525, Müntzer already had a checkered history. He had been run out of Zwickau after repeated fights with the town council and because of a proclivity to interrupt sermons. He believed himself to be a prophet of God, and he had apocalyptic, mystical beliefs. His followers were under constant suspicion for igniting fires, both actual and metaphorical. For Müntzer, the "kingdom of God was at hand," and the Lord had handpicked him to usher in the new era. With these and other grandiose claims, he rose to the leadership of the revolt, even claiming that he could catch bullets in the sleeves of his coat when fired upon by the enemy.[20]

Müntzer organized a secret group he called The League of the Elect. They were his inner circle. They were for radical change and would stop at nothing to institute Müntzer's reforms. In April 1524, they burned down a local convent's shrine to the Virgin Mary. They proclaimed Müntzer to be a "new Daniel" who would dream dreams and usher in the last days. Müntzer's League became an "openly military association . . . convened in order to smite the godless."[21] Müntzer eventually began issuing threats to the local princes that they would either comply or lose their high positions. He acquired unquestioned power in the eyes of his followers, to the point of authorizing executions for those they captured in battle.

In May 1525, Müntzer's men joined with seven thousand fighting peasants near the town of Frankenhausen to overthrow area governments, to implement their reforms, and to purge the church of false clergy. They marched under the banner of a rainbow with the words, "The Word of the Lord remains forever."[22]

When combined militaries from Saxony and Hesse arrived for battle, Müntzer waffled on whether he should negotiate with them. Eventually, he decided to resist, believing God would come to his aid. When his followers noticed a halo around the sun, they took it as an omen from God that they should fight.

The slaughter was ugly and swift. The peasants were decimated. Six thousand of their men were killed, while the armies of Saxony and Hesse only lost six men. Müntzer fled to the town and hid in an attic. When soldiers discovered him in disguise, he acted like he was ill, but his charades failed. He was captured, tortured over several days, killed, and his body impaled and put on display as a warning to other peasants who resisted the long arm of the law.[23]

Today, a great monument stands at Frankenhausen, honoring the peasants for their courage. Müntzer's failed revolt was iconic for the East German government. A huge and ambitious monument—a panorama rotunda painting around four hundred feet long and fifty feet high—stands today for visitors. Created by Werner Tübke, it never enjoyed the adoration for which it was created, for Communist Germany collapsed only weeks after its completion. Today, this massive mural is just a "bizarre" piece of art, seemingly stuck in the Soviet era, off the beaten path of tourism in Germany. It has been called "the largest painting in the world."[24]

Luther: Advocate for the Common Man

At the time, it would have been entirely logical to think that Luther was on the side of the peasants in these disturbances and revolts. In fact, Luther was quite the agitator himself. He, too, rebuked authority. He openly insulted the pope! He refused to back down despite terrific odds against him. Three of his big discoveries were openly embraced by the peasant classes: (1) the priesthood of all believers, (2) the radical freedom of the Christian, and (3) the right of the laity to read the Bible and disagree with the authorities if necessary. These were Lutheran ideals. And peasants, at least initially, thought Luther to be their champion.

Just two years before the tragic finale to the Peasants' War in 1525, Luther wrote a tract entitled *The Rights of a Christian Congregation*. That piece of writing contained within it Luther's doubts that the nobility could bring about reform. It conflicted with his famous 1520 work *Address to the Christian Nobility of the German Nation*, which advocated "church reform on an imperial level through the Reichstag."[25] Evidently, Luther had a change of heart. In 1520, he seemed to say that the Reformation must be spearheaded by the nobility. By 1523, he was growing impatient and advocated a more grassroots approach to reform.

Some suggest that Luther may have been reacting to the refusal of some of the princes to allow Luther's German New Testament to be read in their realms. Luther sensed that without the German Bible he could never "prove"—through *sola scriptura*—his theological arguments over the papacy. Thus, Luther may have wanted to circumvent the nobility and get the Bible into the hands of the people. By advocating their radical freedom and their right to make their own ecclesial decisions, Luther thought he might be able to put pressure on the German nobility. Eventually, he thought, the nobility might capitulate, allowing the common people to access the Bible, read it for themselves, and take reformation into their own hands.

Luther advocated passive resistance in *The Rights of a Christian Congregation.* His tone toward the noble classes was negative and pessimistic. He openly questioned the competence of the nobility on church affairs. He advocated the local churches to hire and fire their own teachers, and he openly condemned the rulers who believed themselves more capable than the local church in determining who their leaders should be. Importantly, he argued that only the local church be authorized to determine what doctrine it should follow. That decision should never be imposed upon them.

The Rights of a Christian Congregation had seeds of revolt within it, although Luther probably did not realize it at the time. For example, he wrote, "Christ takes both the right and the power to judge teaching from the bishops, scholars, and councils and gives them to everyone and *to all Christians equally.*" Luther then quoted John 10:8, "No matter how many of them have come, they are thieves and murderers. But the sheep did not listen to them." Luther then launched a tirade into the papacy and church authorities, accusing them of being the "murderers and thieves" that Jesus was referring to. As usual, he condemned the pope as the antichrist and urged the people to reject the Roman clergy as "perverted and blind masks and true child-bishops," among other insults.[26]

Luther unleashed a whole class of uneducated, untrained preachers who, armed with the Word of God, now felt free to preach, teach, argue their own causes, and air their own grievances. They were empowered, even intoxicated, by the notion that all Christians were priests. All Christians had the authority that comes from Christ alone and not from any man. Luther's teachings made the peasants realize their own worth. They too had a voice. They too had agency. They too could make decisions.

The peasants explicitly identified Luther with their cause. Indeed, in *the Twelve Articles* discussed above, they named Luther and Melanchthon (but not Müntzer) as acceptable arbiters for them. They trusted Luther, and they believed he was squarely aligned with their movement. In their minds, Luther was fueling them. If nobles refused to deal directly with the peasants, then Luther was an acceptable mediator. Luther was one of them. He would stand up for them against tyranny and oppression!

Luther's Change of Heart

As the peasant movement intensified and proliferated, Luther wrote *An Admonition to Peace*, a document that tried to cool escalating tensions between the nobles and the peasants.[27] Luther took a middle road. The revolutionary Luther from just a couple of years ago was absent now. Instead, he chastised the princes for unjust treatment of the peasants, effectively inviting the peasants to revolt. He pointed out that many of the peasants' claims were right and justified. Princes needed to deal more justly with the people, and they must allow the local congregations to enjoy autonomy. However, he argued in equally strong terms that the peasants were wrong to rebel in violent or chaotic ways.

Ironically, and perhaps naïvely, Luther was troubled that the peasants read the Bible differently than he did. How could they? Luther's solution was that large-scale negotiations should take place between the nobles and the common people. Then all would be made well. After admonishing both peasants and nobles, the *Admonition to Peace* concludes with the following dire warning:

> If you do not follow this advice—God forbid!—I must let you come to blows. But I am innocent of your souls, your blood, or your property. The guilt is yours alone. . . . In any case, my conscience assures me that I have faithfully given you my Christian and fraternal advice. God grant that it helps! Amen.[28]

It did not help. The slaughter at Frankenhausen in May 1525 was one of many. Strung together, these local battles and pitiful attempts at revolt by the common people backfired. Around one hundred thousand farmers, low-level workers, and peasants are estimated to have died in the chaos.[29] The stories are brutal. In the end, none of their demands were met. Most scholars agree that they ended up worse off than before. The nobles distrusted them and allowed them no voice in the political process.

In all fairness, Luther tried to prevent these slaughters. As the violence was reaching its height, Luther was "traveling about the countryside and admonishing crowds of peasants to keep the peace." Apparently, the peasants were not persuaded.

Complicating matters was that Luther's great protector, Frederick the Wise, died on May 5, 1525. His death came at a terrible time. Was it possible that Luther feared utter anarchy without such a strong leader in Saxony and indeed in northern Europe? It was a recipe for disaster: peasants revolting, Europe splitting, the Reformation quarreling from within, and the key political leader who had held all things together was dead. After failing to stanch the flowing of blood in many locales, Luther returned to Wittenberg, "dejected and fearful of the future."[30]

Luther's change of heart might well have happened during his preaching tour during April and May of 1525. In one frightful incident, Luther was preaching peace at Nordhausen when some hecklers began to cause a disturbance to the point that they started throwing stones directly at Luther with the clear intention of hurting him. Luther feared for his life during the incident. When he returned to Wittenberg in May 1525, he penned one of his most famous works, *Against the Murderous and Thieving Hordes of Peasants*. On the cover of that tract was displayed an image that summarized Luther's feelings. It showed a peasant holding a sword in one hand and a stolen duck in the other. A banner above the peasant reads "Love God," which would have been an obvious irony to all readers of the tract. A box below the peasant contains the words of Psalm 7:16, "His mischief will recoil upon himself, and his violence will fall on his own head."[31]

It was now clear: Luther was no longer a friend to the peasants. They were his enemies. They were the enemies of civilization. They were thieves. They were killers. They tried to justify their violence in the name of God. But they were wrong, and they must be put down. With Frederick the Wise dead, these thieving hordes threatened the whole of Germany with complete disorder and mass confusion. What Luther failed to realize, however, was this whole episode was largely his fault.

When Luther sat down to write *Against the Murderous and Thieving Hordes of Peasants*, he was convinced that the chiliastic, millennialist, and chaotic methods and beliefs of the peasants were dangerous.[32] Not only dangerous, they were blasphemous. Preaching had failed. Luther, therefore, authorized the rulers of the land to unleash their wrath on the peasants. His language was unambiguous.

> Romans 13 says, "Let every person be subject to the governing authorities." Since the peasants are now deliberately and violently breaking this oath of obedience and setting themselves in

> opposition to their masters, they have forfeited body and soul, as faithless, perjured, lying, disobedient rascals and scoundrels usually do. . . . They doubly deserve death in body and soul. . . . Whoever is the first to put them to death does right and well. . . . Rebellion brings with it a land filled with murder and bloodshed. . . . Therefore let everyone who can, smite, slay, and stab, secretly or openly, remembering that nothing can be more poisonous, hurtful, or devilish than a rebel. It is just as when one must kill a mad dog. If you do not strike him, he will strike you, and a whole land with you.[33]

Luther's wrath was directed not only at their bodies, but Luther damned them also in soul: "Any peasant who is killed is lost in body and soul and is eternally the devil's." Conversely, Luther wrote, "Anyone who is killed fighting on the side of the rulers may be a true martyr in the eyes of God . . . for he acts in obedience to God's word."

Luther uses the strongest of words in his condemnation of the peasants. They are "wicked," they are "damned," they belong to the devil. "Anyone who consorts with them goes to the devil. . . . A pious Christian ought to suffer a hundred deaths rather than give a hairsbreadth of consent to the peasants' cause." Luther's judgment was that these peasants were members of a "devilish league"; indeed, "they are in the bonds of hell and the devil."

In conclusion, Luther reiterates, as if it wasn't already clear enough: "Let whoever can, stab, smite, slay. If you die doing it, good for you! A more blessed death can never be yours, for you die while obeying the divine word. . . . Let every pious Christian say, 'Amen'!"

Luther's specific condemnations were that the peasants had robbed monasteries and castles. They had committed acts of violence. They had disavowed the teachings of Paul in Romans 13 that people should submit to the government. They had also broken Jesus's command (Lk 20:24) to "render unto Caesar that which is Caesar's." He called them blasphemers for their misinterpretation of the word of God. This last charge was critical; Luther simply could not fathom how someone could reach conclusions different from his own when reading the Scriptures. Since they did so in this case, they should pay the ultimate price.

By the time Luther put his pen to paper, the imperial forces—organized under an imperial military known as the Swabian League—had already begun their smiting and slaying.[34] They were extremely successful in putting down the impotent and carelessly executed uprisings of the peasants. When Luther wrote his scornful pamphlet, the battle was almost over. The trigger had already been pulled well before Luther offered biblical justification for the widespread slaughter. It is anachronistic to argue that Luther singlehandedly caused the violence that rained down on the peasants. That decision had been made and was being executed even as he wrote. However, that's not to say that Luther had not already revealed his intentions to write what he did. In other words, it is certain that Luther had *something* to do with the peasant massacres. He certainly offered congratulations to the government for swiftly and violently crushing any more rebellion from among the working classes.

Conclusion: A Turning Point

The Peasants' Revolt was a turning point in the Reformation. Those peasants who survived had been abandoned by Luther, and thus "returned to their parishes to wait for the retribution of their lords." And from this point on, "the Reformation fell subject to the control of the ruling elite."[35]

The German Peasants' War resulted in unspeakable suffering for the common people. Death was everywhere. Men dangled from trees. Women were ravaged and left to die. Children were orphaned and hungry as a brutally cold winter set in during 1525.[36] Cruel punishments were imposed on the survivors: large scale executions, blindings, maimings, crippling fines, and more.[37] And Luther was not about to come to their defense. He had completely turned on his former fans.

Luther became a hero to the upper classes, especially to the nobility, for preserving the status quo. This was incredibly ironic. The man who had wreaked so much havoc on the ruling classes was now hailed as a hero for keeping the peace. The lower classes, however, felt betrayed by him. Many felt Luther was complicit in a horrible and unnecessary slaughter.

Whether he was truly remorseful for his role or simply trying to save his own skin, Luther felt he needed to justify himself. So, only a few weeks after penning *Thieving Hordes*, in June 1525, Luther wrote a tract entitled *An Open Letter on the Harsh Book against the Peasants*. He knew full well that in the minds of some, he had crossed a line of human decency. Clearly, he had allied himself to the political rulers of the day. And, after the massacre, the political rulers—both Protestant and Catholic—frequently cited Luther as being in support of their brutal methods.[38]

Luther fell under verbal attack by many in the aftermath of the war that he helped to foment. Some accused him of abandoning his most coveted doctrinal pillar—justification by faith—when he offered salvation to the princes and their troops if they died on the battlefield while fighting the peasants. To some, this sounded like the papal indulgences during the Crusades![39]

Luther was now beginning to look like a Protestant pope, authorizing massacres, declaring those who differed from him to be heretics, and stepping headlong into the world of politics. His writings were becoming more and more authoritarian and defensive. In his *Open Letter*, he did little to veil his threats against those who disagreed with him: "I must warn those who criticize my book [*Thieving Hordes*] to hold their tongues and to be careful not to make a mistake and lose their own heads."[40] In that same letter, he offered what can only be interpreted as a threat to the nobility as well: "When I have time and occasion to do so, I shall attack the princes and lords, too, for in my office of teacher, a prince is the same to me as a peasant."[41]

By the end of May 1525, the peasants had been defeated, and the princes were busy taking their revenge. Luther came under intense criticism from everybody for how he handled the entire situation. He was accused of being a flatterer of princes and a betrayer of the common man.[42]

Luther's sights, however, were on something else entirely. For merely days after penning his *Open Letter* in defense of his actions during the peasants' revolt, he was busy getting married. Luther was enjoying one of the happiest and most blissful times in his life.

Notes

[1]Lyndal Roper, *Martin Luther: Renegade and Prophet* (London: The Bodley Head, 2016), 233.

[2]Ibid., 233–234.

[3]Ibid., 235.

[4]Ibid.

[5]Ibid.

[6]See Ibid., 237.

[7]Ibid., 243.

[8]Ibid., 244.

[9]See Carter Lindberg, *The European Reformations,* 2nd ed. (Oxford: Wiley-Blackwell, 2010), 150–151.

[10]James Kittelson, *Luther the Reformer* (Minneapolis: Fortress Press, 1986), 190.

[11]Lindberg, 151. See also Michael Baylor, *The German Reformation and the Peasants' War* (New York: Bedford/St. Martins, 2012), 74.

[12]Hubert Kirchner, trans. by Darrell Jodock, *Luther and the Peasants' War* (Philadelphia: Fortress Press, 1972), 3.

[13]C. Scott Dixon, *The Reformation in Germany* (Oxford: Blackwell, 2002), 81.

[14]Lindberg, 152.

[15]See Baylor, 74ff, for various lists, or "articles," expressing peasant demands.

[16]Lindberg, 152.

[17]See Baylor, 74–75, and Lindberg, 156.

[18]Baylor, 76. For sales numbers, see Lindberg, 156.

[19]For "new laws, etc.," see Article Nine, in Baylor, 81.

[20]Kittelson, 189–191.

[21]Dixon, 89.

[22]Lindberg, 148.

[23]For the slaughter at Frankenhausen, see Dixon, 90, and Lindberg, 148–149.

[24]See Stephen Kinzer, "Bad Frankenhausen Journal; A Hero and a Picture From History's Attic," *New York Times*, 1 May 1991, located at: http://www.nytimes.com/1991/05/01/world/bad-frankenhausen-journal-a-hero-and-a-picture-from-history-s-attic.html. The present author visited the Frankenhausen panorama in summer 2016.

[25]The Reichstag is the Diet, or the general assembly of the imperial estates. The Holy Roman Emperor was their authority, and they convened only occasionally until establishing a permanent (Perpetual Diet) meeting place at the Regensburg city hall, which lasted from 1663 to 1806. See James Stayer, "The German Peasants' War and the Rural Reformation," in *The Reformation World*, ed. Andrew Pettegree (New York: Routledge, 2000), 127.

[26]See Baylor, 65–68. Italics mine.

[27]See Kittelson, 191.

[28]Baylor, 113.

[29]Lindberg, 157.

[30]Kittelson, 191.

[31]The cover can be seen in Baylor, 129. For the heckling incident, see Robert Crossley, *Luther and the Peasants' War* (New York: Exposition Press, 1974), 55–56.

[32]See J. M. Porter, *Luther: Selected Political Writings* (Philadelphia: Fortress Press, 1957), 85.

[33]For my quotations of the document, see Robert Schultz, *Luther's Works*, vol. 46 (Philadelphia: Fortress Press, 1967). See *Against the Robbing and Murdering Hordes of Peasants* on 45–56.

[34]See Dixon, 87.

[35]Ibid.

[36]Lindberg, 157.

[37]Baylor, 137.

[38]See the introduction to *An Open Letter on the Harsh Book Against the Peasants*, 59–60, in Robert C. Schultz, *Luther's Works*, vol. 46.

[39]Schultz, 60.

[40]Luther, in Schultz, 60.

[41]Ibid., 75.

[42]Porter, 89.

14

Luther in Love

As Germany's peasants were reeling from catastrophic defeats and receiving their punishments for rebellion, Luther was busy doing what most of the priests-turned-Protestant-preachers were doing. One historian notes, "In the midst of the Peasants' War, Luther seems truly to have been preoccupied by the new phase in his life."[1] That new phase was marriage.

Luther was forty-one years old. Intellectually and career-wise, he was in his prime. All around him, those monks and nuns and priests who supported the cause of the Reformation were getting married. Monasteries and convents were emptying quickly, to the point that "by late 1522, clerical marriage was old news in Wittenberg."[2] Luther's writings against the institution of monasticism were resonating with those who had previously given their lives to chastity.[3]

Naturally, this led many to question Luther's motives, but he was not among the earliest reformers to marry. He waited far longer than most.[4] Not only did he want to avoid rumors that he was upending celibacy simply for the sake of his own lusts, but he also realized he was far too busy—and his life overly erratic—for him to try to settle down and start a family.

Very Melancholy and Much Tempted

The Peasants' War was a terrible time in Luther's life. He was surrounded by suffering, and he knew he had something to do about it. Before the war, he was widely perceived as being on the side of the common man. By the war's end, he was seen as a political player, willing to abandon some of his core principles for political scores. Scholars have typically framed this pivot in Luther's life as something that was necessary. He had to placate the nobles or else lose the momentum he had risked his life to create. But the truth is that Luther abruptly turned on the commoners. Even his close friends thought he mishandled the Peasants' War, notably his *Thieving Hordes* pamphlet, which essentially sanctioned—theologically—the massacre of the peasants. Luther was unwilling to admit culpability. It was the peasants' own demented fault. They were the ones who went wild and, against his wishes, pushed too hard by destroying property and by outright disobeying the governing authorities.

The tumult in Luther's life around the time of the Peasants' Revolt threw him into turmoil. He wrote a friend in March 1525 that he was feeling "very melancholy and much tempted."[5] He was also surrounded by change. In May that year, Frederick the Wise had died; that alone would have caused frightening political disruptions. Additionally, in December 1524, Luther's old mentor—Johann von Staupitz—also died. Both of these men probably would have opposed Luther's marriage.[6] Perhaps their deaths freed him. Plus, Luther also might have wanted to marry to please his father. When Luther went into the monastery years before, one of the reasons his father opposed him was because his eldest son would be forbidden to produce grandchildren.[7] Given Luther's deep desire to please his father, this would have stayed with him.

For several years, Luther insisted to his friends that "he had no sexual desires, and that marriage was not for him."[8] In time, however, this began to change. Why? For one, we know Luther was being pressured to marry to send a signal to all that he was willing to put his money where his mouth was. Luther had written about the permissibility of clergy taking a wife, but was he willing to cross that line himself?

Also, nature's force was powerful. Once Luther began interacting with so many escaped nuns, his latent sexual desires ignited. He wrote to friends about this. Finally, he began to admit that he was "neither wood nor stone."[9]

Luther became a prominent matchmaker in Wittenberg, to the point that even Melanchthon began to worry about his "too frequent and close relations with the fugitive nuns who had come to Wittenberg."[10] While some nuns took up residence in local homes, several ended up staying in Luther's monastery. He would have had ample opportunities to interact with these young women. And, of course, hooking Martin Luther—the champion of reform—would have been appealing to some of them.

Luther's singleness threatened to erupt into scandal. Melanchthon and others close to Luther realized that he *needed* to marry both to save his own reputation and to avoid damaging the Protestant movement. Melanchthon noticed a change in Luther, noting that "the frequent commerce with the nuns had softened and inflamed him, despite all his noble nature and the greatness of his soul."[11]

Runaway Nuns

The life of a monastic was a life given to God. And while both nuns and monks had perks such as respect, opportunities for leadership, and a guarantee that the church would take care of them all of their lives, ample sacrifices also had to be made. Nuns fasted regularly, usually two days per week. And when they weren't fasting, they were allowed only two meals per day. They were expected to remain silent. Laughter was considered worldly. Holy books were read during mealtime to avoid careless talk. They rose for predawn prayers and assembled throughout the day for the canonical hours, which ended after midnight. Theirs was a life of committed devotion.[12]

Martin Luther's future wife—Katherine von Bora—would have lived according to this strict regimen while cloistered as a nun at the Cistercian Convent of Nimbschen, near the German city of Leipzig, about fifty-five miles south of Wittenberg. Around forty nuns were cloistered there, and they were "kept in strict seclusion." Conversation was kept to a minimum, friendships were forbidden, pets were not allowed, and nuns were required to walk "with lowered heads and slow steps."[13]

On the night of April 4, 1523, for unknown reasons, twelve of the nuns of Nimbschen decided to make a run for it.[14] It took great courage, because they had nothing of value with them. Under the cover of darkness, they made a mad dash into the great and wide unknown. This was no trivial matter in the early sixteenth century. One particular nun, Florentina von

Oberweimar from Neuenhelfta Convent near Eisleben, somehow managed to get hold of Luther's writings and wrote him a letter of inquiry. She also attempted an escape, but she was found out. She was punished severely for it: humiliated, stepped upon by the other nuns, confined, chained, and whipped. She finally made it after several botched attempts. She fled to Wittenberg, where she and Luther together published *A Story of How God Rescued an Honorable Nun*. This was yet another dangerous move on the part of Luther and the reformers, since "according to church as well as secular law the penalty for abducting nuns was death."[15]

Who orchestrated the escape of the nuns at Nimbschen? It was none other than Luther. He persuaded his friend Leonhard Koppe and a few others to disguise themselves by making a standard delivery of herring fish and beer, something Koppe regularly did. After the delivery, the nuns—so the story goes—hid themselves in the fish barrels and were thus rolled out of the convent, loaded onto a covered wagon, and safely escaped to Wittenberg.[16]

Almost immediately, Luther wrote about the incident in a tract entitled *Why Nuns May, in All Godliness, Leave the Convent: Ground and Reply*. Luther believed that by publishing the events he would protect the nuns' honor, chastity, and dignity. He encouraged parents to fetch their daughters out of the convents. Several families took him up on it, while others refused due either to opposition to the Reformation or because they simply couldn't afford to support another person. Convents soon were forced to admit that many nuns were being cloistered against their will. Luther freely admitted his role as the instigator of these events and shamelessly defended the rights of monks and nuns to leave their confinement and marry if they so wished. Luther's theology declared that a married life was as godly as a celibate one. Not all nuns were happy with the domino effect happening all around them as nuns fled the cloister. One nun in Nuremberg "planned to stab Luther with a knife," but the plot was foiled.[17]

Luther and others found homes for the young women, but it proved to be a complicated project. Some married almost immediately. Finding employment for them was difficult, so getting married and managing a household was a feasible option. A case in point is Margarethe von Staupitz, the sister of the great Johann von Staupitz. In her late forties, Margarethe was the eldest of the escaped nuns from Nimbschen. She was a talented, capable person, having experience as a choir mistress and organist. Initially, she was to marry Luther's friend George Spalatin, but it fell apart. In late 1524, her brother died, leaving her without an advocate. Luther found her employment at a school in Grimma, near her old convent. He kept an eye on her and came to her defense in 1531 when church officials tried to take her house from her. She finally married a Wittenberg man in 1537, when she was about sixty. She died childless around the age of seventy.[18]

Some of the nuns who escaped from Nimbschen returned to their families. Two sisters wanted to return to their father, but he refused to take them back due to his staunch opposition to Luther and his reforms. Most of them married eventually. One of the ladies—Ave von Schönfeld—initially caught Luther's eye, but for unknown reasons that relationship did not work out. She ended up marrying Basilius Axt, "the personal physician of the duke of Prussia."[19]

Katherine von Bora

Katie von Bora was born at Lippendorf, near Leipzig, on January 29, 1499. Her parents were Hans von Bora and Katharina Haubitz.[20] Her mother died when Katie was only six, leaving behind five children. They were of the noble class, but low nobility. When the mother died, Katie was placed in the care of a convent by her father. A few years later, Katie was moved to Nimbschen, not far away. Her father remarried but made sure that Katie was near relatives and that she received an education.

When Katie escaped the convent, she was twenty-four. Initially, she was put into the upper-class home of Philip Reichenbach, a lawyer who eventually became mayor of Wittenberg. For a more long-term solution, she was then put into the home of Lucas Cranach, the wealthy and famous Reformation artist responsible for nearly all the portraits of Luther.[21]

Katie was a strong person. At first, Luther viewed her as arrogant, but by all accounts she was bright, capable, and confident. She said what she thought, without much hesitation. She was an energetic person, but not beautiful. She probably looked older than she actually was.[22]

Luther tried to connect Katie to a student named Jerome Baumgartner. Katie and Jerome were nearly the same age, and he was from a prominent family. However, he showed little interest in her. She fell in love with him, and he kept her hanging on for a year while he went to Nuremberg to see his family. But in the end he never proposed, probably because his mentor, Philip Melanchthon, had recently married and was not enjoying matrimony at all. For whatever reasons, Baumgartner decided not to return to Wittenberg, despite Luther's attempts to lure him back through letters.[23] Obviously, his feelings for Katie were not as strong as hers for him.

Next, Luther tried to connect Katie with Caspar Glatz, a doctor of theology who served as the rector of the university and worked as a pastor. She wanted nothing to do with him, however, thinking he was too old for her. She suggested in a letter to Nicolaus von Amsdorm—another prominent reformer in Wittenberg—that she would rather marry him or Dr. Luther.[24]

Luther the Groom

Sometimes the picture is painted that Katie was the rejected nun who was finally picked up by Luther out of pity. This is not altogether true. While Luther joked with friends that Katie was the last of the nuns who remained single, this was common comedic fare in the sixteenth century. Instead, Luther noticed Katie's gifts. She was industrious and steady. She had made a name for herself. By all accounts, she was an extremely competent person. Historical consensus is that Luther struck gold when he secured Katie's hand in marriage. She turned out to be "the best wife the difficult man could possibly have found."[25]

On the evening of June 13, 1525, Luther and Katie rather suddenly and quietly exchanged vows, without any fanfare whatsoever. They were wed in the Augustinian monastery—their new home.[26] They married on a Tuesday, the customary day of the week for weddings. It surprised everyone in Wittenberg. Even many of his friends were caught off guard. Melanchthon was outright offended, accusing Luther of "indulging himself and compromising his good reputation at a time [during the Peasants' War] when Germany needs his spirit and authority."[27] Luther was unfazed. Looking back about fifteen years later, he told some friends that to get engaged for a long period is unwise, for it threatens to "make a whore" out of a woman: "One should not hesitate for long [between the engagement and marriage]. I did it the right way, got everything done in one evening. The devil is too evil, he must always support trash. . . . I never advise anyone to delay even a day."[28]

Luther likely did want to protect the honor of Katie, but he was a decisive man, so there is something rather true to form in his sudden decision to marry.

The wedding ceremony for Luther and Katie was performed by Johannes Bugenhagen, one of the prominent Wittenberg preachers. Luther was forty-one years old, and Katie was twenty-six. Katie had no dowry to offer, and they did not exchange rings until later. But when the rings—commissioned by Cranach—finally were produced, they were marvelous. Katie's was gold with a ruby, decorated with the crucified Christ, a spear, and a crown of thorns. Engraved on the inside of the ring were their names and the wedding date. Luther's ring was large, mounted with a diamond and ruby and bearing the initials of the couple. There was also a passage from Matthew: "What God has joined together, let no man put asunder."[29]

Sixteenth-century weddings in Germany were "ribald occasions." The newly married were expected to make love under a sheet or duvet in front of the guests, as a way of publicly declaring the marriage to be official. However, it was normal for couples to consummate the relationship in the weeks leading up to the wedding. Thus, Luther and Katie were certainly not virgins when it came time to perform for the onlookers. Indeed, Luther wrote to his friends and bragged about how he had already proved his manhood to Katie before the wedding banquet.[30]

By marrying, Luther also proved his manhood to his father. Hans and Martin mended their fractured relationship at the wedding banquet. Extremely relieved by this reconciliation, Luther wrote, "My father took me into his favor, and I became once more his dear son."[31]

Several prominent people donated money to Luther on the occasion of his wedding, including one of his enemies, Cardinal Albert von Mainz. The new elector—John the Steadfast—who had succeeded his brother Frederick the Wise just a month before the wedding, also made a significant donation to Luther. The town of Wittenberg donated cash as well as a large barrel of Einbecker bock beer—brewed in Germany continuously since the fourteenth century. Today, Einbecker is one of the oldest breweries in the world.[32]

Martin Luther's marriage to Katherine von Bora was one of the most significant marriages in Western history since it opened up the possibility of clerical marriage once again. The Roman Catholic Church had mandated celibacy for clergy since the Second Lateran Council in 1139.[33] Luther's marriage to Katie, however, overturned that for Protestants. Obviously, other Protestant pastors had wed before Luther, but Luther's marriage sealed the deal. His life was the bellwether for the entire Protestant movement. As a result, Katie was the archetypal wife for Protestants. Had their marriage failed, Protestantism would have been dealt a crippling blow. Thus, everybody was watching this marriage.

From day one, Katie von Bora was under intense scrutiny. In the minds of some, she was nothing but an escaped and reprobate nun who tempted a priest to marry. "She had to suffer a great deal of ridicule." One pamphlet vilified her by calling her a "nymphomaniac . . . who jumped into bed with all the students."[34] One publication referred to Katie as Luther's "supposed" wife, "an unfaithful, perjured, runaway prostitute."[35] Even Melanchthon accused Luther of having been "snared by the former nun." Duke George of Saxony questioned Luther's salvation; in his mind, the marriage proved Luther was a fallen monk who had caved in to the deadly sin of lust.[36]

Katie the Housewife

Perhaps the most enduring information about Katie von Bora was that she was full of energy. She was herculean in her abilities and accomplishments throughout their twenty-one years of marriage. Luther grew to love her deeply, although he soon noticed her "quick tongue"—probably a sign that she was able to stand up for herself.[37] He also noted how she would interrupt his work with what he considered to be trivial matters.[38] Mostly, however, Luther doted on Katie. He was pleasantly surprised to notice her pigtails on his pillow in the morning, and he considered himself to have gained the riches of kings by marrying her.[39]

Luther gave Katie a whole host of affectionate names in his writings, evidence of a warm companionship. He labeled her the "Doktorissa," which probably had something to do with her influence in the cloister. He called her "my dear rib," "my lord Katie," and "the boss of Zulsdorf" (referring to her childhood home). He often called her his "morning star."[40] In his *Table Talks*, he said he "wouldn't trade my Katie for France or Venice," and praised her for her fidelity and respectfulness to him.[41] He once commented, "Next to God's Word there is no more precious treasure than holy matrimony. God's highest gift on earth is a pious, cheerful, God-fearing, home-keeping wife, with whom you may live peacefully, to whom you may entrust your goods and body and life."[42] Katie earned this kind of praise. She worked hard to keep up with Luther's many plates spinning.

Luther had full confidence in Katie as she managed the house and the finances. This was probably wise, because Luther's generosity could be unrestrained at times. Katie had a more frugal nature. On one occasion, Luther gave away some of their wedding goblets to a person in need. Katie hid the rest so that he couldn't find them. Luther was happy to give away his coat to strangers, and dinner guests were always expected.[43] The Luthers struggled financially due to his generosity, his constant employment of numerous domestic servants, and his dislike of accounting. Katie, however, fixed some of that with her philosophy: "a penny saved is more valuable than a penny earned."[44] It is easy to forget that Luther received little money for his books, nor was he paid a salary for preaching in the town church.[45]

The Luthers lived in the old Augustinian monastery, and Katie kept them afloat financially by renting out rooms (former monastic cells) to boarding students, travelers, and guests. She was an excellent provider for them. She kept a garden and looked after a fish pond stocked with pike, bass, and trout. She raised farm animals and maintained a brewery (her beer enjoyed a good reputation). She oversaw an orchard and a vineyard. She kept bees for honey. She grew flowers. And in only a few months she was pregnant, which became her usual state since they went on to have six children. They also raised eleven orphans—children belonging to Luther's sisters who had died relatively young.[46] It took a unique person to keep pace with Luther, but Katie was fully capable.

Parenthood

The Luthers welcomed their first child, Johannes (named after Luther's father), in 1526. Elisabeth was born in 1527. Magdalene came in 1529. Martin arrived in 1531. Paul was born in 1533. And, finally, Margarethe was added to the family in 1534. Luther was utterly ecstatic when he received his firstborn: "From the most precious woman, my best of wives, I have received, by the blessing of God, a little son, Johannes Luther, and, by God's wonderful grace, I have become a father."[47]

The Luther children were loved deeply by their parents and enjoyed a happy home. The couple were devastated, however, when their Elisabeth died as an infant and when Magdalene succumbed to illness as an early teen, passing away while in her father's arms. Johannes studied law and became a court advisor. Martin Junior studied for ministry but was always rather sickly. He died in his thirties. Paul became a successful physician to the elector of Saxony. Margarethe married into a prominent and well-to-do aristocratic Russian family.[48]

Luther was in his early forties when he started having children, which might explain his intimate involvement in their lives—something that was not customary for the time. His utter sadness over his two daughters' deaths suggests that he was emotionally attached to his children. He would write long letters to his children when he traveled. Some of these letters are preserved, and they are extremely tender and loving.[49]

Martin and Katie Luther became the first family of Protestantism—an archetype for Protestant families to follow. Catholics at the time did not have anything like this, since priests were unmarried. Luther blazed a trail here. His roles as husband and father were examples for the students who came to Wittenberg, and this explains why so much was written about Luther's family life in his *Table Talks*. People were intrigued to see a priest with a wife and children. What Luther did, the rest of the Protestant world mimicked.

Luther's influence was unmistakably powerful on how Protestants would conceive of marriage, child-rearing, the treatment of women, and carrying out one's domestic responsibilities. His earthiness—his allowing so many people to come into his home—was revolutionary. People ate and drank with him. They listened to him tell stories and play his lute and sing. He was accessible in a way that clergymen had not been before.

Everybody could see that Luther took his domestic roles quite seriously. He was good to Katie. His love and care for his children were obvious to all who visited Wittenberg. Luther made sure his children were educated, and—particularly advanced for the time—he advocated education for girls, "where the girls could hear the Gospel for an hour every day." As a result of Luther's pioneering efforts, "the cause of female education was pursued in all of the subsequent Lutheran church orders."[50]

Katie the Widow

Luther was anything but easy to live with and look after. As he aged, he became sick and irritable. Katie worried about him during his final years, knowing his death would jeopardize her livelihood and potentially imperil her existence. She reacted to his declining health with "unconcealed anxiety" in their correspondence.[51] When Luther passed away in 1546, Katie wrote to her sister-in-law that she could "neither eat nor drink. Nor again sleep." She grieved deeply that God had taken her "dear master" from her, and not just from her "but from the whole world—this dear and worthy man."[52] She confessed that she was so overcome by grief that she could hardly speak.[53]

Katie's great fears for her own welfare in a life without her husband proved to be rational and justified. While Luther left everything to her in his will, the document was "invalid according to the laws of the land."[54] The elector of Saxony—by that time John Frederick I—intervened to help her by offering her a pension. However, shortly after Luther's death, great upheaval ensued. The Schmalkaldic War between Protestants and Catholics broke out, and the promised pension often "failed to materialize."[55] After a period of traveling to various cities because of the war, Katie returned to Wittenberg, where she was forced to start taking more and more boarders into her home. The Melanchthon family saved her from destitution.[56]

Eventually, the violence closed in on Wittenberg and on Katie, with three of her children. Both the Luther and the Melanchthon families were forced to flee. They managed to reach Magdeburg, a city in Protestant hands. Soon, they had to run for their lives again toward Torgau. Katie was thrown from the wagon and severely injured. She was bedridden for three months and succumbed on December 20, 1552. Her daughter Margaret—by then eighteen years old—nursed Katie until she died.[57] She was buried in Torgau, in the town church of Saint Mary, where she remains to the present day.

Notes

[1]Lyndal Roper, *Martin Luther: Renegade and Prophet* (London: Bodley Head, 2016), 281.

[2]Scott Hendrix, *Martin Luther* (New Haven: Yale University Press, 2015), 140.

[3]By 1525, Luther had already written several works that promoted clerical marriage and the inherent goodness of sex within marriage: *On Monastic Vows*; *The Seventh Chapter of St. Paul's Epistle to the Corinthians*; *The Estate of Marriage*; and *The Babylonian*

Captivity of the Church; and *Why Nuns May, in All Godliness, Leave the Convents: Ground and Reply*. For more discussion, see Martin Brecht, trans. by James Schaaf, *Martin Luther*, vol. 2 (Minneapolis: Fortress Press, 1990), 91–100.

[4]The first reformer to marry was Bartholomaus Bernhardi in August 1521. Karlstadt also married in 1521. Justus Jonas and Johannes Bugenhagen found wives in 1522. Wenzeslaus Linck—the Vicar General of the Augustinian Order—married in 1523. From there the floodgates were opened to convents and monasteries in addition to the already-marrying priests. See Roper, 278.

[5]Hartmann Grisar, *Martin Luther* (Westminster: The Newman Press, 1950), 290.

[6]See Grisar, 291.

[7]See Roper, 277.

[8]Ibid., 274.

[9]Heinrich Bornkamm, trans. by E. Theodore Bachmann, *Luther in Mid-Career 1521–1530* (Philadelphia: Fortress Press, 1983), 401.

[10]Brecht,196.

[11]Roper, 279.

[12]See Martin Treu, *Katherine von Bora: Luther's Wife* (Lutherstadt Wittenberg, Germany: Drei Kastanien Verlag, 2003), 12.

[13]Richard Friedenthal, trans. by John Nowell, *Luther: His Life and Times* (New York: Harcourt Brace Jovanovich, 1967), 435.

[14]Some historians put the event on April 5, but Brecht claims it was April 4, on Easter Eve. Some historians say it was nine nuns, but Brecht clarifies: twelve escaped to the homes of relatives, but the remaining nine made it all the way to Wittenberg. See Brecht, vol. 2, 100.

[15]See Mary Helene Rasmussen Jackson, *Daughter of the Reformation* (Minneapolis: Huff Publishing, 2014). See also Larry Mansch and Curtis Peters, *Martin Luther* (Jefferson, NC: McFarland, 2016), 153. See also Treu, 17–18.

[16]No one knows for certain how much of the story is true, as the legend grew over time. See Brecht, 100, and Bornkamm, 258–259.

[17]See Bornkamm, 259–261, and Treu, 16–18.

[18]Treu, 19.

[19]Brecht, vol. 2, 197.

[20]Hendrix notes it was either Haubitz or Haugwitz. See 141. In this paragraph, I have used his biographical information of von Bora.

[21]Jackson, 165.

[22]See Grisar, 294, Treu, 27–28, and Bornkamm, 261, 404, 407.

[23]Hendrix, 143–144, and Bornkamm, 403.

[24]It is not clear how old Glatz was at the time. See Bornkamm, 403–404.

[25]Friedenthal, 437.

[26]See Brecht, vol. 2, 198.

[27]Treu, 31–32. See also Brecht, vol. 2, 199.

[28]Martin Luther, May 6–16, 1540, in *Off the Record with Martin Luther*, trans. and ed. by Charles Daudert (Kalamazoo, MI: Hansa-Hewlett Publishing, 2009), 59.

[29]Mansch and Peters, 157.

[30]Roper, 280.

[31]Friedenthal, 438.

[32]Treu, 30.

[33]See Dyron Daughrity, *To Whom Does Christianity Belong* (Minneapolis: Fortress Press, 2015), 227.

[34]Friedenthal, 434, 437.

[35]Treu, 33.

[36]Brecht, vol. 2, 199.

[37]Ibid., 198.

[38]See Daudert, 50.

[39]Mansch and Peters, 158.

[40]Jackson, 179, 182–183.

[41]See Daudert, 36.

[42]James Atkinson, *Martin Luther and the Birth of Protestantism* (Baltimore: Penguin, 1968), 247–248.

[43]Jackson, 183.

[44]See Daudert, 56. On his dislike of accounting, see Friedenthal, 443.

[45]Atkinson, 252.

[46]Mansch and Peters, 157; Jackson, 175; Friedenthal, 441; Treu, 48.

[47]Jackson, 187.

[48]See Atkinson, 248, and Jackson, 187–192.

[49]See Andrew Pettegree, *Brand Luther* (New York: Penguin, 2015), 257. For a preserved letter, see Atkinson, 249.

[50]Pettegree, 265–266.

[51]Treu, 67.

[52]Hendrix, 286.

[53]Treu, 70.

[54]Friedenthal, 447.

[55]Ibid.

[56]Hendrix, 287.

[57]Ibid., 288.

15

The Protestant Pope

To insinuate that Luther became a pope-like figure in the Protestant churches seems blasphemous, but it is true. Luther continuously mocked the pope as an ass and as the antichrist, but he, too, wanted to be in charge of his movement. He became prickly when anyone else tried to go toe to toe with him in a debate, or when others tried to rival his leadership in the Reformation. Luther was bitter with those he perceived to be a threat, hardly more friendly to Protestant competitors than he was to the papists he excoriated with regularity.

But there was no denying that Luther was the leader of the Protestant world. Since the outrage caused by his *Ninety-Five Theses*, he was the point man and Wittenberg was ground zero—like a Protestant Rome. As Luther's vision of reform crescendoed, he became the father figure in the movement—certainly in Germany. He worked hard to make this movement his.

Luther's Increasing Authoritarianism

Earlier, we noted that while Luther was hiding in Wartburg Castle after the Diet of Worms in 1521, his leadership of the Reformation had begun to slip into the hands of Andreas Karlstadt. And we saw how outraged Luther was when he walked back into Wittenberg a year later and saw Karlstadt's reforms. Everyone knew this new movement was Luther's baby, though, so it didn't take him long to regain control.

Luther's teaching seemed to democratize Christianity, so his explicit goal probably never was to establish himself as the unquestioned authority of the Reformation. But his actions spoke otherwise. He would not countenance disagreement. If someone challenged him, he became volatile. Often, he outright insulted them, especially in print, and everyone knew that Luther was the king of media. The printing presses saw Luther as their darling because of the glut of business he secured for them. By controlling the media, Luther controlled the people around him.

In that late-medieval world, the church and the state were not separate entities. They functioned together and held significant sway in each other's realms. The two entities were deeply enmeshed in ways modern Westerners—especially Americans who early on separated church and state—can hardly fathom. So when Luther and his colleagues attacked the papacy, they were attacking the social order. And this led to a deep crisis among the people. Who was in charge? Was Luther some kind of new pope? Was the Roman pope to be challenged so overtly? What if the pope was able to unleash the civil authorities and clamp down on the Wittenberg reforms? Would supporters of the Reformation go to jail or worse? Questions like these caused acute anxiety in Wittenberg, and Luther was the only person capable of navigating this extremely delicate social and political reality.

Even while Luther was still in hiding—as Junker Jörg—he asserted himself in various ways. His frequent letters to Wittenberg would have been pored over carefully each time one arrived. His already voluminous writings gave the reformers plenty of guidance. After all, by 1521, Luther had penned some of the Reformation's most influential documents. So, even without Luther's physical presence, his writings, which *caused* the Reformation, exacted obeisance from his colleagues and followers.

Luther's influence turned out to be profound. For example, in 1521, his rival, Cardinal Albrecht of Mainz, announced a major campaign to sell indulgences for those who visited his relic collection (he needed the money). Luther caught wind of the plan and threatened the cardinal, telling him he would "show to all the world the difference between a bishop and a wolf." Luther wrote to this high-ranking clergyman that he had previously used restraint toward the elector but would do so no longer. He accused Albrecht of erecting an "idol which robs poor simple Christians of their money and their souls." In brutally harsh terms, Luther railed against Albrecht and demanded that the cardinal stop the indulgence selling and stop harassing priests, monks, and nuns who decided to marry. If Albrecht did not comply, Luther promised to humiliate him in the same way he had destroyed John Tetzel. Luther threatened to go public with information related to the "harlots" Albrecht and other bishops kept in secret.

Incredibly, Luther thus was able to hold Albrecht hostage. If the cardinal did not comply, then Luther would spill the beans about the cardinal's whores. Luther's letter was caustic. He called Albrecht "insolent." He called him a tyrant. More than a dozen times in the letter, Luther threatened him, saying he would publicly dishonor Albrecht's name. Luther issued a fourteen-day deadline to the cardinal. "If after this appointed fortnight no public answer should appear, my little book *Against the Idol at Halle* will be released." Finally, Luther boldly warned the cardinal: "You haven't yet wiped out all whom Christ has raised up against your idolatrous tyranny."

This letter is not surprising for its vitriol; that was common for Luther. What is surprising is the clearly authoritarian aura Luther assumes in the letter. He wrote to the cardinal—an elector of the emperor no less!—as a superior would write to someone ranked way down the totem pole. It was a reprimand. And the result? Obviously, Luther won this clash, for in a very short time "the cardinal apologized and told Luther it would stop."[1] Luther's authority—even after he was condemned as a heretic by the pope of Rome—was unquestioned. He could make the highest authorities tremble, even while he was confined. Not even the pope could stop him. Once Luther had escaped the clutches of his enemies at the Diet of Worms, his power was unleashed. That he was fully aware of his power can be seen in the unapologetic way he communicated with people in the highest echelons of church and state.

Another display of Luther's increasing authoritarianism was his acrimonious falling out with Karlstadt, which we looked at in Chapter Thirteen. Karlstadt had seniority and held high offices at the University of Wittenberg before Luther arrived on the scene. But Luther's superior intellect allowed him to dominate the man. Karlstadt respected Luther for leading him to new discoveries in Augustine's theology. As a result, Karlstadt joined Luther in his task of reform, but Luther later crushed him and his "unauthorized" reforms.[2]

Yet another sign of Luther's move to become a kind of Protestant pope was his evolving approach to other Reformation movements, such as the Anabaptists. In 1528, he wrote, "It is not right, and it pains me greatly, that people kill, murder and burn these poor folk so horribly." By 1529, however, Luther had fallen under the influence of Melanchthon's view that Anabaptists should be dealt with harshly and severely; indeed, he said they should die for their position on baptism.[3] Anabaptist leaders were "brutally tortured and executed in January 1536, their remains put in iron cages hung from the tower of St Lambert's Church, where the cages can still be seen." Luther thought they had it coming because of their "contempt for true doctrine."[4] He was not opposed to persecuting those who misunderstood or defied his position as a Protestant pope. His willingness to persecute opponents was most evident in the Peasants' Revolt in 1525, but this disposition stayed with Luther until his death.

Luther's hope for a united Protestantism rapidly diminished as new visions of reform were introduced all across Europe. He had to consolidate his gains, however, if his own version of Protestantism—"Lutheranism"—was to survive. He was now making the kind of crucial decisions that usually fall to political leaders and high-ranking clergyman. Ironically, Luther's previous championing of concepts like the "priesthood of all believers" had to be dramatically curtailed. People simply couldn't be trusted. They would almost inevitably create new interpretations of the Bible that Luther could not countenance. And Luther's newfound muscles enabled him to force his detractors to comply, either through torture, public humiliation, or getting rid of them altogether.

A Church of His Own

As churches, towns, and political rulers began to split from Rome, Luther's leadership was in higher demand than ever before. By the late 1520s, Luther's movement had turned political, and the task of figuring out how Germany was to function without Rome for the first time since Charlemagne's crowning in the year 800 fell to Luther. He was up to the task.

> Over the next few years, and through a series of polemics, pamphlets, letters, disputes and negotiations with his rivals, Luther tacitly abandoned the project of reforming *the* Church. Instead he began to create a church of his own. . . . The man who had been convinced, in 1520, that all believers were equally priests now had to decide questions about authority and structure within the Church.[5]

Luther's fingerprints were all over his new church, from its organization to its theology, from its relationship with the state to the specific songs that were sung in worship services.

One of the most lasting elements of Luther's influence on his movement is in the realm of theology. It did not have to be this way. For instance, Karlstadt preferred to emphasize regeneration rather than justification. There is a critical difference here. A movement that emphasizes regeneration is a movement focused on behavior, evidence of holy living, and outward change. A movement emphasizing justification is more cerebral.

Luther found his satisfaction in the cross. Jesus's death on the cross justified the believer; one's pure lifestyle and moral choices could never accomplish salvation, since all humans are self-condemned. Luther's cues came from Paul and Augustine. These ancient debates go back to the early church, and Luther chose to go with a faith that takes place most crucially in the mind rather than in the outward person. Some have accused Luther of being soft on sin, and he certainly was in comparison with other reformers such as John Wesley, who tended to privilege purity of life over cerebral exactitude.

Other notable changes that Luther brought into his movement were the allowance of clerical marriage and its consequence—a virtual abolition of monasticism in Protestant circles. He changed forever the idea of what it means to be a priest: one probably does it best as a husband rather than as a solitary individual. He also allowed laypeople to take the Eucharist in both bread and wine, a practice considered anathema by the Roman Catholic Church at the time.

Through it all, Luther seemed convinced that his interpretation of the Bible was the best—a shockingly naïve idea today. He was utterly dumbfounded when other reformers deviated from his pattern. Luther was a bona fide celebrity, with all the arrogance this often entails. After his victory at the Diet of Worms, he rarely seemed to doubt himself.

One area where Luther's ideas had immediate import was in the role of women in church leadership. Not only did Luther allow women into the homes of priests to be wives and mothers, but his entire philosophy of women led to deep Roman Catholic suspicion. One of Luther's most outspoken critics, Johannes Cochlaeus (1479–1552), expressed horror that Luther's theology might lead to women priests! He thought Luther was flirting with changing the rules of Christianity in a way that seemed cavalier at best and downright blasphemous at worst.

Luther's political ideas surfaced early in the Reformation when in 1523 he published *Temporal Authority: To What Extent It Should Be Obeyed?* In it, he essentially argued that Christians should obey the government unless they felt their consciences were being coerced. Luther's thinking in that text set the tone for a Lutheran approach to politics that could easily be characterized as accommodationist. Many historians have drawn a direct line from some of Luther's tendencies—especially in his dealing with the Peasants' Revolt—to the horrors of the holocaust. Historian Lyndal Roper writes: "His . . . willingness to make compromises with political authorities, even when they were acting in an unchristian manner, provided the theological underpinnings of the accommodation many Lutherans would reach centuries later with the Nazi regime."[6]

Luther seemed to be naturally gifted when it came to politics. He knew the value of negotiation and compromise, which seems ironic for a man who is most famous for his "Here I stand" speech. But there is no doubt that his political savvy is a big reason that Protestants now make up 40 Percent—and growing—of the market share of the world's 2.5 billion Christians.

To craft a church of his own, Luther not only had to flex his muscles from time to time and make difficult alliances with government. He also had to win the hearts and minds of the people, and this is where Luther excelled most. What made Luther different than virtually all other religious leaders of his day was that he had "the people" in mind when he took up his pen. So his catechisms are easy to read and almost rhythmic in such a way that they are easily memorized. The word *catechism* derives from the Greek word meaning "to sound over." It is meant to be taught by word of mouth.[7] Luther realized that if he could reach the children, the mothers, and the farmers, he could grow his church from the ground up. It was a brilliant strategy. Luther's *Small Catechism* is today generally recognized as "the most influential of Luther's works over the past five centuries."[8]

By authoring catechisms, Luther enabled the people to learn the Bible and the core doctrines of faith. It was a sleight of hand that helped him keep the area preachers in check. He was offering to the untrained masses "the tools by which to hear, understand, and even judge the preacher's sermon."[9] This was the democratization of religion—yet underneath the authority and watchful eye of Martin Luther.

Perhaps more than any Christian leader before him, Luther insisted on getting his message to children. He poured tremendous energy and resources into the establishment of schools. It was common for Luther to require churches to add a school if they became Protestant. This linking of education with the church was "revolutionary," as it trained thousands of children across Germany to think like Lutherans rather than Roman Catholics from the moment they started their formal education. In 1530, Luther published *A Sermon on Keeping Children in School* that made clear his motives: "The chief purpose of schooling was to train up a new generation of ministers." Melanchthon realized it was not wise to marginalize the future lawyers and businessmen, so he later modified Luther's stance in one of his tracts, when he wrote that schools are "for raising up people who are skilled to teach in the church *and* govern the world." Emphasis on education for both girls and boys in Luther's Saxony increased dramatically. Literacy rates soared. Protestant universities were established. "By 1600 Württemberg had 401 schools . . . or one for every thousand in the population. Luther's goal of universal provision, if not universal attendance, was now close to being realized."[10]

The 1526 Diet of Speyer

As Luther's forays into social order and politics increased, he found himself reliant on political players to help him sustain his movement. Frederick the Wise had been extremely helpful to Luther in the earliest years of the Reformation. When Frederick died in 1525, Luther needed other high-ranking nobles to step up for the cause. Luther found such a person in Philip of Hesse (1504–1567), an influential ruler in Germany who became one of the most enthusiastic champions of the Reformation. Luther also relied on the support of the new elector of Saxony, the younger brother of Frederick the Wise, who was even more committed to the Protestant cause than his brother had been. He came to be known by Protestants as John the Steadfast. With Philip of Hesse and John the Steadfast, Luther had firm commitments of support from two of the most powerful men in Germany.

Philip of Hesse joined the Protestant movement in 1524 and began to rally other political leaders for the cause of reform. He was a prominent voice in 1526 at the Diet of Speyer. The first Diet of Speyer was meant to overturn the decisions made at Worms in 1521—that Luther was an outlaw and that his supporters would be punished. Forbidding the Reformation was no longer a tenable position to hold in several parts of the empire. Luther's movement had grown too large too fast. When the Diet of Speyer lifted the official ban on Luther, Protestantism was officially unleashed.

However, it turned out not to be so simple. Protestantism was starting to take a different form in other places. In Zurich, for example, Ulrich Zwingli was the Protestant leader, and Luther resented him deeply. The biggest complaint Luther had against him was on the nature of the Eucharist. Luther was unwilling to relinquish the notion that Christ was actually chewed and drunk. This is why, on one occasion, when the Communion wine was spilled onto a woman's jacket during church services, Luther "licked it off her coat" and "went so far as to cut out the bits of the jacket they had been unable to clean." He then cut sections off the affected pew and burned it to avoid desecrating the blood of Jesus. Zwingli's followers—who were known by Luther as the "sacramentarians"—thought the Lutherans were acting like cannibals when they claimed to eat Christ's flesh and drink his blood. They mocked the Lutherans for worshiping "a baked God."[11] All of this caused the Reformation-friendly political leaders great alarm. They wanted Luther and Zwingli to unite for the sake of a common defense against the powers of southern Europe. Splintering into several different factions would be a disaster for them militarily. Then they would be no match for a southern alliance united in their Roman Catholic faith.

The 1526 Diet of Speyer opened on June 25. Emperor Charles V was unable to attend due to a serious spat with Pope Clement VII. In fact, just a year later, Emperor Charles sacked Rome, and his soldiers violently looted the city for months. Thousands were killed. In other words, the Holy

Roman emperor and the pope were by no means united, and this proved quite favorable to the reformers at Speyer.

Charles V sent his younger brother, King Ferdinand, to lead the 1526 diet and represent the wishes of the crown. Ferdinand had been instructed to do everything in his power to prevent any major religious decisions. The goal was to buy some time until a general council could be called by the pope.[12] However, the result was dramatically different. The diet concluded that every estate was free to make a responsible decision about Luther and the Reformation. Naturally, the Protestant estates thought they had been given "the right to make reforms or introduce the whole Reformation."[13] Pro-Reformation rulers John the Steadfast and Philip of Hesse were determined to use this decision to expand Protestantism in their lands. It was now official—Lutheranism was becoming a state church in parts of Germany.

Another major issue helped to procure a highly positive outcome for the reformers at the 1526 Diet of Speyer: the invasion of the Turks from the East. Emperor Charles V and his brother King Ferdinand needed cooperation from all of Germany if they were going to prevent the Muslims from bursting through Hungary. Ferdinand became king of Bohemia and Hungary in 1526; it would be disastrous for him to lose a war to the Turks the very year of his coronation. That is precisely what happened, however, in 1526 at the Battle of Mohacs. The Ottomans won. Suleiman the Magnificent earned his title as a major power in central Europe. Muslim armies used Hungary as a base to launch new incursions into Vienna, Austria, and a possible conquest of western Europe.

Thus, at the Diet of Speyer in 1526, the reformers had all the leverage. Charles and Ferdinand needed Germany more than Germany needed them, so concessions were made to the reformers. And the reformers did not squander the opportunity to spread Lutheranism throughout their lands.[14]

The 1529 Diet of Speyer and the Origin of "Protestantism"

The 1526 Diet of Speyer was not the final word on Luther's movement by any means. Another Diet of Speyer was called in 1529, and it had lasting consequences. At that diet, the term "Protestant" was derived. Again King Ferdinand presided, but this time he was in no mood to negotiate with Luther's supporters. He came down hard on them and strove to remove any latitude they might have interpreted from the 1526 diet. He forcefully declared, with support of the emperor, that the Edict of Worms was still in place until a general council was called by the church. In other words, Luther was still considered an outlaw, and rulers who supported him were breaking the law and were subject to punishment.

The 1529 Diet of Speyer had two major items on the agenda: what to do about Luther and his movement, and how to counter the Ottoman siege of Vienna. King Ferdinand and the Catholics argued that the reason the Muslim armies were having so much success was because God was displeased with the Lutheran heresy. In Ferdinand's view, both the Turks and the Protestants should be defeated. Then God's favor would return to the Holy Roman Empire. Unfortunately for the Lutherans, "the vast majority of those present agreed with Ferdinand, at least in principle."[15]

Almost immediately, Philip of Hesse and Elector John (the Steadfast) of Saxony "protested" the decisions. They argued that to outlaw the reform movements was to unlawfully abrogate the decisions made at the 1526 diet. And this time they were joined by others: Margrave George of Brandenburg, Duke Ernest of Brunswick, and Prince Wolfgang of Anhalt. In addition, thirteen Zwinglian cities stood with them in the protest. These "Protestants" began planning an alliance just in case their protests incurred hostility from the Catholic states. This Lutheran alliance set the stage for a Protestant political and military force. They called themselves the Schmalkaldic League—named after a town in Germany not far from Luther's old stomping grounds in Eisenach and Erfurt.[16]

So "Philip of Hesse and Elector John had some allies, but precious few. Against them stood all the other princes, cities, and prelates."[17] They realized that if they persisted in their Protestant rebellion, Charles V might come up from Spain and force them into submission. In the emperor's mind, this was no time for a divided empire. Defeating the Turks was too much a priority. Sometimes enemies are forced into friendship for the sake of taking on a greater foe. For the Protestants, the handwriting was on the wall: they could either grow their alliance to include more estates, or face certain destruction by the highly capable armies of the Holy Roman Empire. With the Turks coming from the East, it was a potential disaster for Christendom.

When Luther realized the outcome of the 1529 Diet of Speyer, he penned *Concerning War Against the Turks* (1529). In that book, he was his typical defiant self, arguing that if Ferdinand wanted God's support against the Turks, then he should stop causing trouble for the Reformation in Germany and in Switzerland. On another front, however, Luther and Melanchthon realized that for defensive purposes they badly needed the Zwinglian cities. This set into motion an earnest attempt to reconcile the two largest strains of the Reformation: Lutheranism and Zwinglianism.

The Marburg Colloquy (1529)

Philip of Hesse agreed that Luther and Zwingli needed to unite to prevent a great crack in the united front of Protestantism. He urged the two sides to iron out differences at a meeting in the city of Marburg in October 1529. Virtually all the major reformers were there, and Philip of Hesse presided.

For all three days of the colloquy, Luther was intransigent. The core issue at stake was the Eucharist. Luther believed that when Jesus said, "This is my body," he was being literal. Zwingli and his cohorts argued that Jesus's words of institution were figurative. Just as when he said, "I am the vine, you are the branches," Jesus did not mean he is an actual plant. Similarly, Jesus was not saying that he was an actual loaf of bread. Luther, however, insisted. Using chalk, he wrote on the table in the room the words of institution, "This is my body," and covered them with a sheet, as if they were the elements on the altar.[18] Luther was a master debater, and his opponents were novices compared to him. He used all his rhetorical devices to show that Jesus meant what he said—the Communion bread *is* Christ. Zwingli would not agree. Luther dismissed his interlocutors as heretics. He wrote a letter to his wife, telling her that Zwingli's supporters were "simple-minded and inexperienced debaters."[19]

So what was the outcome of the Marburg Colloquy? In many ways, it was a success, but in that one key area it was a colossal failure. "Although everyone in the room agreed on fourteen points of doctrine—including fundamental issues such as infant baptism, justification by faith, and belief in the Trinity—agreement proved impossible on a fifteenth point: the sacrament of the Eucharist."[20] In the end, the two types of Protestantism became more deeply entrenched than before. Luther and Zwingli hurled insults at each other, creating lasting wounds that would never heal, even among their followers.

As the Marburg Colloquy was ending, Zwingli asked that they all take Communion together. Luther "flatly rejected." And four hundred years later, in 1929, at the anniversary of the colloquy, the scene played out again as the Lutherans refused to Commune.[21] Protestantism was officially and perpetually divided.

The Diet of Augsburg (1530)

Emperor Charles V was perturbed that the two Diets of Speyer failed, so he called for another in the city of Augsburg, Bavaria, in 1530. Gossip said his plan was to formally denounce Protestantism and perhaps even try to put an end to Luther. All Luther's advisors warned him to lie low, so he went into hiding in the Coburg Castle, also in Bavaria. The imperial ban on Luther was still in effect, so he was an outlaw in the mind of the emperor. Consequently, Melanchthon—Luther's most trusted colleague—became the point person who would represent Lutheranism at Augsburg.[22]

In preparation for the diet, Melanchthon spearheaded the writing of a defense—an apology—that attempted to explain that the Protestant reforms were never meant to split the church; rather, their motive was simply to correct abuses. Melanchthon was much less fiery than Luther, and there were hopes that perhaps he could do what the boisterous and bold Luther could not. The first draft of *The Augsburg Confession* was presented to the assembly on June 25, 1530. It was a great coming-out party for Melanchthon as the successor to Luther. When Melanchthon sought Luther's opinion on certain matters, Luther wrote back in a fatherly way, saying Melanchthon should feel free to be strong and independent, for Luther trusted his judgment. Luther was particularly pleased with Melanchthon's *Confession*, realizing his mentee was fully competent to represent the Lutheran cause.[23]

The Catholics were not impressed, however. In defiance of Melanchthon and Luther, they put together a document of their own, the *Confutation*. That document was merely a refutation of virtually all Lutheran ideas. Luther wrote to Melanchthon, advising him to stand firm and avoid any compromise. Melanchthon never had the fortitude of Luther, though, so he continually wrote to his mentor asking his opinion on how he should handle the proceedings. He held onto hope that a compromise could be negotiated between the reformers and the Catholics. Eventually, though, Luther had enough of this nonsense, and he wrote a treatise to be read at

Augsburg: *Articles against the Whole Synagogue of Satan and All the Gates of Hell*. Luther's continued intransigence was on full display, to say the least.

The 1530 Diet of Augsburg ended in late September and failed to produce results, other than the emperor's threat that he would take "forcible action" if the Protestants did not capitulate to his will by April 15 of the following year. Melanchthon's *Augsburg Confession* was flatly rejected. Evangelical writings were condemned and future publications forbidden, which incensed Luther. He responded in black-and-white terms: the Catholics were of the devil and the Protestants were of God. He said the Reformation had "pure grace" on its side, while the Catholics had incurred "pure wrath" from the Almighty.[24]

The emperor received the results of the diet and made it clear that he would use the Imperial Supreme Court to try anyone who persisted down the path of Protestantism.[25] This was a very real threat to the Protestant princes because they were the signatories of the *Augsburg Confession*. Melanchthon had been only an advisor at Augsburg; it was chiefly the princes who were being warned by the diet's strongly Catholic conclusions.[26] Luther was intensely frustrated that he was unable to play the lead role at Augsburg, but it could have been disastrous had he shown up. Politically, the Diet of Augsburg made one thing manifest: Protestants and Catholics were now at "a complete political impasse."[27]

The Schmalkaldic League

Philip of Hesse had by 1530 turned firmly against the emperor. He knew he had bargaining power when it came to his military because Philip knew how much Emperor Charles V needed it. Philip figured piecing together a strong Protestant military force could dramatically increase his worth in the eyes of the emperor, who was contending with the Ottoman Turks as they ravaged Vienna.

The Schmalkaldic League was formed in early 1531 in the city of Schmalkalden, Germany. It employed the *Augsburg Confession* as its standard for membership, which effectively cut out the Zwinglians. Saxony Elector John the Steadfast and Philip of Hesse were the leaders of this defensive alliance. If the emperor attacked one Protestant region, they pledged, he would have to contend with all of them. This was a brilliant political maneuver, because Emperor Charles did not have the resources to wage war with Protestants in the north *as well as* with Suleiman in the east. Other leaders joined, and in a few short years the Schmalkaldic League became a major force.[28]

Interestingly, Luther was not at first enthusiastic about the League. He thought that by building a military arm the princes were trusting in their weapons and not trusting God.[29] However, Luther was in no position to thwart the political moves of Philip of Hesse and Elector John of Saxony when his safety and security rested squarely in their hands. Eventually, he approved of this evangelical military alliance.

The Schmalkaldic League protected Protestantism long enough for it to get firmly entrenched in northern Europe. It placed the Protestant princes in a remarkably powerful position for negotiation with the emperor. As a result, Emperor Charles entered into a treaty with them—the Peace of Nuremberg—in 1532, securing "a kind of informal toleration" between Protestant and Catholic heads of state.[30] For the time being, the threat of war was removed, and Protestants could go about the business of evangelizing the citizens of their lands.

The Schmalkaldic League barely outlasted Luther's death in 1546. The following year, the League was crushed by imperial troops in the Schmalkaldic War. A united Christendom, however, was no longer possible, and in 1555 the Peace of Augsburg was signed by Emperor Charles V and the Schmalkaldic princes. The famous conclusion of that treaty was *cuius regio, eius religio* (whose realm, his religion). In other words, if you live in a Protestant land, live as a Protestant; if you live in a Catholic land, live as a Catholic.

It was official: Lutheranism was legal and permitted. However, the Holy Roman Empire was now formally divided into Protestant and Catholic. Despite its defeat in 1547, the Schmalkaldic League deserves much credit for the growth of the Lutheran faith from "an amorphous evangelical movement" into an officially recognized and established political entity.[31] The League might have continued longer were it not for a sexual scandal that engulfed its leader, Philip of Hesse. At some point in the 1530s, Philip made it clear to Martin Luther that, unhappy in his marriage, he had fallen in love with a teenager named Margarethe von der Saale. On December 10, 1539, "Melanchthon and Luther signed a memorial . . . in which they agreed that the landgrave [Philip] could marry his concubine in secret, while remaining publicly married to his wife."[32] Luther cited the Old Testament patriarchs and the silence of the New Testament to argue that in Scripture bigamy was not forbidden. The scandal became well known and public opinion began to turn against Philip. Luther, meanwhile, urged Philip to simply shut up and, if questioned, just "deny everything." However, Emperor Charles saw the scandal as an opportunity. Thus, he made a deal in 1541: if Philip would stop all opposition, then the emperor would not bring charges against Philip for bigamy, a crime punishable by death. With Philip thus severely limited in what he could do, "the Schmalkaldic League became increasingly less powerful and the advance of the Reformation into new territories was halted."[33]

This was, of course, not the only high-profile divorce during Luther's life. King Henry VIII (1491–1547) had a similar predicament when he soured on his wife Catherine of Aragon for not producing a male heir. Henry wanted to marry Anne Boleyn, but Luther never gave any indication that he would support a divorce. Presumably, Luther would have been open to the bigamy option for Henry. This episode "poisoned English relations with Saxony," and when the Schmalkaldic League was forming, a huge opportunity was missed not to have the English on board.[34] The League, with the addition of the English, would have survived longer than it did.

Notes

[1]Carl Lindberg, *The European Reformation,* 2nd ed. (Oxford: Wiley-Blackwell, 2010), 93.

[2]See Ibid., 89–91.

[3]Lyndal Roper, *Martin Luther: Renegade and Prophet* (London: Bodley Head, 2016), 348.

[4]Ibid., 349–350.

[5]Ibid., 343–344.

[6]Ibid., 321.

[7]See Timothy Wengert, "The Small Catechism (1529)," in *The Annotated Luther,* ed. Mary Jane Haemig, vol. 4: *Pastoral Writings* (Minneapolis: Fortress Press, 2016), 201.

[8]Timothy Lull, "Luther's Writing," in *The Cambridge Companion to Martin Luther,* ed. Donald McKim (Cambridge: University Press, 2003), 46.

[9]Wengert, 208.

[10]Italics mine. See Andrew Pettegree, *Brand Luther* (New York: Penguin, 2015), 262–265. For Luther's sermon, see *Luther's Works*, ed. Helmut T. Lehman, vol. 46: *Christian in Society III* (St. Louis: Fortress Press, 1955).

[11]Roper, 354–355.

[12]Heinrich Bornkamm, *Luther in Mid-Career 1521–1530* (Minneapolis: Fortress Press, 1983), 615.

[13]Bernhard Lohse, *Martin Luther* (Philadelphia: Fortress Press, 1986), 82.

[14]Pettegree, 253–254.

[15]James Kittelson, *Luther the Reformer* (Minneapolis: Fortress Press, 1986), 221.

[16]Hartmann Grisar, *Martin Luther* (Westminster: The Newman Press, 1950), 346–348.

[17]Kittelson, 221.

[18]Larry Mansch and Curtis Peters, *Martin Luther* (Jefferson, NC: McFarland & Co., 2016), 177.

[19]Pettegree, 248.

[20]Carlos Eire, *Reformations: The Early Modern World, 1450–1650* (New Haven: Yale University Press, 2016), 242.

[21]Richard Friedenthal, *Luther* (London: Weidenfeld and Nicolson, 1967), 505–506.

[22]See David Whitford, "Luther's Political Encounters,"in *The Cambridge Companion to Martin Luther,* ed. Donald McKim (Cambridge: Cambridge University Press, 2003), 187.

[23]Martin Brecht, *Martin Luther,* vol. 2 (Minneapolis: Fortress Press, 1990), 395–396.

[24]Ibid., 406–407.

[25]Whitford, 187.

[26]Lohse, 83.

[27]Roper, 343.

[28]Ibid.

[29]Lohse, 36.

[30]Roper, 343.

[31]Thomas Brady, "Emergence and consolidation of Protestantism in the Holy Roman Empire to 1600," in *The Cambridge History of Christianity,* ed R. Po-Chia Hsia, vol. 6: *Reform and Expansion 1500–1660* (Cambridge: Cambridge University Press, 2007), 21.

[32]Roper, 358–359.

[33]Lohse, 78.

[34]Roper, 358.

16

Luther the Writer

Perhaps more than any other figure since the dawn of the printing press, Martin Luther's success was directly tied to his writing and publishing prowess. He participated in debates, preached innumerable sermons, sat around his dining room table to converse with colleagues and students, counseled people privately, and enjoyed the company of nobility. But it was his writing and publishing abilities that catapulted him onto the world stage. Through writing, he changed the church. Through the written word, he changed the course of Western civilization and, indeed, the course of the world.

Martin Luther was a writer. He was a powerful, creative, at times brutal, and most persuasive writer. No contemporary could keep pace with his literary output. It is difficult to find writers throughout history who not only published so much, but who influenced the minds and hearts of people as much as Martin Luther did through the written word. This chapter takes a broad look at his written corpus.

Luther's literary gifts were many. His interpretation of the Bible was pioneering for its day and often impacted readers deeply. Many great Christian thinkers have been transformed by Luther's biblical commentary, leaders such as the founder of the Methodist Church, John Wesley. While in

London in 1738, he heard someone reading Luther's *Preface to the Epistle to the Romans*, and suddenly Wesley felt his heart "strangely warmed," he said. He went on to lead one of the most important movements in Christian history.[1]

Luther's gift for translation is widely acknowledged. He seemed to grasp more fully than most how language works, how it is most effective, and how it can change minds. Luther's mastery of German is particularly noteworthy. He was able to communicate so effectively with the common person. His obvious advantage over other popular writers of his day, or even since, was that he was able to write for such a wide array of audiences. He could pen erudite theology, hymns, instruction manuals for children, sacred liturgies, personal letters, and scathing speeches within days of each other. All his manifold forms of writing became highly popular for academicians as well as for the common people.

What was Luther's secret for his journalistic success? What was he doing that others were not doing? History's foremost Luther scholar, Martin Brecht, boiled it down to this: "Luther was not so much interested in the poetic shaping of his writings as in straightforwardly giving his ideas to the public."[2] Put another way, Luther wrote his theology for the people. He understood that to impact more than a few academic minds or perhaps a small cohort of clergy, he needed to write for the common man, the common woman, the common Christian. Luther wrote for the people. This was his genius. This is why we are still talking about Martin Luther's writings five hundred years later.

Luther's Early Works

Devising a way to divide Luther's works is difficult, not just because there are so many of them, but also because his writings tended to blur the lines of literary genres as we understand them today.[3] He was constantly challenging literary boundaries. For example, one of his important early writings, *On Christian Freedom* (1520), "is partly a sermon, partly a treatise, and partly a work of polemic against the 'bondage' of the church in his time—a sequel to the *Babylonian Captivity* of earlier that same year."[4]

Luther's works were rarely stand-alone volumes due to his prodigious literary output. People were reading his works constantly and feverishly, so there was a perpetual and fluid story being told by Luther as people read him. About the time they got their hands on one of his publications, another was waiting in the wings. Today, it is difficult for us to grasp the rapidity of events as they were occurring during Luther's life. Times were changing, and Luther was the point man. His writings provide us a track record of the events, but today we cannot comprehend the immense importance of Luther's impact on the people and the events occurring right then and there. There was no disconnect between Luther's ubiquitous publications and history's unpredictable flux. It was an unfolding drama, a revolution, and Martin Luther was the prime mover of all these events.

Luther's earliest works are dominated by his studies of Scripture. He began working on Bible commentaries in 1513 at the age of thirty while he was a young professor at the University of Wittenberg, and he continued this work to the end of his life in 1546. He published many of his Bible class lectures as well as hundreds of his sermons on biblical texts. His earliest studies were on Psalms, Romans, Galatians, and Hebrews, the biblical books that dominated his thinking between 1513 and 1518. Luther was already showing signs of innovation in his writing as "he abandoned the traditional form of interpreting scripture" in favor of a more continuous approach that followed the text verse by verse. His novel approach "brought things out of the Bible that had not been heard before" and became "one of Luther's lasting literary influences."[5]

It is interesting that in 1517—the year Luther's *Ninety-Five Theses* came onto the scene—he also published *The Seven Penitential Psalms*, which were "strongly meditative in nature."[6] Throughout Luther's career, his piety went alongside his contentiousness.

Early Disputations and Confrontations

Among Luther's earliest works are his disputations, a side of Luther that quite accidentally propelled him to great fame and infamy. His *Ninety-Five Theses* (also known as the *Disputation on the Power and Efficacy of Indulgences*, 1517), *Heidelberg Disputation* (1518), *Proceedings at Augsburg* (1518), *Leipzig Disputation* (1519), and his famous encounter at Worms (1521) demonstrate a remarkable ability to provoke, argue, and critique in the most trenchant yet effective of ways.[7]

Luther's ability to pick a fight sent him often into the fires of controversy. Not mere attempts to undermine authority, these disputations were predicated on Luther's theology, so clearly at variance from the theology of his day. Luther saw these literary confrontations as an effective way to teach. His facility with words put him at an obvious advantage. Further, publishing accounts of his proceedings gave Luther an opportunity to stay ahead of his opponents. Publishing his own versions first was critical to his success, since he was able to put words into his opponents' mouths. Using this method, Luther was able to claim victory in his various confrontations. And later he could point to the publications—which he controlled—as evidence of his triumph over his enemies.

Martin Luther was truly at his best (or worst, depending on one's perspective) when he was arguing. He was able to escalate tension and create drama with tremendous effectiveness. Many people were recruited to the cause of reform when they read his published confrontations of the church. Luther was able to control the talking points of the controversies while everyone else simply played catch up. *He* set the tone for the debates. *He* was the chief interpreter of the events happening all over Germany. *He* was able to stay on the offensive because he was always two or three publications ahead of his critics.

Luther's disputations forced him to think in short, pithy sentences. He had to critique large ideas, such as the deficiencies of scholastic theology or the immorality of selling indulgences, in pointed ways. Luther had a knack for shocking readers. He was excellent at one-liners. He would be a Twitter genius today! He could create irony with a poignant phrase. He could harpoon his opponent with such ferocity that only a fool would try to take him on toe to toe. Luther was a master at this, and everyone who tried to keep pace with his insults and war of words lost. Not only lost, but lost badly. Luther was not satisfied just to defeat opponents with his sharp wit, but he mocked them to the point that they did a disservice to themselves by even trying to play defense. Any response to Luther would simply attract more of his venom. Opposing him was a losing battle, especially considering the wild popularity of his publications. Over and over again, we read about how many editions Luther's writings went through in comparison to the abysmal sales of his opponents' works. Luther had all the momentum, and to take him on publicly was to lose before you started.

Embedded in Luther's rebuttals, theses, polemics, and defenses were his theological innovations and contributions. He was uniquely gifted at tearing down his opponent in few words and then quickly offering what he thought was a better alternative. This method played to his strengths because his opponents were almost always too long-winded. Luther's attacks were calculated and precise: "He concentrated on a few salient points, and then broke off the debate" rather than allowing the opponent to set the tone.[8] Yet, in these quick maneuvers, he would make new proposals. The *Ninety-Five Theses* are a good illustration of this. Luther's succinctness works like biblical proverbs; it takes a while to digest what he is saying, but when it sinks in, the truth of his claims appears to be obvious.

Why were Luther's disputations so successful and persuasive? First, Luther was a gifted debater. He was as impressive in person as he was on paper. People talked about his performances long after he delivered them. This is a rare quality for any academician.

Second, by reacting so strongly to Luther, the Catholic Church made things worse for itself. Had they ignored Luther, he might have become only a disgruntled professor in Germany. Where the church miscalculated was in thinking they could treat Luther like they did the antagonists before him: the louder the church screamed, the less confident the antagonists would become. This simply was not the case for Luther. His courage outpaced the vociferousness of the pope.

Third, as we have noted earlier, Luther had an uncanny ability to appeal to the common man. When his accusers were pretentious or abstruse, Luther was plain and sensible. And this is where his publications served him well. People responded to Luther's earthiness. His language was often foul. His constant references to breaking wind, his labeling the pope as an ass, or his insults to his critics in the most demeaning of terms seemed to endear Luther to the working classes. An obvious example is Luther's 1521 published letter to one of his detractors—Jerome Emser—whom Luther called "the goat in Leipzig" because of his coat of arms: a shield and helmet adorned with a goat. "My greetings to the goat in Leipzig," Luther began his reply to Emser. In what Luther called "glaring letters that everyone must see," Emser had referred to his goat symbol and had threatened to butt Luther. Luther jumped on the metaphor. "Your entire nature certainly reveals you to be a goat," Luther replied, and he proceeded to use the goat metaphor to belittle and insult Emser. "You can hardly express what is on your mind in German, for your words roam about so clumsily, so helter-skelter, and in such disorder," Luther demeaned the man. "Never mind, dear goat," Luther concluded. "It does not help to look for anything good in you."[9] Commoners ate up this stuff, and Luther knew it. That's how he was able to win big in the court of public opinion: he entertained his readers.

Luther's style is still exhilarating to read. His sentences have "rhythm and timber," his vowels have melody, his use of dissonance and alliteration is genius, his analogies and associations are relevant and often funny, and his images are rich.[10] His teachings, for example his catechisms, were so well written that they were "easily committed to memory and recited."[11] This was in contrast to the late-medieval philosophers and theologians, who tended to be cold and rational, "well-polished and neatly packaged," using recondite, academic formulas.[12]

Luther's Treatises

Luther dealt often with specific themes in his published sermons and treatises. When chaos ensued following his *Ninety-Five Theses* in 1517, he published *On Indulgences and Grace* (1518) to unpack his theology. A short piece, only twenty paragraphs, and crafted as a sermon, it was Luther's way of opening up his rather academic *Ninety-Five Theses* to a conversation that was more comprehensible to the common man. It became so popular that "it was reprinted twenty times in runs of 1,000 copies each."[13] In it, Luther ripped the idea that by buying indulgences one could purchase their own salvation. He also clarified that he was not attacking the pope; rather, he was refuting John Tetzel, the indulgence salesman.[14] He also called out those who were wont to declare him a heretic: "I do not consider such monotonous screeching very seriously, since those who make the accusation are dimwits who have never even smelled the Bible."[15]

As the critiques of Luther poured in during the aftermath of the *Ninety-Five Theses*, Luther used Tetzel as a punching bag for his various sermons and treatises. For example, in his *Freedom of the Sermon Touching Papal Indulgence and Grace*, he mocked Tetzel, using animals—a common tactic for Luther. "Tetzel strummed the scriptures as a pig plays the lute," he wrote. He then sarcastically challenged Tetzel to come to Wittenberg: "Here I am at Wittenberg. . . . Is there a heretic hunter who dares devour iron and scale?"[16]

Then in late 1520, Luther penned his three masterpieces: *Address to the Christian Nobility of the German Nation*, *The Babylonian Captivity of the Church*, and *On Christian Freedom*. In these works, Luther unpacked more of his theological agenda. For example, he began to envision what Christianity would look like without a pope at its head. He appealed to the German nobility to come together and help carry out much-needed reforms. He redefined the sacraments and argued that they should be reduced from seven to two or three—only baptism and Eucharist, and possibly penance. He delved into what became, perhaps, his most famous teaching: justification by faith alone (*sola fide*).

In *Address to the Christian Nobility of the German Nation*, Luther argued three main ideas:

1. The laity should not be dominated by the clergy.
2. The pope was not the only person who could interpret Scripture authoritatively.
3. The pope was not more authoritative than church councils.

It should be kept in mind that by 1520 Luther was determined to reform the church, and he saw the clergy in general—and the pope in particular—as obstructing the necessary reforms. Thus, in Luther's mind, if the clergy neglected their duties, then laypeople were authorized to be leaders in the church and interpreters of Scripture. This idea has come to be known as Luther's doctrine of "the priesthood of all believers," which he based on 1 Peter 2:9: "You are royal priests, a holy nation, God's very own possession." Luther argued that all Christians are priests based solely upon their baptism.

Clearly, he was playing with fire. In essence, he was intimating that anyone's interpretation is as valuable as anyone else's—including the pope's! Luther went on in the book to address the exorbitant wealth of the church and its hierarchy, including its lust for more—as evidenced in the indulgence controversy. Luther's prime motive was not kept hidden: Germany needed to escape the clutches of Rome. The Roman hierarchy was unnecessary for a German national church. Indeed, in Luther's mind, Rome's impact on the German church was corrosive. He referred to the papal officers as "a crawling mass of reptiles."[17] This book was a huge success, selling out all four thousand copies of the first edition in just two weeks.

In *The Babylonian Captivity of the Church*, Luther once again critiqued the Roman hierarchy. As he did in *Christian Nobility of the German Nation*, he wrote in German so his compatriots would be in the know, although his remarks were directed primarily at clergymen. The book attacked Rome's sacramental system, especially how the clergy abused and manipulated the people through them and by withholding them. Luther argued that humans are saved by grace and not by sacramental works and that by using Christ as a threat the institution had become "identical with the kingdom of Babylon and the Antichrist itself."[18] It was a radical and angry document, railing against the sacramental system in excruciating detail. In this book, more than any other, Luther put the axe to the root, attempting to sever the German church from the Roman Catholic institution. "To begin with," he wrote, "I must deny that there are seven sacraments, and for the present maintain that there are but three: baptism, penance, and the bread. All three have been subjected to a miserable captivity by the Roman curia, and the church has been robbed of all her liberty."[19] This book was dangerous and subversive. Luther's larger agenda was now on full display.

On Christian Freedom, published in November 1520, addresses the paradoxical ideas that Christians are free, subjected to none but Christ, but they are also to be dutiful servants to all. There is tension here, and Luther engages the tension through a discussion of love. He argues that while Christians are free, they are to be people of great love. Indeed, love is the clear sign of a Christian. And the Christian life is a life of good works to others, motivated by love for them. Luther makes it clear that salvation comes by faith, but love and good works flow naturally out of the person who is truly saved. Good works can never save a sinner, but the sinner whose faith is in Christ can rest assured in his or her salvation. Luther describes this condition as *simul justus et peccator*—"always sinning, yet always justified, at the same time."[20]

Old and New Testaments

Earlier, we detailed how Luther translated the New Testament from Greek into High German in 1521 while at Wartburg Castle. It was first published in September 1522 and therefore became known as the September Testament.[21] A magnificent piece of work, it singlehandedly transformed the German language. His word choices were beautiful, sharp, and forceful. "Expressions such as scapegoat, decoy, stopgap, or eaves trough were his creations." When Luther felt he was unable to do justice with his translation, he used marginal notes to explain.[22]

Luther began his Old Testament translation shortly after finishing the New, but it took him much longer to complete. He wanted to publish the Old Testament in three parts to keep it affordable. Thus, the Pentateuch was published in 1523; the historical books (Joshua to Esther) appeared in early 1524; and the poetic books (Job to Song of Songs) in the autumn of 1524. Although he completed the prophets in 1524, their publication was delayed until 1532. Luther's Old Testament was not exclusively his; he headed a team that included his friends Melanchthon and Spalatin. Luther consulted Jerome's authoritative Latin Vulgate (fourth century) throughout but felt that his translation was better and was constructed from superior manuscripts, which it certainly was.[23]

Luther's Sermons

Luther started preaching at Wittenberg's City Church in 1514.[24] He was dedicated to his role as preacher and considered it not only a labor of love, but also necessary to carry out his program of reform.

Luther's preaching was "distinguished by great freshness and practicality." His famous maxim about preaching was "Ascend the pulpit, open your mouth, and then stop." He preached forcefully, and his topics were always relevant, though laced with biblical references. Once the Reformation began, he railed against Rome much of the time, but even then his "diversity of thought" was impressive and unique for the age.[25]

Luther's sermons were often very creative. For example, on Palm Sunday in 1518, he preached on the righteousness of Christ being transferred to humans "in a way which had earlier been totally unknown."[26] In that sermon, he said Christ was the groom who transferred his righteousness to the bride—the repentant sinner. It was brilliantly crafted and resonated with marital customs of the time. He was able to take a difficult theological subject and bring it down to the commoner's level with great ease.

Luther realized that he held great influence over the proliferating crop of preachers who were joining the Reformation. So, in 1521, he published his *Church Postil*, which became critical for helping pastors determine what and how to preach. That resource served as a model for preaching within the Lutheran church for centuries. Luther preached often through books of the Bible, for example a series on Psalms or on the Gospel of John. However, he preached topical sermons frequently as well, tackling such topics as marriage, what age to marry, keeping children in school, how to pray, how to handle miscarriage, preparing for death, baptism, fleeing to escape the plague, and countless others.[27] He preached through the liturgical calendar, especially near Christmas and Easter.

One of the key and recurrent themes in Luther's sermons was liberation. As in much of his writing, Luther sometimes acted like he was wiping away fifteen hundred years of church tradition that had built up like residue. He felt he was setting people free by removing the shackles the church had placed on its members through centuries of canon law. His teachings on marriage were highly unconventional, such as his belief that "it is no disgrace to recognize a vow [celibacy] one cannot keep and should not have made in the first place." Luther felt he was liberating marriage from its inferior status in the church. He said the church had placed hindrances and limitations on marriage that should not be there. In his mind, marriage was not in the hands of clergyman; rather, it was "under the protection and promise of God."[28]

Hymns, Worship, and Prayers

Luther was enthusiastically engaged in the pursuit of meaningful Christian worship. He had gifts in the arts, particularly in music. He played the lute and sang often. Some of his hymns are still being sung in churches today.

Luther wisely realized that he needed church music because of its ability to penetrate the Christian's heart. He adapted many of the medieval church hymns by rewriting lyrics to reflect a more biblical focus. For Luther, it was imperative to draw the minds of worshipers to the Word of God. And he was never satisfied to have a church choir, as had been common throughout church history. Rather, he advocated congregational singing, where every believer played a role. Luther began publishing hymnals in 1524, and they were highly influential for Protestant worship services. His first hymnal consisted of twenty-five hymns, fifteen of them written by Luther himself. In 1529, one of his hymnals was published containing the classic Lutheran song, "A Mighty Fortress Is Our God."[29] Luther's hymnals were extremely successful, both in churches and in schools. Well over one thousand editions of his hymnals were published in the sixteenth century alone.[30]

Luther recreated the entire church liturgy, baptizing everything in Protestant theology and heavily biblical themes. He revised the baptismal liturgy, the service for marriage, ordination, and the structure of the Mass.[31] Luther left his marks all over the German Protestant worship services. His *German Mass* was the culmination of his life's work of adapting the Christian worship service to decidedly Lutheran sensibilities. Not inflexible in how he envisioned worship, he did advocate local variation to some extent.

Perhaps Luther's most durable writings are his *Large Catechism* and *Small Catechism* (catechism means "church teaching"), both published in 1529.[32] The catechisms are vintage Luther. They are essentially his version of what a Christian needs to know, a confession of faith. Luther's catechisms are sheer mastery in their breadth, depth, and absolute command of the German language.[33] One leading scholar of Luther, Tim Lull, wrote: "The most influential of Luther's works over the past five centuries has been his *Small Catechism*." Luther wrote the catechisms after learning that many Saxony church members—especially in the rural parts—were wholly ignorant on fundamental aspects of Christian faith such as the Creed, the Lord's Prayer, the Ten Commandments, and the sacraments. Thus, his language in the *Small Catechism* was clear and simple, written in such a way as to be easily memorized.[34]

The *Small Catechism* was a huge success. It was "published as a wall chart" for schools, and quickly was translated into Latin, French, Dutch, Danish, and Low German.[35] Luther realized that the teaching of the catechism was central to his movement, especially in the quality of Christians it produced. In Luther's mind, the rural people were living "as if they were pigs and irrational beasts." He believed they "had mastered only the art of abusing evangelical liberty"—meaning they took Luther's "Christian freedom" ideals and misused them as a license to live however they wanted. Luther and the pastors recognized this situation to be an "urgent emergency." They became extremely motivated to ensure that pastors were teaching people—especially the youth—what it meant to live as Christians. They used the *Small Catechism* to accomplish the task.[36]

Luther's *Large Catechism* was also known as the *German Catechism* (*Deudsch Catechismus*). It was directed to pastors and heads of households. Approximately half of it was devoted to the Ten Commandments, for Luther believed that "anyone who really understands the Ten Commandments has mastered the entire Bible." The rest was devoted to the Apostles' Creed, the Lord's Prayer ("Our Father"), baptism, and the Eucharist. In the introduction,

Luther said that he read and recited the catechism every day, religiously, like a child. He was careful that he did this daily, and "gladly." He believed the Holy Spirit was present when a person recited the catechism, and evil thoughts were expelled from the mind. Luther believed that "the beginning of the Lord's Prayer brought him into communion with the almighty God, made Christ his brother, and the archangels his servants." Luther's beginning to the section on the Decalogue is memorable: "What is it to have a god? What is God?" His famous answer was, "A god is that to which we look for all good and in which we find refuge in every time of need. To have a god is nothing else than to trust and believe him with our whole heart."[37]

The *Large Catechism* was intended to be a "theological handbook" for pastors. It was an aid for preaching and teaching about the Christian faith. In 1537, Luther referred to it as one of his best writings.[38] It was of such high quality and real clarity that it could—and probably should—have been an ecumenical document to unite the various strands of Protestantism that were then proliferating in Europe. However, as we noted earlier, Luther's non-negotiable teaching on Christ's "real presence" in the Eucharist prevented a unified Protestant movement from happening. His teaching on the sacrament was "closer to the Catholic teaching on the matter, actually, than any of the other Protestant explanations."[39]

Consolidating His Gains

Luther's later years were spent reiterating his core teachings and defending them, which meant writing disputations against those he disagreed with. His literary output was still impressive, but his main ideas of reform were established, and it was now time for him to consolidate the gains he had fought for throughout his long and turbulent career.

In 1530, a milestone in what we now know as "Lutheran" theology was reached when the famous *Augsburg Confession* was presented to the Diet of Augsburg—the legislative assembly—at the city of Augsburg in Bavaria. It was a summation of Lutheran thought, arranged into its final form by Melanchthon. It "set forth, in plain style, the common ground that Protestants found with Catholicism while at the same time articulating their doctrinal differences."[40] This work, consisting of twenty-eight articles, became one of the critical Reformation documents and is still used by Lutherans today. When the Catholic Church drafted a *Confutation* against it, this only angered Luther and convinced him that any level of reconciliation with the Roman church was a waste of time. Luther's attempt to consolidate his gains was a mammoth enterprise that consumed him and his publishers until his death. Petegree notes the following:

> Catechisms and prayer books, Bibles and hymnals, sermons, church orders, and commentaries: the work of church building generated a huge volume of print, both for the use of the churches in Saxony and elsewhere in Germany. For the Wittenberg printing industry this was a golden period. . . . Between 1530 and 1546 [Luther's Death] Wittenberg's presses turned out over sixteen hundred editions. . . . At its heart was Martin Luther, still ceaselessly active in writing, apportioning work among the firms and seeing books through the press. . . . In the last fifteen years of his life, Luther exercised an extraordinary influence over the output of the German press.[41]

Luther was an amazing wordsmith. Few—if any—authors in history have accomplished his level of output and influence. More than anyone else, Luther understood the implications of the printing press and its influence over hearts and minds, and he took full advantage.

But what may be easy to forget is that Luther's writing was not what set into motion the unstoppable force that we call the Reformation. It was his beliefs. Many people throughout history have had a literary gift. Great writers come and go, but they do not rend civilization in two. What caused the Reformation was not necessarily Luther's writing; it was his ideas. And Luther's most important ideas are what we turn to next.

Notes

[1]Frederick Dreyer, *The Genesis of Methodism* (Bethlehem, PA: Lehigh University Press, 1999), 27.

[2]Martin Brecht, *Doctor Luther's Bulla and Reformation: A Look at Luther the Writer* (Valparaiso, IN: Valparaiso University Press, 1991), 2.

[3]The critical edition of Luther's writings is the Weimar Ausgabe, containing 68 volumes. The American edition, entitled *Luther's Works*, contains 55 volumes. These are by no means complete collections of Luther's writings, however. See Timothy Lull,

"Luther's Writings," in *The Cambridge Companion to Martin Luther* ed. Donald McKim (Cambridge: Cambridge University Press, 2003), 39.

[4]Lull, 41.

[5]Brecht, 2–3. The literary changes were technical in nature. Luther's innovation was that he *combined* grammatical, linguistic, historical, and theological statements into one continuous text rather than using the gloss method wherein scholars interpreted the text with words or short statements between the lines or in the margins. For the "brought things out" quotation, see Bernhard Lohse, *Martin Luther* (Philadelphia: Fortress Press, 1986), 98.

[6]Lohse, 103.

[7]*Luther at the Diet of Worms* (1521) was clearly published to bolster Luther's cause, although it is unclear who exactly wrote it. It has been suggested it might have been Luther's good friend Justus Jonas, with the help of Luther and a few other close companions. See *Luther's Works* (Philadelphia: Muhlenberg Press, 1958), vol. 32, 103.

[8]Brecht, 3.

[9]*To the Goat in Leipzig*, in *Luther's Works*, vol. 39, 111–115.

[10]Lohse, 98.

[11]Brecht, 5.

[12]Gerhard Brendler, *Martin Luther* (Oxford: Oxford University Press, 1991), 63.

[13]Larry Mansch and Curtis Peters, *Martin Luther* (Jefferson, NC: McFarland & Co., 2016), 69.

[14]Scott Hendrix, *Martin Luther* (New Haven: Yale University Press, 2015), 64.

[15]Brendler, 120.

[16]Ibid., 126.

[17]Mansch and Peters, 101.

[18]James Kittelson, *Luther the Reformer* (Minneapolis: Fortress Press, 1986), 152.

[19]*Babylonian Captivity of the Church*, in *Luther's Works*, vol. 36, 18.

[20]Mansch and Peters, 106.

[21]Ibid., 128.

[22]Martin Brecht, *Martin Luther*, vol. 2 (Minneapolis: Fortress Press, 1990), 49.

[23]Ibid., 55.

[24]Ibid., 4.

[25]Hartman Grisar, *Martin Luther* (Westminster: The Newman Press, 1950), 471–472.

[26]Brecht, 4.

[27]Luther and Katie "had taken in so many who were stricken that their home remained under quarantine even after the Plague left the city." See Kittelson, 210.

[28]Heinrich Bornkamm, trans. by Theodore Bachman, *Luther in Mid-Career* (Philadelphia, PA: Fortress Press, 1983), 109–111.

[29]Grisar, 478.

[30]Andrew Pettegree, *Brand Luther* (New York: Viking, 2015), 322.

[31]Lull, 51.

[32]See Timothy Wengert, "The Small Catechism," in Mary Jane Haemig, ed., *The Annotated Luther*, vol. 4: *Pastoral Writings* (Minneapolis: Fortress Press, 2016), 201.

[33]See Brecht, 5. The original title was *Small Catechism for Ordinary Pastors and Preachers*. See Brecht, 275.

[34]Lull, 46.

[35]Pettegree, 261–262.

[36]Brecht, vol. 2, 275.

[37]Ibid., 277–278.

[38]Ibid., 278–279.

[39]Kirsi Stjerna, "The Large Catechism of Dr. Martin Luther," in Stjerna, ed., *The Annotated Luther,* vol. 2: *Word and Faith* (Minneapolis: Fortress Press, 2015), 283.

[40]Mansch and Peters, 184.

[41]Pettegree, 267, 275.

17

Luther's Core Beliefs

Martin Luther was a medieval man. His thoughts and his faith were in line with the university-trained people around him: a rather unquestioned belief in the God of the Bible, a theological outlook that had been nurtured by a millennium of Roman Catholic theology, and a preoccupation with the status of his soul—whether he would spend eternity in heaven or hell. Where Luther differed from those around him was his unique historical circumstances and his willingness to innovate despite powerful opposition. And, while it is reasonable to suggest that Martin Luther's career represents a shift from a medieval mindset to a modern one, these two categories are problematic. Luther certainly had a hand—perhaps even the leading role—in changing the political and ecclesial structures of his day, but intellectually and spiritually he was far closer to his detractors than he was to, say, the Eastern Orthodox. He was a medieval man in western European Christendom. His ideas were not so much novel as they were creative. It was his courage that propelled his interpretive innovation, leading to a real breakthrough in theology, philosophy, authority, and epistemology. Luther has been credited with putting into motion such paradigm shifts as the Enlightenment, the modern world, and secularization. Whether he was the critical force in them is debatable. What is not debatable is that he is widely seen as that force.

The Problem: Sin

Like virtually all theologians of his day, Luther understood the "fall" of Adam and Eve to be an actual, historical event. Luther also believed that a real serpent tricked Eve to eat the forbidden fruit. In his *Lectures on Genesis*, Luther described Satan as a "natural serpent . . . a most beautiful little beast" who became poisonous and ugly only after the first sin.[1] That sin, which entered the world through Adam and Eve, continued throughout human history as "hereditary sin," or "natural sin," in the mind of Luther. In one of his New Year's Day sermons, he said the following:

> Hereditary sin or natural sin or personal sin is the truly chief sin. If this sin did not exist, there would also be no actual sin. This sin is not committed, as are all other sins; rather it *is*. . . . This natural sin is the only one to which God pays attention. It cannot be driven out by any law or any punishment. . . . Only the grace of God, which makes nature pure and new, can sweep it out. The law . . . does not help against sin.[2]

This "natural" sin is commonly referred to as "original sin." And Luther—like all theologians of his time—accepted it as true.

"In Luther's view, when we speak theologically, sinfulness is the very essence of what it means to be human."[3] Humans are sinful at their core. In Luther's formal defense of his *Ninety-Five Theses*, number thirty-one reads, "A righteous man sins in all his good works."[4] Humans are therefore in a predicament. They have sinned against God, and they can do nothing about it. This is where Luther's Christology rescued him from despair: "Jesus Christ, the Lord of life . . . has snatched us, poor lost creatures, from the jaws of hell, won us, made us free, and restored us to the Father's favor and grace."[5] In other words, humans cannot do anything about their sins, but God in his grace has saved humans.

This is where modern thinkers struggle to understand Luther. On one hand, he argues that humans can do nothing, but on the other hand, he argues that humans have to trust in Christ to receive salvation. Some have argued that Luther's ideas of predestination come to the fore here. In other words, God will save some and he will refuse to save others, completely at his discretion. Humans all deserve eternal punishment, according to Luther. But to those who trust in Christ, God will be merciful and will redeem them from the human predicament.

Luther ended up despising indulgences because, in his mind, they offered nothing. They were a scam because only God could offer salvation. Human beings simply received God's offer of salvation. They could not *buy* it. Luther is difficult for modern thinkers to understand on this. He seems to say that humans can't do anything to obtain salvation, but *how they believe* is precisely where salvation can be found. While humans are powerless to expunge their condemnation, if they believe in Christ the way Luther thinks they should, then they will receive salvation. Is saving faith cerebral activity a work? Luther argues no.

It could be argued that Luther had a more robust idea of sin than the church had. He saw human sin as an element of our nature that is impossible for us to overcome. Luther thought the Roman Church was minimizing sin. Humans cannot eradicate their sins with offerings. To say they can was not only unscriptural, he taught, but it downplayed sin's gravity. Only Christ, the Son of God, could purchase human salvation from the clutches of the devil. The transaction was a divine one. God paid the penalty by sending Christ. Humans are able to enter into that divine transaction by believing it to be true, by trusting in Christ rather than in money. Luther labeled this idea *sola fide*, "faith alone."

But, again, reading Luther can be confusing, because he seems to say that humans must only believe, but then he goes on to explain—in excruciating detail—not only what a Christian needs to believe, but how a Christian should respond to the transaction God has made in Christ. Therefore, salvation is perhaps not as easy as it initially sounds with *sola fide*. Yes, faith is required, but Luther had in mind a particular kind of faith. It was a faith that precluded indulgences, for one thing. And it was faith that required *true* repentance rather than simple payments to the church in the form of indulgences.

Since money helped no one to merit salvation from sin, Luther advocated that the money spent on useless indulgences, relics, and pilgrimages should be spent on charity or on one's own family.[6] Later in his career when the Reformation was fairly well established, Luther argued strongly in favor of Christians using their money to build and establish schools that would teach Lutheran theology.

The Solution: Faith and Sacrament

Raised in the Catholic Church, Luther inherited the notion of seven sacraments: baptism, confirmation, Eucharist, reconciliation/penance/confession, anointing of the sick, marriage, and holy orders. Luther's understanding of the sacraments was "entirely conventional" in 1517 when he launched the Reformation.[7] In time, however, he deviated dramatically from the medieval teaching he was raised and educated in.

For Luther, the sacraments consisted of three elements: a physical and outward sign, a divine promise toward which the sign pointed, and the individual's faith to receive the promise. In Luther's mind, this last element—faith—was crucial. It was "of all things the most necessary, for it is the ground of all comfort." In other words, the sacrament itself was devoid of power without the individual's faith. After 1517, Luther's theology of the sacraments began to deviate from the medieval, scholastic notion of *ex opera operato* (the sheer performance of the act brings about the effect, the infusion of grace). Luther came to repudiate that idea in favor of the primacy of the believer's faith. Faith became, for him, the "constitutive element" in the sacraments, and this impacted his theology deeply.[8] For the medieval mind, the sacrament *in itself* provided grace to the recipient. Luther, however, saw a more active participation by the believer. God's grace comes to human beings who have faith.

This step in the direction of faith was a key ingredient in Luther's protest when he posted the *Ninety-Five Theses*. "Already in October of 1517, Luther's attack on indulgences bore within it an implicit critique of the sacrament of penance."[9] He began to use Paul's writings to take the position that faith is greater than the sacraments themselves. In Luther's mature thinking, sacraments are valuable, just not absolute. And without faith, they become impotent. He taught that sacraments are useful to the believer but not necessary for salvation, and this is where Luther was often reproved by Catholics. He seemed to be making light of bedrock Catholic tradition and practice.

Luther often is said to have sanctioned only two sacraments—baptism and Eucharist—when he occasionally referred to a third: penance/confession.[10] In 1519, he wrote to George Spalatin that he would not admit any of the other four sacraments "until someone shows me by what [Bible] passage I can prove it." In that same letter, Luther began to describe the other sacraments as manipulative fabrications by the church to exert control over the people.[11] Still, baptism and Eucharist remained for him "the solid ground on which the certainty of a Christian's faith rests."[12]

Baptism

For Luther, baptism was a combination of divine action with an act of faith. It was extremely potent spiritually, for it was "the driving out of the old man and the birth of the new."[13] Baptism was covenantal for Luther, a "joyful exchange," because through it the recipient "receives the righteousness of Christ and Christ takes over his sins."[14] The person who receives baptism "becomes guiltless, pure, and sinless, while at the same time continuing full of evil inclinations." Indeed, through baptism, God "pledges . . . not to impute to you the sins which remain."[15]

Luther often criticized the Anabaptists for arguing that infant baptism was invalid. In their view, baptism should only be administered to a person old enough to make their faith their own. Luther rejected Anabaptist views strongly on the grounds that they distorted the sacrament, "transforming it from the work of God into the work of man."[16] Luther thought of baptism as a great gift, a treasure given to the person in their infancy.

However—and this is where it got tricky for Luther—infants are unable to have faith. Luther was never clear on how he was able to get around this problem. On some occasions, he seems to attribute to infants the ability to have faith. At other times, he seems to indicate that "the faith of the parents and sponsors substitutes for the infant."[17] Luther's position on infant baptism was ambiguous, and he was never quite able to resolve the tension. In *Defense and Explanation of All the Articles*, he pointed to "Christ's saying in the last chapter of Mark, 'He who believes and is baptized will be saved.'" Faith must always come before baptism, he reasoned, citing the Acts 8 story where Philip agreed to baptize the eunuch only after the man professed his faith. "On the basis of this faith and confession, the sacrament of baptism is administered," Luther insisted.[18]

Luther seemed to be unable to resolve this ambivalence. The Anabaptists used Luther's views against him when they accused him of going beyond the written word. Luther, however, argued that the Scriptures were silent on infant baptism. He wrestled with this issue, however, evidently realizing the vulnerability of his position.

The Eucharist

Luther invested much more energy into the sacrament of Eucharist than into baptism. Today, we marvel that he was willing to break with all other Protestants over this one issue. For him, the Catholic understanding was correct. The bread *is* the body of Christ, he insisted. Any who challenged Luther on this idea received his wrath. Luther may today serve as a dividing line in history between medieval and modern, but his views on the Eucharist were very much in line with the medieval perspective on it. Luther's "lifelong conviction" was that in the Eucharist "the divine mysteriously becomes present to us."[19]

Two top Protestant leaders who faulted Luther on his view of the Eucharist were Zwingli and Johannes Oecolampadius (1482–1531). Zwingli's view was that when Jesus said "is" ("This *is* my body"), he meant "represents." Oecolampadius argued that when Jesus used the word "is," he meant "is a sign of." Luther repudiated them in his 1527 treatise *That These Words of Christ, "This Is My Body."*[20] He argued that Christ is present everywhere, but not in a literal way. In the Eucharist, Christ is "present for you."[21] Luther scathingly mocked his opponents for their caricatures of his position. He argued that some of his detractors on this matter should be punished by the civil authorities. "They know nothing about what they are saying but speak blasphemy anyway." Calling his opponents insulting names, Luther railed, "Listen now, you pig, dog, or fanatic, whatever kind of unreasonable ass you are." And he blasted them with his conviction that Christ was present in the bread and wine of the Eucharist.[22] Something about the Eucharist brought out the worst in Luther. He was consistently bitter when challenged on this issue, but he was altogether unclear on the matter.

Luther would not tolerate the other reformers who wanted to turn the Eucharist into a memorial or the elements into symbols only. His detractors rightly saw little difference between Luther and the official position of the Roman Catholic Church. Luther always held that Zwingli and the others did not understand his position. They accused him of being too literal. Luther defended himself in another work entitled *The Sacrament of the Body and Blood of Christ—Against the Fanatics.* When the other reformers said he was being illogical, Luther countered that just as God could impregnate Mary, he could also make himself really present in the Eucharist.[23]

Luther did break Catholic tradition when he extended the cup to the laity. Part of his reasoning was his priesthood-of-all-believers idea. We're all priests, so we all are entitled to the cup, he said. He also argued that the elements were gifts, and it was wrong to prevent God's gifts from being distributed to his own children. Just as priests must not forbid a family to baptize their infant, they may not forbid Christians access to both the bread and the wine.[24]

Penance

Penance, or confession, was the third and final of Luther's list of sacraments. Sometimes he included it and other times he did not. For him, penance certainly did not hold the weight that baptism and Eucharist did, but Luther thought it important for true Christian piety. His *Ninety-Five Theses* were an attack on the entire system of confession—particularly on the notion that one could do penance through indulgences. Luther was troubled by the corruption surrounding this sacrament, but he was also repulsed by the notion that people were not truly repenting for their sins. They were relying on the church's system of penance for absolving their consciences, even when their hearts were not pure or remorseful.

Luther's critiques on penance attracted the ire of the church. "Sixteen of the forty 'errors' censured by Pope Leo X's bull *Exsurge Domine* had to do with penance, and thus Luther's reply dealt at length with the issue."[25] In his response, entitled *Defense and Explanations of All the Articles*, he said he regarded penance/confession to be a sacrament, but he critiqued the church for abusing it, notably by withholding it from those who refused to conform to the church.

Luther saw the church as exerting power over people by withholding absolution from them during their time of need. Papists, Luther argued, wanted to keep people feeling guilty so the church could extract obedience and money from them. Letting people's consciences be absolved, Luther charged, "would undermine the honor accorded to the clergy, dry up financial contributions, and generally disempower the clergy."[26]

Moreover, Luther argued, penance was a return to one's baptism.[27] In baptism, one becomes purified from the stain of original sin. Similarly, when the individual confesses sin and means it, he returns to a purified state. This "return" notion was the root cause behind Luther's waffling over whether penance/confession should even be regarded as a full-blown sacrament.

Luther's ambivalence about confession appears often in his writings. Perhaps it was most clearly expressed in a line of his famous book *The Babylonian Captivity of the Church,* published in 1520.

> As to the current practice of private confession, I am heartily in favor of it, even though it cannot be proved from the Scriptures. It is useful, even necessary, and I would not have it abolished. Indeed, I rejoice that it exists in the church of Christ, for it is a cure without equal for distressed consciences. . . . There is just one thing about it that I abominate, and that is the fact that this kind of confession has been subjected to the despotism and extortion of the pontiffs.[28]

Incidentally, Luther practiced private confession to the end of his life. He found the practice helpful in his older years. In his youth, he was fixated on his own sins, and thus he confessed to his mentors but rarely encountered a feeling of absolution in his heart. His conscience was left "wallowing in uncertainty."[29] He argued later that our absolution comes only through Christ's death. It is not dependent on a priest's whims.

The Other Sacraments

When it came to the other four sacraments of the Roman Church—confirmation, marriage, holy orders, and extreme unction/anointing for the sick—Luther rejected them as unscriptural. He claimed confirmation was only a ceremony. Yes, the apostles laid hands on people, but that was not grounds for declaring it sacramental. The apostles did many things. Peter cut off a person's ear and had visions, but those are not somehow sacramental just because he did them. For something to be a sacrament, the Lord had to institute it specifically.

Similarly, Luther found no scriptural warrant for considering marriage a sacrament. First, Jesus did not institute marriage; it was instituted by God when he created man and woman. Second, Scripture does not attribute divine grace to matrimony. Third, marriage is not something that should be patrolled or controlled by the church. Both Christians and non-Christians can marry. It is not peculiar to Christianity. Marriage is a good institution because it is good for people not to be alone, but it is not an institution that should be sanctioned only within the confines of the church.

Luther's skepticism toward holy orders is well known, and he heaped vitriol on the institution. It "was invented merely to increase the distance between the clergy and the laity and to give hierarchy a privileged position. . . . We are all equally priests in so far as we are baptized."[30] The priesthood of all believers was perhaps his best-known teaching. Luther considered the clergy to be "an invention of the church of the pope. . . . Not only is there nowhere any promise of grace attached to it, but there is not a single word said about it in the whole New Testament."[31] Luther also lambasted priestly celibacy as an equally fallacious ploy to make certain people look more holy. He said it was all a sham.

Extreme unction was, in Luther's mind, just another way for the church to exert control over people. In itself, the practice of anointing the sick is scriptural (James 5), but Luther said it was hijacked by the church. It was *helpful*, not *sacramental*. Besides, the church rarely used it for healing, as the Bible makes clear. Rather, it was used almost exclusively for those who were all but dead, hence the expression *extreme* unction.

How Then Should We Live?

Since the sacraments had been abused by the church, and most of them were never sanctioned by Christ, Luther steered people away from them. He urged people to allow Scripture to determine what they did with their lives. This is what Luther meant by the Latin expression *sola Scriptura*. For him, the Scriptures were sufficient for the Christian. The duty of the Christian was to examine the Scriptures for oneself and conform to the standard found in its pages. This was empowering and intoxicating for many during Luther's day. No longer did they turn to a person—a clergyman—for direction; they could find that direction themselves in the pages of Holy Writ. One's conscience could then become reconstructed by the assurance of God's word rather than man's. And, as Luther memorably pronounced at Worms in 1521, "To go against one's conscience is neither safe nor right."

Luther unleashed a powerful curiosity in people to understand the mind of God. Literacy spread due to Luther's insistence that people come to understand the Bible's contents instead of trusting the interpretations of the popes, bishops, and priests who had proven themselves untrustworthy. Luther's work ultimately elevated the status of Scripture in the eyes of Christians. His critique of the church hierarchy was accompanied by a conviction that "the Bible's authority for believers is unique, final, and definitive."[32] In his estimation, "Scripture alone is the true lord and master of all writings and doctrine on earth."[33] The obvious irony noted by all scholars of Luther, however, is that he struggled mightily to influence people's interpretation of the Bible. Often, it was not so much *sola Scriptura* at play as it was Luther's interpretation of Scripture.

Indeed, even Luther's definition of Scripture departed from church tradition. He had his own "canon within a canon." Paul's Epistle to the Romans could be understood as Luther's "center," for it explained how people were made acceptable to God. Any biblical book that supported Luther's belief that "the gospel" was at the center of Scripture could be affirmed. The four Gospels, of course, received high praise from Luther, especially the book of John.

He departed from tradition, however, when he raised serious doubts about several biblical books including Hebrews, Jude, Revelation, and especially James—"an epistle of straw."[34] His chief problem with James was that it "is flatly against St. Paul and all the rest of Scripture in ascribing justification to works [2:24]. . . . St. Paul teaches to the contrary." Equally problematic was that James "does not once mention the Passion, the resurrection, or the Spirit of Christ."[35] Luther seemed to prefer to exclude these books from the biblical canon, but he could not bring himself to do so out of respect for tradition. He did place the intertestamental books—often called the Apocrypha—into a separate section in his Luther Bible.

Sola Fide

During Luther's upbringing, he understood God to be a tyrannical figure, angry and destructive. Luther thought he had come into contact with the true gospel—the "good news"—when he realized that God is not like this. Rather, God is loving and merciful and gives grace to those who love him. God's gifts are free. We *receive* them rather than earn them, as the church had erroneously prescribed. When we put our faith in God, we enjoy an abundance of grace that only God can provide. These ideas are what Luther called *sola fide* (only faith) and *sola gratia* (only grace). We are saved by God's grace simply by having faith in God's promises. It is unmerited.

Luther saw faith in Christ as the key to salvation. This is often considered his "breakthrough" idea.

> In my heart there resides this one doctrine, namely, faith in Christ. From it, through it, and to it all my theological thought flows and returns day and night; yet I am aware that all I have grasped of this wisdom in its height, width, and depth are a few poor and insignificant first-fruits and fragments.[36]

Luther felt he had rescued the true gospel from the clutches of a church overcome by legalism. The genuine gospel offers freedom to the person who walks by faith. Luther urged, over and over, that his readers get this straight. We are saved by faith. And all our good works pale in comparison to the great power and grace that come down to us if only we have faith. Faith liberates a person from the inadequacy that arises when one realizes his or her works might not be *enough*.

Christ justifies, and his justification is what liberates the human being from sin. Indeed, faith in Christ destroys sin. Faith is the process that allows a person to be justified because he or she is unable to achieve salvation alone. Only by cerebrally tapping into that power can a person become justified. When that person trusts Christ for this salvific process, then God imputes righteousness to the believer. Then, God no longer sees the sinful human being; he sees Christ, his only begotten Son. Luther repeatedly spoke of the justified person as being righteous and a sinner at the same time. Faith in and of itself is not what justifies. Rather, it is faith in Christ.[37]

Celibacy and Sex

Not only did Luther call into question the Roman Church's sacramental perspective on marriage and holy orders, he rejected it radically. Priests could marry, celibacy was no longer praised, everybody was potentially a priest, and sex no longer reduced someone to an inferior status. All this had deep impact on the sexual ethics of the sixteenth century and beyond. The traditional link between sex and shame was severed. Luther and the reformers emphasized the dignity of human sexuality and the nobility of a committed sexual relationship within the confines of marriage. While the

Roman Catholic Church had emphasized Bible passages that praised chastity, the Protestants pointed to Genesis' command, "Be fruitful and multiply."

Initially, Luther's ideas were exceedingly controversial, as celibacy was the sacred cow of Catholic hierarchical thinking. Luther's views were "highly offensive" even to lay sensibilities that thought sexual passion sullied one's holiness. Luther, however, turned all this on its head when he argued that "sexual drives were a divine force or even God's vital presence." Luther found great encouragement for his revolutionary views on sex and marriage in Genesis, which he preached and wrote on frequently. He delved deeply into the Hebrew text to better comprehend his most decisive passage on this topic: "It is not good that the man should be alone; I will make him a help meet for him" (Gen. 2:18). Luther's exegesis of this passage was "truly epoch-making."[38]

By the time Luther finally took Katie von Bora's hand in marriage, he had convinced himself that he was doing no wrong. Earlier, Luther had hedged, and even when he married there were detractors. Ultimately, however, Luther found great encouragement in the Bible's positive view of marriage. He began to teach that marriage and sex are "natural and necessary,"[39] that the basic need for sex by both men and women is as deeply rooted in nature as eating, drinking, and sleeping.[40]

True celibacy is an exceedingly rare gift. Women and men can scarcely keep the vows of chastity; they burn with passion and lust, and even compromise themselves sexually when they are claiming to be celibate. Luther wanted to rescue these women and men from the guilt and shame of such a state, such a terrible inward battle that so often was a losing one. Luther said, "Consider the one side of this misery. The majority of young women in nunneries are robust and healthy, created by God to be wives and to bear children. But they are not strong enough to remain in this state." Burning with passion, they compromise their vows.

So Luther gave the following advice to those who knew of nuns who were struggling with their passions: "If you have a daughter or a friend who has fallen into such a state, you should help her out of it, if you are honest and devout, even if you had to risk all your property, life, and limb to do so."[41] Luther totally turned the tables on sexuality among Protestants. Allowing someone to remain celibate was harmful to their health and probably to their soul. For Luther, the institution that should be doubted and even shamed was celibacy, not marriage!

The normative medieval views on celibacy and sexuality were undermined by Luther's attack on authority. By rejecting a priestly class, he abolished hierarchy and leveled the church to a body of equals. He ripped several privileges out of the hands of the clergy: the giving of absolution, the administration and distribution of the sacraments, the presiding over the Mass, divine rights, and more. Luther attacked clerical hierarchy as "an invention of the church of the pope" and offered an egalitarian religion in its stead.[42] The wall separating clergy and laity should fall, he said. The papacy was the president of this devilish nonsense, and Luther saved his most vicious attacks for the pope at Rome. Luther's shorthand for the pope was almost always "the antichrist."

Priests and Purgatory

Luther's democratization of religion meant that the word "Christian" was essentially a synonym to the word "priest." In Luther's powerful treatise *The Babylonian Captivity of the Church*, he wrote, "Let everyone, therefore, who knows himself to be a Christian, be assured of this, that we are all equally priests, that is to say, we have the same power in respect to the Word and the sacraments." Luther cautioned, however, that "no one may make use of this power except by the consent of the community or by the call of a superior."[43] All baptized Christians are given "sacerdotal status"; therefore, whoever "comes crawling out of baptism has thus been consecrated a priest, bishop, and pope."[44] Luther emphasized that everyone, even so-called clergymen, were laypeople. The word "lay" comes from the Greek word *laos*, which simply means "people." Yes, priests are people (lay, or laity) as well. They are no better or worse. Like the rest of us, they are, simply, people.[45]

Luther's views on afterlife were also revolutionary. He began to tug on the threads of established medieval norms when he critiqued the practice of selling indulgences to reduce one's time in purgatory. Eventually, Luther abandoned belief in purgatory altogether. At first, he refused to come down too forcefully on these matters because the Bible was far from clear.

We first see Luther's views about afterlife in the *Ninety-Five Theses*.[46]

> #16: Hell, purgatory, and heaven seem to differ the same as despair, fear, and assurance of salvation.
>
> #18: Furthermore, it does not seem proved, either by reason or Scripture, that souls in purgatory are outside the state of merit, that is, unable to grow in love.
>
> #22: As a matter of fact, the pope remits to souls in purgatory no penalty which, according to canon law, they should have paid in this life.
>
> #27: They preach only human doctrines who say that as soon as the money clinks into the money chest, the soul flies out of purgatory.
>
> #29: Who knows whether all souls in purgatory wish to be redeemed, since we have exceptions in St. Severinus and St. Paschal, as related in a legend.

Here Luther condemns indulgences, but he is far from denying the existence of purgatory.

Luther begins to show clear doubts about purgatory in his work *Defense and Explanation of all the Articles*.[47] The thirty-seventh article is confusing. The title of that article is: "That there is a purgatory cannot be proved by those Scriptures which are authentic and trustworthy." However, the text of this 1521 article reads:

> The existence of a purgatory I have never denied. I still hold that it exists, as I have written and admitted many times, though I have found no way of proving it incontrovertibly from Scripture or reason. . . . In short, I myself have come to the conclusion that there is a purgatory, but I cannot force anybody else to come to the same result.

By 1528, however, Luther rejected the existence of purgatory as a teaching from the devil. In his work *Confession Concerning Christ's Supper*, he wrote: "Vigils and requiem Masses and yearly celebrations of requiems are useless, and are merely the devil's annual fair. Nor have we anything in Scripture concerning purgatory. It too was certainly fabricated by goblins. Therefore, I maintain it is not necessary to believe in it."[48] In 1530, in his work

Exhortation to All Clergy Assembled at Augsburg, Luther listed purgatory as one of the false teachings of "the pretended church."[49] It seems all but certain that he held to this view until the end of his life.

In one of Luther's most tender and pastoral works, *A Sermon on Preparing to Die* (1519), he wrote the following words for people who were about to walk through the valley of the shadow of death:

> So then, gaze at the heavenly picture of Christ, who descended into hell [1 Pet. 3:19] for your sake and was forsaken by God as one eternally damned when he spoke the words on the cross, "Eli, Eli, lama sabachthani!"—"My God, my God, why have you forsaken me?" [Matt. 27:46]. In that picture your hell is defeated and your uncertain election is made certain. If you concern yourself solely with that and believe that it was done for you, you will surely be preserved in this same faith. Never, therefore, let this be erased from your vision. Seek yourself only in Christ and not in yourself and you will find yourself in him eternally.[50]

Luther's intention never was to completely undermine purgatory, but he seems to have abandoned it himself. He certainly saw it as an idea that had become utterly objectionable because of how it had been abused by the church authorities. But Luther focused little on purgatory or hell, since he believed that those whose faith was in Christ had only to think of the bliss and joy they were to encounter when they entered heaven.

Notes

[1]See "Lectures on Genesis," in *Luther's Works*, vol. 1, 152.

[2]See "The Gospel for New Year's Day," undated, in *Luther's Works*, vol. 52, 152.

[3]Denis Janz, *The Westminster Handbook to Martin Luther* (Louisville, KY: Westminster John Knox Press, 2010), 124.

[4]See "Defense and Explanation of All the Articles," in *Luther's Works*, vol. 32, 83.

[5]See Luther's "Large Catechism," in *The Annotated Luther*, vol. 2 (Minneapolis: Fortress Press, 2015), 357.

[6]See Luther's *Ninety-Five Theses*, numbers 43, 45, and 46. See also Heiko Oberman, *Man Between God and the Devil* (New Haven: Yale University Press, 1989), 77.

[7]Janz, 10.

[8]See Janz, 119, 85.

[9]Ibid., 120.

[10]See Robert Fife, *The Revolt of Martin Luther* (New York: Columbia University Press, 1957), 531, 538.

[11]Ibid., 460.

[12]Oberman, 227.

[13]Fife, 461.

[14]Oberman, 227.

[15]See Luther's "Holy Sacrament of Baptism," in *Luther's Works*, vol. 35, 34–36. See also Janz, 10.

[16]Oberman, 231.

[17]See Luther's "Holy Sacrament of Baptism," in *Luther's Works*, 73. See also Janz, 11.

[18]See *Luther's Works*, vol. 32, 14.

[19]Janz, 85.

[20]This work is located in *Luther's Works*, vol. 37, 13ff.

[21]Ibid., 68.

[22]Ibid.

[23]This work is located in *Luther's Works*, vol. 36, 335ff. The quotation is on 341.

[24]See Fife, 531.

[25]This quote is from Janz, 105. For Luther's reply, see "Defense and Explanation of All the Articles," in *Luther's Works*, vol. 32, 7ff.

[26]Janz, 106.

[27]Ibid., 105–106.

[28]See "The Babylonian Captivity of thc Church" in *Luther's Works*, vol. 36, 11ff. For Luther's understanding of Confession, see 86.

[29]See ibid. For Luther's understanding of Confession, see ibid. 86. See also Janz, 106.

[30]Fife, 537.

[31]In "The Babylonian Captivity of the Church," in *Luther's Works*, vol. 36, 106–107.

[32]Janz, 15.

[33]See *Luther's Works*, vol. 32, 11–12.

[34]See Luther's New Testament Preface, located in *Luther's Works*, vol. 35, 362.

[35]See Luther's preface to James in *Luther's Works*, vol. 35, 395–396.

[36]See Luther's preface to his 1519 edition of "Lectures on Galatians," located in *Luther's Works*, vol. 27, 145.

[37]See Ian Siggins, *Luther* (New York: Barnes and Noble, 1972), 166. On Luther's "Discovery of Justification," see Walter Altmann, *Luther and Liberation* (Minneapolis: Fortress Press, 2015), 73ff.

[38]Oberman, 273.

[39]See "The Estate of Marriage," in *Luther's Works*, vol. 45, 18.

[40]See "Against the Spiritual State of the Pope," in *Luther's Works*, vol. 39, 297.

[41]See Ibid., 296–297.

[42]See "The Babylonian Captivity of the Church," in *Luther's Works*, vol. 36, 106.

[43]See *Luther's Works*, vol. 36, 116.

[44]Oberman, 227.

[45]Altmann, 218.

[46]I have used *Luther's Works*, vol. 31, 25–33.

[47]See The Thirty-Seventh Article in *Luther's Works*, vol. 32, 95.

[48]See *Luther's Works*, vol. 37, 369.

[49]Purgatory is listed at number 4 of 37 false teachings. See *Luther's Works*, vol. 34, 54.

[50]See Mary Jane Haemig, ed., *The Annotated Luther,* vol. 4, Pastoral Writings (Minneapolis: Fortress Press, 2016), 296.

18

Missed Opportunities: Erasmus and Zwingli

Martin Luther's beliefs were radical for his day, and he had no shortage of people eager to challenge him. He was almost always willing to engage in the debates because they fueled him. They attracted people to his message. They gave him an enemy, something Luther seemed to need all through his turbulent life and career. Without fail, Luther referred to himself as being on the right side and his long line of opponents as being with the devil.

As we have seen repeatedly, Luther was a successful debater, particularly on paper. His public debates must not be underestimated, for they pointed people to his published texts. Luther was able to control the outcomes of the debates due to his writing prowess. When he or his friends published one of his formal debates, inevitably he came off as the winner. His publications and rhetorical contests were a one-two punch that few could counter. This brilliant strategy explains why his campaign for a new form of Christianity succeeded.

Luther trained generations of preachers to argue their way toward reforming the church. His legacy was a quarrelsome one. One must always be willing to take a stand against any person one might disagree with. Protestantism has been saddled with this phenomenon for five centuries now. But, like so many other aspects of Luther, while this tendency to critique and dispute has served the movement well, it has also proven to be an Achilles' heel. Embedded in Protestantism are myriad seeds of protest. The term "Protest-ant" is an accurate one. Protestants protest. They quarrel. They test and challenge. In some ways, this is good. Protestantism constantly reforms, upgrades, and keeps itself relevant in a changing society.

Sometimes, however, the Protestant proclivity to argue turns inward, causing great division and infinitely more fractures within itself. This is, and probably always will be, the greatest Protestant predicament.

In this chapter, we will discuss two of Luther's high-profile quarrels with people who could have expanded his movement exponentially: Erasmus and Zwingli. At the end of the chapter, we will make a few observations about John Calvin's brand of Protestantism and how it managed to surpass Lutheranism in some key ways. Had Luther not burned bridges with the Swiss during his career, he would have had a much better chance of recruiting the extremely talented Calvin to his cause.

Nevertheless, by understanding Luther's clashes with two other titanic personalities of the Reformation, we can see more clearly how he was able to define the borders of his movement. By the end of his life, Luther had built a truly impressive Protestant ecclesial empire. But he had also burned many bridges due to his inability to negotiate. The flipside of conviction is compromise. Luther excelled in the former but was severely lacking in the latter. Had he been more effective in managing his relationships with Erasmus and Zwingli, his movement would have become even more expansive than it already was. These were Luther's biggest missed opportunities.

The Loss of Erasmus

Desiderius Erasmus (1466–1536) was one of the few intellectual equals Luther faced. Through the force of his personality and the sheer volume of his writing, Luther was usually able to overpower any who got in his way. Not Erasmus. Erasmus was not intimidated by Luther because he was Luther's superior when it came to understanding the Reformation's primary source: the Bible.

Erasmus was about seventeen years older than Luther. He was a Dutchman, a theologian, and a Roman Catholic priest. His command of Latin was unparalleled in his day, and he was known as the "Prince of the

Humanists." He is among history's greatest scholars of the Bible due to his mastery of New Testament Greek and his high-quality publications of Greek versions of the text. Luther was a great admirer of Erasmus's work. In fact, he used the scholar's Greek New Testament to compose *Luther's Bible.*

Erasmus seemed to be headed down the path of reform earlier in his career. Like Luther, he was able to see huge discrepancies between the Bible and the beliefs and practices of the church. Their relationship at first held great promise: Erasmus, the careful and erudite scholar, and Luther, whom Melanchthon called the "Charioteer of Israel."[1]

Erasmus and Luther broke onto the public scene at nearly the same time. In 1516, Erasmus made a monumental contribution to scholarship when he published the first Greek New Testament—just a year before Luther nailed the famous theses to the Castle Church door. Luther seemed to think Erasmus would get behind his ideas for reform, but Erasmus remained committed to Rome to the end of his life. As the two men came to understand one another and critique each other's work, however, their promising partnership turned into a bitter parting of ways.

The Luther and Erasmus breakup was a missed opportunity for many reasons. First, both men were great scholars who truly wanted to use their scholarship for the benefit of the church. Second, both were highly critical of the dire state of the church during their time, yet both seem to have had the best of motives—to reform it. Third, both were extremely public figures, and with their alliance they could have accomplished even greater things than they did.

Their differences, however, were deep-seated and, with time, began to surface in irreconcilable ways. Already in 1516—when Erasmus's Greek New Testament was published—Luther noticed that the two men had differing interpretations of the writings of Paul. Erasmus—the quintessential humanist—had a high regard for a person's moral capabilities. His theology sometimes seemed to allow humans a measure of free will. Luther, however, focused intensely on Paul's teachings on justification, especially the notion that humans are depraved.[2] Luther was also a strong believer in the doctrine of predestination. For Erasmus to open himself up to the possibility of free will, Luther felt, would have been to compromise his own integrity as an exegete of the Bible. Conversely, Erasmus was convinced that Luther's idea—"that everything a person does on his own is sin"—had to be false.[3]

Erasmus never wanted to have a public controversy with Luther, and he "thought his critique of the church was generally justified." In 1520, Erasmus even tried to intervene and help settle Luther's dispute with Pope Leo X. This caused some Catholics to think that Erasmus might be turning Protestant. This fear, however, was never grounded in reality. It demonstrated the high level of suspicion on both sides. Winning Erasmus would have been a huge victory indeed for Luther, and losing Erasmus would have been catastrophic for the Catholics. Erasmus, however, steered a middle course. He kept his distance from Luther, which angered Luther. Luther accused Erasmus of being duplicitous and malicious toward the movement of reform. And, as with virtually all his opponents, Luther eventually accused Erasmus of being "the devil's agent."[4]

Erasmus thought Luther's approach was hostile and extreme. Erasmus was a much more balanced and moderate man. His concern was for the unity of the church. He agreed with Luther that the church needed reform, but he disagreed with Luther's caustic and uncompromising approach. He felt Luther lacked an "evangelical gentleness" that should be evident in a Christian. It is also important to realize that in 1522 a Dutchman rose to the papacy and took the name of Adrian VI (or Hadrian VI). He was the only Dutchman in history to hold that position, although he died less than two years after being elected. Erasmus had been one of that pope's students years earlier, and the two had good relations. Thus, Erasmus was careful not to damage the Dutch pope when he offered critiques of the church. Luther viewed Erasmus as a traitor since Erasmus earlier had seemed relatively friendly to the cause of the Reformation. As time went on, Luther's attacks left Erasmus no room but to reject the reformer.[5]

Between 1517 and 1524, Luther and Erasmus were locked in a Cold War. Each had deep suspicion of the other, but neither resorted to public attacks on the other. The Catholic princes tried to persuade Erasmus to condemn Luther, but he refrained, for in ways he sympathized with Luther's cause.[6] In addition, he thought a public quarrel with Luther would be ineffectual.

But then, in 1524, Erasmus broke the stalemate and attacked Luther and Melanchthon in a publication entitled *A Diatribe on the Freedom of the Will*.[7] He essentially argued that Luther's assault against the church was also an attack on the councils, the richness of church tradition, and the universities. He thought Luther was jettisoning all authority, and he warned

Luther to take a more humble approach. He also ventured into the free will/predestination debate by asserting that "there is some sort of power of free will." Erasmus was concerned about purity of life, righteous conduct, and public morality. He thought that these deep theological discussions should not be debated in front of the masses of commoners. These were issues for theologians to settle. And he believed Luther was being fanatical in asserting his own opinions as "the truth" and casting them before the uneducated masses for consideration, hoping to win an audience. To Erasmus, "fanaticism about one's opinions was repugnant." Luther needed to settle down, debate with scholars, and resist dividing the church. Besides, these centuries-long debates—such as free will versus predestination—were "inscrutable," and the bottom line was that humans just could not know for sure how God really felt about such things.[8]

Luther and Erasmus were very different in their understanding of the human being's innermost self. Luther thought humans were depraved and self-condemned due to their own sinfulness. Erasmus, however, "firmly believed that there was a pliant, good nucleus within a man."[9]

In December 1525, Luther tore into Erasmus with one of his most famous publications, *The Bondage of the Will*. In the introduction, Luther said that replying to Erasmus was a waste of time since Erasmus's written defense of free will was so incompetent. He pointed out that if Erasmus—supposedly one of the great thinkers of the age—could not offer a better defense of the doctrine of free will, then Luther had no reason to consider it true. "In his masterful way Luther left no doubt that he considered Erasmus theologically unqualified." Luther reiterated his bedrock belief that man could do *nothing* to help his own salvation; it was purely a gift from God.[10]

Erasmus had argued that the Bible is not clear on these issues. Some passages seem to advocate free will while others seem to advocate predestination—that humans have no power over whether they are saved. Luther disagreed, however, and accused Erasmus of doing "the work of Satan" by saying the Scriptures were ambiguous. He asserted that Erasmus was an atheist, a despiser of the Bible, and an enemy of the Christian faith.[11] Luther was unambiguous: the Bible is very clear in its explanation of how humans are saved.[12] Deeply hurt by Luther's viciousness, Erasmus wrote two very academic responses to Luther's charges, but their debate deescalated when it became clear that Luther saw no need to respond again.

The Bondage of the Will is a most important piece of work for Luther and for his legacy. With its publication, "Luther laid the grounds for the fundamental Lutheran understanding of the infallibility of Scripture and its centrality in Lutheran theology."[13]

The Break with Zwingli

Ulrich Zwingli was one year younger than Luther. Born in Switzerland and groomed for the priesthood at an early age, he was in the new humanist tradition. He became a priest in 1506 at the age of twenty-two.

Zwingli began preaching for reform around the same time Luther did, although his rise to fame was not meteoric like Luther's. His reforms "progressed more slowly and cautiously on a small stage." The young cleric began preaching against the corruptions of the church as early as 1516, a year before Luther's *Ninety-Five Theses*.[14]

Zwingli had a fiery personality, just as Luther did, and he took great offense when people began to accuse him of being a "Lutheran." Zwingli thought he preached "straight from the Bible" with no influence whatsoever from Luther. He became testy when, during his own Reformation movement in Zurich, people began associating his work with Luther's. The crowd noted, "You must be a Lutheran . . . for you preach exactly the same way as Luther writes. My reply is this: I preach exactly the same way as Paul wrote; why don't you call me a "Paulist," then? Yes, I preach the word of Christ; why, then, don't you call me a "Christian?" Zwingli never lost this defensiveness toward accusations that he was merely a clone of Luther. In fact, Zwingli was as Swiss as Luther was Saxon in his "personal quirks or predilections."[15]

Part of the disagreement between Luther and Zwingli was that Zwingli was a great admirer of Erasmus. Around 1515, Zwingli even traveled to Basel to meet Erasmus. He devoured the famous Dutch scholar's writings and was transformed by Erasmus's agenda for reform, which included a humanist "back to the Bible" orientation, a Christocentric perspective, and revulsion at the sordid state of the Roman Catholic Church. He was also enthralled by Erasmus's herculean work of producing a top quality Greek New Testament.[16]

Zwingli was indeed impacted by Luther's early writings, especially his notion of justification by faith alone, although he was reluctant to admit it openly. In fact, "Luther's works would certainly have been freely available in Zurich through their numerous Basel reprints."[17]

Zwingli's Reformation is often associated with a debate involving sausages. During the Lenten season in 1522, some church leaders in Zurich ate smoked sausages. Eating meat during Lent went against church laws, and although Zwingli did not partake, in his sermons he defended the actions of his colleagues. Zwingli used the kerfuffle to state his position that the church's regulated fasts were unscriptural.[18]

Like Luther, Zwingli inspired the common man toward civil disobedience. But Zwingli had no figure comparable to Frederick the Wise protecting him. And whereas Luther was able to disassociate himself from the Peasants' Revolt, Zwingli jumped in headlong and acted impulsively—and violently—on occasion. For example, when the Anabaptist movement rose up, Zwingli was quick to pick up the sword, arguing that they should be put to death for their disavowal of infant baptism.[19] He was also an iconoclast, believing all church images should be taken down and smashed. In this reaction, he was like Karlstadt in Wittenberg. Luther opposed such iconoclasm, arguing that it was too radical.

The most important difference between Zwingli and Luther, however, had to do with the Eucharist. Their debate lasted about five years, from 1524 to 1529.[20] It had to do with the "real presence" of Christ in the Eucharist. To the end of his life, Luther held that Christ was physically present in the Eucharist, although he was not always clear about what he meant. What *was* clear was that Zwingli thought any notion of the real presence to be sheer superstition. He argued that Christ had been resurrected and was thus seated at the right hand of God. Luther, however, believed Christ could be in two realms at once—in the heavenly as well as the earthly realms—since "my Lord Jesus Christ can easily do what he wishes." Luther used the analogy of a mirror to explain the phenomenon of the real presence. He said that when a mirror is broken, what was once one mirror becomes many, since each fragment now reflects the image that was formerly singular.[21]

Zwingli disagreed. He believed that when Jesus instituted the Lord's Supper, he was saying, "This signifies my body," rather than, "This *is* my body." Luther was outraged by this metaphorical interpretation and accused Zwingli of heresy. As usual, Luther dismissed his opponent as "simply an emissary of the devil." Zwingli retaliated by calling Luther a cannibal. At stake was a vague biblical passage, a saying of Jesus from John 6:63: "The Spirit gives life; the flesh counts for nothing. The words I have spoken to you—they are full of the Spirit and life."[22] Zwingli emphasized "the flesh counts for nothing." However, Luther emphasized Christ's words of institution: "This *is* my body." Luther was unwilling to compromise. When Jesus said "is" he meant "is." He did not mean "represents" or "signifies"; otherwise he would have used those words.

The two brilliant theologians lowered themselves to hurling abuse at one another over this issue. When they could not figure out a compromise, they began to insult each other's character and publicly call into question one another's integrity, even Christianity. "This exchange, and subsequent volleys through 1527 and 1528, was immensely destabilizing to the evangelical movement."[23] The Marburg Colloquy was held in October 1529 to reconcile the two positions, but it failed. Those in attendance left "with the profound sense of an opportunity lost." Regrettably, "the two wings of the Reformation would go their separate ways, and the cities of southern Germany would be forced to choose, often with difficulty and acrimony, which route to follow."[24] After the Marburg Colloquy, there was a "Lutheran" way to be Protestant, and a "Reformed," or Zwinglian, way.

Zwingli died on the battlefield while fighting against Catholics during the Kappel War of 1531. Afterward, they burned his body, since he was considered a heretic. Luther considered it to be punishment from God because of Zwingli's blasphemy against the body and blood of Christ in the Eucharist.

Zwingli's extremely capable successor, Heinrich Bullinger, took the reins of the Zurich Reformation and provided truly admirable leadership. A few years later, in the late 1530s, John Calvin began working with the Protestant church in Geneva. These two stalwarts of the Protestant Reformation turned much of Switzerland into a Protestant Mecca for many generations. Reconciliation between Luther and the Swiss Reformed Christians remained elusive, however, and attempts at unity did not bear much fruit until the twentieth century.

No one will ever know how the Reformation would have unfolded had the Germans, Swiss, and English united in the cause of reform. It is tantalizing to think what might have been accomplished both politically and religiously had the Lutherans, Anglicans, and Reformed Christians united northern Europe for a common Protestant cause.

Conclusion

In hindsight, we can only wonder how successful Protestantism would have become had Zwingli and Luther reconciled. What is quite plausible is that John Calvin's amazing work in Geneva probably would have built bridges all over the Protestant world. As it happened, however, the Germanic forms of Protestantism—including northern Germany and Scandinavia—went on a different trajectory than the Reformed churches to the south. As a result, western Europe fragmented with various factions of Protestantism in Europe's north and a fervent and militant Catholicism in the south. The whole region descended into hostility and war in the wake of the Reformation.

After Luther, John Calvin (1509–1564) probably offered the last best hope for unifying Protestantism. Calvin and Luther were contemporaries for a time. Luther was twenty-six years older than Calvin and was in ill health just as Calvin's career was hitting its stride in Geneva in the 1540s. Calvin was a new breed of reformer. He was never an ordained priest. He was not formally trained in theology. He was from northern France, and somehow—scholars still do not understand—he came under the influence of Protestantism just as the reformers were being persecuted intensely in and around Paris. He moved to Basel, Switzerland, where he plunged himself into the study of Luther and Augustine. He already had a good knowledge of Greek, and he immersed himself in the Scriptures.[25]

Calvin and Luther shared much in common theologically, such as the issue of predestination. It was clear that Calvin had read Luther carefully. Where they differed was in all the other ways: disposition, culture, method, and temperament. Luther was an open book; Calvin was tight-lipped about his personal life and background. They also differed substantially in their emphases. Whereas Luther emphasized *sola fide*, *sola gratia*, and *sola Scriptura*, Calvin emphasized God's sovereignty and man's chief duty—to glorify him.[26]

When reading Luther and Calvin today, it is clear that Calvin was much more precise. He had been trained as a lawyer, and his writing was indelibly stamped with a rationalistic, precise, and orderly approach. Calvin was systematic, as if he were putting together a legal textbook of Protestant belief and practice. Luther, on the other hand, appealed to emotion and was prone to crassness. Calvin was much more restrained, although his critiques of Rome were every bit as fervent, just colder, more rational, more logical and cerebral. Calvin's truly extraordinary accomplishment—perhaps the most important summary of Protestant faith ever written—was *The Institutes of the Christian Religion*, first published in Latin in 1536.

Calvin's magisterial manual of Protestant faith resonated with people outside Germany in ways that Luther's writings never did. The *Institutes* were not so linked to one culture. Whereas Luther's writings had been aimed at Germans, Calvin's elegant prose seemed to be aimed at Protestants in general. As a result, Calvin's systemization of the Christian faith expanded to new frontiers, while Lutheranism came to be associated with Germany and Scandinavia. Calvin thought outside his own culture. He built bridges where Luther seemed only to focus on his own Germanic people. Luther was a German leader for a German nation. Calvin, however, brokered good relations with the Swiss, French, Dutch, Scottish, and British. Part of Calvin's success was because he was able to learn from Luther's mistakes, since he was active two decades later and lived for nearly two decades after Luther's death.

One final missed opportunity was Luther's burning of the bridges that might have existed between Germany and England. King Henry VIII put his name in our history books by wanting a divorce from his wife Catherine of Aragon. Henry had been a loyal son of the church in his younger years, even to the point that Pope Leo X awarded him the title "Defender of the Faith" because of Henry's public opposition to Luther. Henry condemned Luther for making himself "chief" of his own church. This proved to be terribly ironic, for Henry later broke with Rome and declared himself to be the "Supreme Head of the Church of England."[27]

Luther fiercely rebuked the king in 1522 with a treatise called *Against Henry, King of England*. In that work, Luther mocked Henry as "the lying king of England" and claimed Henry's accession to the throne in 1509 had been illegal. It was a bitter, caustic letter, and "even today people find Luther's sharp tone hard to understand."[28]

When Henry later broke from Rome in the 1530s, he did not turn toward Luther. Rather, he considered Luther to be a threat to the stability of his empire due to Luther's *sola Scriptura* idea, which Henry rejected. The two men exchanged acrimonious letters from 1525 to 1527. At first, Luther had high hopes that something good would come out of it. However, the wounds from their squabbles a decade earlier had permanently severed any respect Henry might have had for Luther. So when Luther read the English monarch's reply, he was saddened to see nothing but patent hostility.

In the mind of Henry VIII, Luther would destabilize his empire just as he had thrown the Holy Roman Empire into divisive chaos. Henry had watched the Peasants' Revolt from afar and abhorred the results of it. Luther's ideas bred revolt, class warfare, and outrage among the commoners. Henry needed to avoid that mayhem at all costs. Further, Henry viewed Luther as an errant monk who broke his monastic vows to God by getting married. Thus, Henry made it clear that he would walk a middle path—a *via media*—between the Catholic Church and Protestantism. What was certain was that he would not need the services of Martin Luther. Characteristically, Luther understood Henry's invective to be "a work of the devil."[29]

Had Luther kept his spiteful tongue in check, he might have won over the king of England. Had he compromised just a little on the "real presence," he might have prevented the Swiss from breaking off and forming their own brand of Protestantism—a brand that traveled far and wide, indeed all over the globe, due to the genius contributions of John Calvin. And had he massaged his relationship with Erasmus more, he quite possibly could have won the support of the most gifted intellect of the era. But Luther missed those opportunities. Yet the deeper theological ideals of his movement lived on, even in the minds of those who, ostensibly, opposed him.

Notes

[1]See Martin Brecht, trans. by James Schaaf, *Martin Luther*, vol. 3 (Minneapolis: Fortress Press, 1999), 377.

[2]Martin Brecht, trans. by James Schaaf, *Martin Luther*, vol. 2 (Minneapolis: Fortress Press, 1990), 213.

[3]Brecht, vol. 2, 215–216.

[4]Ibid., 213–215.

[5]Ibid., 217.

[6]Ibid., 219.

[7]James Kittelson, *Luther the Reformer* (Minneapolis: Fortress Press, 1986), 204.

[8]Brecht, vol. 2, 220–221.

[9]Ibid., 222.
[10]Ibid., 226.
[11]Ibid., 236.
[12]Kittelson, 205–206.
[13]Volker Leppin, introduction to "The Bondage of the Will (1525)" in *The Annotated Luther,* ed. by Kirsi Stjerna, vol. 2: *Word and Faith* (Minneapolis: Fortress Press, 2015), 156.
[14]Carlos Eire, *Reformations* (New Haven: Yale University Press, 2016), 218.
[15]Ibid., 219, 221.
[16]Ibid., 223.
[17]See Andrew Pettegree, *Brand Luther* (New York: Penguin Press, 2015), 246.
[18]Pettegree, 246, and Eire, 228.
[19]Richard Friedenthal, trans. by John Nowell, *Luther* (London: Weidenfeld and Nicolson, 1967), 500.
[20]See Bernhard Lohse, *Martin Luther* (Philadelphia, PA: Fortress Press, 1986), 69–71.
[21]Kittelson, 207, and Friedenthal, 504.
[22]Friedenthal, 504.
[23]Pettegree, 248.
[24]Ibid., 249–250.
[25]For this summary of Calvin, I have used Robert Kingdon, "The Calvinist Reformation in Geneva," in *The Cambridge History of Christianity,* vol. 6: *Reform and Expansion 1500–1660* (Cambridge: Cambridge University Press, 2007), ed. by R. Po-Chia Hsia, 92–93.
[26]Eire, 288–290.
[27]See Eire, 319.
[28]Brecht, vol. 2, 86.
[29]Ibid., 347–348.

19

Luther on the Jews, Turks, and Eastern Orthodox

Martin Luther had three archenemies: Jews, the pope, and the Turks. He went to great lengths in his career to demonize this "unholy coalition."[1] Throughout this book, we have looked repeatedly at Luther's conflicts with popes, but in this chapter we will focus on the other two.

It is widely known that some of Martin Luther's writings are anti-Semitic, especially his famous text *On the Jews and Their Lies*. It is also known that Germany's Nazi party in the mid-twentieth century used Luther's writings to bolster their cause.

What is perhaps less known is Luther's perspectives on the Turks, who were a constant menace during his lifetime. While Jews were an annoyance to Luther, the Turks represented a real threat. Luther feared the end might be in sight, especially if the Turks succeeded in their conquest of Austria, and perhaps in time, of Christendom itself. In the twenty-first century, it is easy to forget how close Islamic forces came on several occasions to obtaining victory in the West, as they had done over Spain and Portugal, as well as over the Christian Byzantine Empire. For many centuries, Islam had the upper hand, and in many instances the Christian world witnessed their homelands turn from Christian to Muslim. Luther feared that possibility when the Turks successfully invaded Hungary and began to conquer Vienna.

Probably even less well known is the Lutheran-Eastern Orthodox correspondence that occurred shortly after Luther's death. We will not unpack this story in detail, but it is an important one. Luther's close friend, Philip Melanchthon, was perhaps the person who understood Luther's intentions best, and his exchange of letters with the patriarchs of Constantinople is a fascinating chapter in history that sheds much light on early Lutheranism.

Luther and the Jews

Perhaps no other topic in the life of Martin Luther stirs such emotion today as his writings on the Jews. In preparation for the 2017 quincentenary of Luther's *Ninety-Five Theses,* German historian Hartmut Lehmann addressed this most painful topic in a critical essay. He first makes the claim that putting Martin Luther on center stage in the celebrations is "a most problematic decision." He continues:

> Since the 1970s, more and more Germans have begun to understand fully that the Holocaust was no less than a complete rupture of civilization, a complete turning-away from basic human values. . . . Everyone studying the Nazi policy of racial extermination sooner or later comes across Martin Luther's vitriolic anti-Judaic writings. Those studying this topic find out that the Nazis used Luther's writings in their anti-Semitic propaganda, that the Nazi pastors reprinted parts of these writings shortly after the November pogrom of 1938, and that some Protestant Nazi pastors were eager to help the perpetrators. Is this a case of an irreconcilable clash of cultures of remembrance? How might we celebrate Luther and remember the catastrophe of the Holocaust at the same time?[2]

This awkward tension exists not only for Germans, but indeed for all who look to Luther as the originator of their Protestant faith.

Two obvious problems, however, arise when we try to implicate Luther, directly, in the Nazi Holocaust. First, we have no way of knowing how Luther might have handled the reality of mass extermination of Jews four hundred years after his life. He might have opposed it. Indeed, many prominent Lutherans such as pastors Dietrich Bonhoeffer and Martin Niemöller not only spoke out but took action to oppose Hitler. Bonhoeffer was hanged in a concentration camp due to his efforts to murder Hitler. Niemöller famously spoke out against Hitler with his widely quoted poem:

> First they came for the Socialists, and I did not speak out—
> Because I was not a Socialist.
> Then they came for the Trade Unionists, and I did not speak out—
> Because I was not a Trade Unionist.
> Then they came for the Jews, and I did not speak out—
> Because I was not a Jew.
> Then they came for me—
> and there was no one left to speak for me.[3]

These are but two of many Lutheran leaders who opposed the Nazi horrors.

A second problem with directly implicating Luther in the Holocaust is that by no means was he unique in his disdain for Jews in church history. Many of the church fathers were hateful toward Jews in their polemic, such as the series of sermons by John Chrysostom in the fourth century entitled "Against the Jews." Christendom could be brutal in its punishment of Jews at many points in history. Two major expulsions of Jews from England took place in 1215 and 1290, and two more in France in 1315 and 1348. Many massacres and forced conversions of Jews happened in the years leading up to the Spanish Inquisition in the late fifteenth century. The major expulsion of Jews from Spain occurred in 1492. They were expelled from German free imperial cities between 1480 and 1500. These expulsions continued throughout the sixteenth century, for example in Prague from 1541 to 1543.[4]

These are but a few of hundreds of examples of Christian mistreatment of Jews throughout history. Luther was a product of his time. His writings were at times undoubtedly anti-Semitic, but it would be inaccurate to think that he was unique in the history of Christianity in his views toward Jews. Nor were his actions more barbaric than the above examples.

Nevertheless, scholars today are divided over Luther's influence on the Nazi party. Some argue that Luther was complicit in the murder of six million Jews, and their view must be respected and heard.[5] It goes beyond the scope of this biography, however, to detail Luther's influence on anti-Semitism during the last four centuries. That story needs to be told, but this present chapter focuses on his posture toward Jews during his own life and in his writings.

Luther interacted with many Jews, and he was always perplexed over how they could continue in their Jewry since the appearance of Christ. He interpreted the destruction of the Jewish Temple in AD 70 as evidence that God had "cast them off" and no longer considered them his holy people. They had rejected his Messiah and, in doing so, had lost their place of privilege.[6]

Curiously, Luther's earlier writings often are held to be rather favorable toward Jews. For example, in his 1523 work *That Jesus Christ Was Born a Jew*, there is a rather "benevolent, paternalistic" attitude; it is not vitriolic at all. It has been described as "relatively positive" with its promotion of "humane treatment" of Jews.[7] In that text, Luther argues that Christians have always treated Jews "like dogs," so it is no wonder they have never converted to Christ. If Christians could do their evangelism of Jews in a spirit of kindness and Christian love, he argued, "it might be possible to instruct them from Scripture, proving to them that Jesus was the Messiah." Indeed, in that work by Luther, "anger and bitterness are largely absent" and one can notice even "a kind of respect." The Jews are our cousins, he argued. They are brothers to Christ. Importantly, Luther needed Jews for various reasons, for example, to help him with his Hebrew grammar, especially for his translations of the Old Testament into German. He relied on them heavily for his *Lectures on Genesis*, which he published between 1535 and 1545. His deep resentment of Jews seems to have arisen later in life.[8]

Many of the Jews Luther interacted with were converts to Christianity, and he always seemed a little suspicious of them for various reasons. In 1530, he advised a pastor to be wary when baptizing a Jewish girl to make sure her intentions were honorable. In 1532, he reported the baptism of a Jew in Wittenberg who seems not to have taken it very seriously. Luther advised Protestant ministers to be wary of potential Jewish converts. Luther supported one Jew who converted to Christianity, a man called Bernard. Both Luther and Melanchthon helped this man, who always seemed to struggle financially. Occasionally, Luther trusted Bernard as his personal courier and "felt obligated to do good to Bernard as a member of the Jewish church."[9]

Luther believed that the plight of the Jews over fifteen hundred years of Christian history was evidence of their being rejected by God. He thought it utterly incomprehensible that God would allow his chosen people to exist in such vulnerable and pitiful conditions for so long. His only resolution was that God must have handed them over to the devil for refusing the gospel.[10]

During Luther's lifetime, the ridiculous "blood libel" conspiracy theory was in full steam—the accusation that Jews kidnapped Christian children to use their blood in the celebration of Jewish holidays, particularly in the making of matzah bread. In 1544, Luther showed his belief in this myth during his Lenten lecture on Isaiah 53: "The Jews still kill Christ daily, not in the sense that they merely desire to do so, but rather in fact. For they slaughter many Christian infants and children. In short, they are killers forever."[11]

Much of Luther's hostility toward Jews ultimately may stem from the controversial passage in Matthew that has been used for centuries to bolster the theory that Jews killed Jesus—that Jews essentially cursed themselves when they declared at the trial of Jesus, "His blood is on us and on our children" (Matt. 27:25). Some historians have argued that Luther's increasingly hateful attitude toward Jews was motivated by his declining health and overall grumpiness in later years. Others have claimed that Luther equated Jews with Roman Catholic legalism. Still others believe that Luther was, in the end, frustrated that more Jews had not come to Christ in the aftermath of his own teachings.[12]

Luther detested the Jewish belief that they were God's chosen people. He felt that if they were still chosen, then all Gentiles must thereby be damned. He had worked hard to come to his conclusions that humans were saved by Christ alone, and Jewish narratives of chosenness directly contradicted his life's work. This helps to explain why Luther's venom against Jews became much more toxic as he aged. This also helps to explain why Luther hated the book of Esther so much—a book that celebrates the chosenness of the Jews.[13]

Was there any real threat that some Christians might be tempted to convert to Judaism? Indeed, "there may have been some grounds for such hope" on the part of some Jews. One historian points out that "the breakup of the Roman Church's monopoly in matters of Christian faith seemed to a certain extent to favor religious dissidents and outsiders." Furthermore, as reformers and humanists encountered Hebrew studies, they seemed to gain some sympathy toward them. Luther and his colleagues were sometimes accused by Catholic leaders of being "Judaizers," intent on destroying Christendom and the Roman Catholic Church from within. Some Jews hoped Luther's break with Rome might "trigger a conversion of Christians to Judaism." Luther's 1538 book *Against the Sabbatarians* may betray concern on the part of Luther that some Protestants were opening themselves to Jewish teaching, in this case on when to observe the Lord's day.[14]

Rich Jews in particular were a threat to Luther and to his society in general because some of them proved to be immensely gifted in business and "made great profits from usury (excessive taking of interest)," causing competitive resentment.[15] Jews were seen to be financially exploitative of Gentiles. Luther said he had "watched the common man being robbed of all he had by the Jews." His perception here had a history. "'Out with the Jews' was a common rallying cry in the streets and from the pulpits" since well before the Reformation.[16]

Throughout his career, Luther had been exposed to "strident anti-Christian" literature composed by Jews. These writings that had been around since the Crusades (twelfth century) "satirized Christian beliefs, attacked Christian exegesis, and longed for the destruction of the enemies of the Jewish people." They also insulted Jesus and Mary "with shameful names," including the accusation that Mary was a whore and therefore Jesus was a bastard.[17] Luther was deeply offended by all of this and felt he was defending his own Christian faith by taking on this Jewish polemic often comprised of vicious lies. This was a normal strategy of Luther. When he was offended by someone's writings, he took up the pen as a soldier would take up the sword. He could be merciless in his critiques of anyone he countered, whether pope, Anabaptist, indulgence salesman, Turk, or Jew. And those often vicious writings are an unmistakable part of Luther's corpus. Their context—theological, historical, and polemical—must be kept in mind, however.

Luther's invective against Jews was not always shared by all his colleagues. While most in his circle probably saw nothing unique in his critique of Jews, a few did take issue. Justus Jonas, Andres Osiander, and Philip Melanchthon all "mildly criticized the reformer for his harshness" against Jews.[18] Even Luther's wife, Katie, "was among those close to Luther who were offended by incitement of persecution. She stood up to him, quoting Scripture in Latin, to which he made feeble reply."[19]

Nevertheless, Luther was the bellwether of the Reformation, and there can be little doubt that his virulent attitude toward Jews spread among his readers. Luther's most notorious writing, *On the Jews and Their Lies*, published in 1543, showed his rising animosity. After reading this text, few can doubt that Luther "advocated that the government take action against the Jews."[20] In the fourth section of this lengthy treatise, he makes seven severe recommendations concerning Jews:

1. Their synagogues and schools should be burned to the ground.
2. Their houses should be "razed and destroyed."
3. Their "prayer books and Talmudic writings" should be confiscated.
4. Their rabbis should be "forbidden to teach henceforth on pain of loss of life and limb."
5. They should be denied safe-conduct on the highways.
6. They must not be allowed to practice usury (charge interest), and their gold, silver, and cash should be taken from them.
7. Finally, they should be subjected to harsh labor as retribution for their laziness.[21]

Surprisingly, this work may not have been the most bitter of Luther's writings against Jews. His work *On the Ineffable Name and on the Lineage of Christ* "sinks to even lower depths of polemical rhetoric. . . . Nothing in the earlier Luther can prepare the reader for the venom of this work. It is not difficult to imagine why it was not published in English translation until 1992."[22]

To think that Luther's writings were bereft of occasional kindnesses toward Jews would be a mistake, however. For example, he considered one Rabbi Josel of Rosheim to be his "friend." In 1537, even later in his life when he is thought to have been rabidly anti-Semitic, Luther wrote to Rabbi Josel: "My opinion was, and still is, that one should treat the Jews in a kindly manner."[23] In another place, he exhorted his readers to "practice Christian love toward them and pray that they convert."[24] In Luther's very last sermon, preached in 1546, he "urged Christians to forgive Jews if they converted and if they ceased their offenses against the Christians. If not, he wrote, then they should neither tolerate nor suffer them to remain in the territory."[25] Thus, we can observe that while Luther did allow a little leniency toward Jews occasionally, it was always accompanied by a deep-seated hope for their conversion to Christ.

Luther scholar Scott Hendrix has argued, "It is not historically accurate, however, to draw a direct line from Martin Luther to the Holocaust." He notes that several have indeed made this connection, but it is anachronistic because the misuse of Luther's theological writings for race-based anti-Semitic theories does not arise until after World War I. Luther argued on theological grounds, not on much later notions of race-based, pseudo-scientific theories such as eugenics and the like. Hendrix also argues that while *On the Jews and Their Lies* certainly contains deplorable material, it should be emphasized that 85 percent of it is devoted to "arguments that Jesus was the messiah prophesied in the Old Testament."[26]

Luther and the Turks

Islam was a constant menace to Christian Europe during Luther's lifetime. Ottoman armies were successfully advancing into western Europe, and the possibility of a catastrophic defeat of Christians at the hands of Islam was a legitimate possibility. In Luther's mind, and with justification, the future of Western civilization was hanging in the balance. It was no exaggeration to think that Christianity's days were numbered in Germany, so close to Vienna—where Suleiman the Magnificent had anchored his troops.

Suleiman's Siege of Vienna in 1529 is a historic moment in the annals of Western civilization for two reasons. First, it represents the culmination of a 150-year relentless incursion of the Ottomans into Europe that seemed almost destined to finally overtake the Christian world. Second, it represents a turning point, as the 1529 siege is the moment when Christendom finally proved itself capable of defending its eastern border—even though Suleiman conquered Hungary "and brought it under his rule" in 1540.[27] Despite a successful, albeit temporary defense in 1529, the Ottoman Empire continued to declare war on the Christian West for another 170 years, until 1699—when the Treaty of Karlowitz solidified Christian control of Hungary and signaled the end of Islamic military expansion into Europe.

The larger context of the Siege of Vienna went back to 1453—to the Turkish conquest of Constantinople and the final defeat of the Christian Byzantine Empire. Ever since, Muslim armies had proven themselves to be superior to Christian ones as they advanced steadily westward.

Luther knew only three religions: Christianity, Judaism, and Islam. And while he understood something about Islam, his knowledge was "derived primarily from medieval literature."[28] In addition to having read various writings on the religion, he became well-acquainted with Islam's holy text after 1542. He and Melanchthon wrote prefaces for a revised Latin translation of the Quran in 1542, as it was the first complete version of it that they had ever seen.[29] His knowledge of Islam, however, was doubtlessly tainted by the fear that the religion might one day break through the dam of central Europe and come spilling into Saxony. This scenario frightened Europeans, especially those in lands connected to Hungary and Austria, where Islam had made great gains.

Luther was astounded "that rational human beings could give credence" to the Quran. In his mind, it was "a book filled with nonsense and self-contradictions." He was amazed that humans could have been so duped for nearly a thousand years, and he blamed it on sheer "human stupidity." In his mind, the Quran "sanctions the basest human instincts: greed, cruelty, murder, and sexual license."[30] In Luther's view, it was full of false teaching, and he studied it to warn the Christian world of those teachings.[31]

In Luther's 1543 preface to the Quran, he wrote that his motive was to expose and "refute the pernicious beliefs of Muhammad" so that "all pious persons will more easily comprehend the insanity and wiles of the devil."[32] He wished to equip his readers to be prepared to refute Islam in case Islam conquered all Christendom. "I write that those who are now or in the future under the Turk might protect themselves against Muhammad's faith, even if they are not able to protect themselves against his sword."[33]

Luther's belief was that if he could make the Quran available for Christians to read and explore for themselves, it would "expose the falsehood of Islam."[34] In his mind, Islam was an inherently violent faith that spread itself "by the sword and killing."[35]

Luther's writings depict Muhammad as an "utterly immoral fraud."[36] He openly and unashamedly deviates from the teachings of the prophets and apostles, Luther charged. Luther noticed that Muhammad did not perform signs and wonders, and he said this was the key reason that Muhammad should not be trusted.[37] The teachings of Christ and the apostles were accompanied by signs and wonders that established the credibility of the teachings; Islam offered no such vindications of its truthfulness.

Furthermore, any teachings in the Quran that might be useful were undermined by Muhammad's "condoning of violence, his open adultery, and especially the Quran's licentious description of paradise."[38]

Indeed, Luther accused Islam of being merely "a patchwork of three religions: Judaism, Christianity, and paganism." It borrows Christianity's story of Jesus, the apostles, and the saints. From Judaism, it adopts dietary laws and fasts on certain days, but the largest part of Islam comes from paganism. To put it bluntly, Luther was surprised that "some people believe and accept such a blasphemous religious faith."[39]

In 1529—the year of the Turkish Siege of Vienna—Luther published two important works against Islam: *On War Against the Turk* and *Army Sermon Against the Turk*. These texts were "part warning, part encouragement, and part call to arms."[40] More than anything, they were pastoral instruction to Christians that they should fight Islam, and if conquered, they should have a competent understanding of the Christian faith.[41]

Luther's critiques in these meandering treatises can be summarized by four larger principles. First, Luther believed that Islam is essentially a revival of the Arian heresy—that Christ is not God; rather he is merely a creature. Second, Muslims are idolatrous because they misinterpret God; they do not see Christ as God's final revelation. Third, Islam is subject to the same criticisms that cripple Judaism and Roman Catholicism: they rely on self-salvation. They are works-based and not grace-based. Paradise is a reward for those who work hard, rather than a gift for those who place their trust in Christ. Fourth, Islam contains many immoral commands such as robbery, murder, and wanton lust.[42]

Luther saw the threat of Islam to be a threat against true faith and a threat against the estate of marriage due to its promotion of polygamy, its rather loose divorce laws, and its repressive treatment of women.[43] It was a threat against Christian civilization due to its advocacy that the lands it conquered should be ruled by Islam. Most fundamental, Islam threatened the true gospel: "the incarnation, death, and resurrection of Christ as the Son of God."[44]

Luther's comments on the Turks were not all bad. He spoke of their often commendable lives that put many Western monks to shame. He wrote of the Muslims' constant prayers that were "disciplined, quiet, and beautiful." Turks were often people of "integrity and honesty." They refrained from alcohol and did not live lavish lives like many Christians. They did not curse with their mouths, and they kept their private lives in order. Luther concluded these praises with the caveat, however, that it was better to be a wine-drinking Christian than to live a life like a Muslim—without hope in Christ.[45]

Luther advocated a defense of Christian civilization, but he was repulsed by notions of crusading in the name of the church or in the name of Christ.[46] Nevertheless, the Christian soldier should go to war against the Turk with full assurance that "God is calling him."[47] However, he seems to have resigned himself to the prospect of living under Turkish rule. He urged Christians to teach their children the catechism. Then, if they were conquered by Islam and taken captive, they would at least have Christian teaching in their hearts.[48] This gave rise to accusations that Luther was "more concerned with Christians at home than with the Turk." Lutherans were characterized as reluctant to fight for the cause of Christendom against the Turkish advance.[49] There is certainly some truth to the charges, as Luther and his supporters had their hands full defending themselves against Catholic rulers and against constant political pressure from the south of Europe. Of course, he was reluctant to join a cause that might have put his soldiers under papal command.

But as a theologian, Luther's chief concerns were theological in nature. He fundamentally opposed Islam because its mission "was chiefly to supplant all other religions." And while Islam views Jesus positively, it "totally re-envisions the person and work of Christ" as a mere prophet sent to reiterate the original message given to Adam. Islam holds it was Muhammad who restored the aboriginal message of God to its purest form. These were ideas that Luther outright rejected.[50]

For Luther, the pope was the antichrist, but Islam is "the devil, the Gog of Daniel 7, the horrible sixth angel of Revelation."[51] In his *Table Talks*, Luther frequently equated the Turkish threat with the apocalyptic end to humanity, which he believed was coming very soon. The Turks were essentially God's agents of punishment and wrath on humankind for their sins.[52] However, they were also servants of the devil. They were a force for Christians, as were the Babylonians for the Israelites, sent to chastise and discipline those who had lost their way. In Luther's mind, "the real culprits then were not the Turks, but the 'papists and false Christians.'" Christians must, therefore, repent of their sin, pray, and trust in the mercies of God to save them, both in body and soul.[53] For Luther, the Turkish threat was quite possibly the "end of history," and Christians should therefore prepare themselves.[54]

Lutheranism and the Eastern Orthodox

A fascinating and little-known chapter of history occurred shortly after Martin Luther's death. What happened is in many ways another missed opportunity. Some of Luther's followers initiated a written correspondence with the Eastern Orthodox Church in Constantinople. I call this a missed opportunity because one can only imagine the implications of a Lutheran-Eastern Orthodox union. While the correspondence eventually came to nothing, at one time both parties must have been supremely intrigued, and historians are left with a fair bit of intrigue still today. How would Christianity have developed if the Lutherans had decided to join the Orthodox?

Luther was quite mindful of the Eastern Orthodox Churches. He felt like his churches had something in common with them since both were condemned by Rome. In addition, Luther had high admiration for the Orthodox, writing, "The Greeks and Bohemians are not heretics and schismatics but the most Christian people and the best followers of the Gospel on earth."[55]

Undoubtedly, Philip Melanchthon was aware of Luther's admiration of the Orthodox, and he "devoted his entire personality to the task" of proving to everyone around him the "true catholicity of the Lutheran Church."[56] Like Luther, Melanchthon was also aware of the real possibility that Islam could eventually break through Vienna and conquer Western Christian civilization, just as the Orthodox had finally lost their precious capital of Constantinople in the year 1453. Islamic conquest was too real to them, as they had come under Islamic rule in recent memory. Melanchthon saw these Christians in the East as allies against the Turks, and he figured it could be advantageous to establish an alliance between Wittenberg and the orphaned Christians who still survived in the Ottoman Empire.

Melanchthon died in 1560, about fourteen years after Luther. During that decade and a half, however, he took initial steps to investigate whether any sort of constructive work was possible between the reformers and the Orthodox. The first evidence of contact was in 1543 when a Greek humanist named Antonios Eparchos wrote a letter to Melanchthon in Wittenberg. Eparchos was residing in Venice, Italy, due to Ottoman advances in his homeland.[57] While in Venice, he encountered some writings from the German Protestants. In his letter, he reached out to the reformers hoping to start a conversation that might lead to diplomatic ties between Germany and the Orthodox. According to one historian, Eparchos's motives were not chiefly theological. He was most concerned with the destruction of the Orthodox Church by the Turks. "Unity of Christendom is the demand of the hour. Christians must not argue about doctrines while the enemy is steadily advancing. Christians must concentrate their attention on the Turks, 'that we may not lose the earth while searching for heaven!'"[58]

Melanchthon was "deeply moved," but instead of dealing with the letter himself, he handed it to his close colleague, Camerarius of Leipzig, who wrote back, arguing that "Rome does not have the truth on its side. The truth is found among the Evangelicals, who are persecuted by the pope just as the first Christians were persecuted by pagan Rome."[59] Camerarius pointed out that some Christians were allying themselves with the Turks to defeat other Christian princes. He was outraged by this development and argued—in all likelihood to the delight of Eparchos—that "no compromise is possible" with the Turks. And with that reply, the first wave of Orthodox-Protestant contact ended.

A second major wave of contact occurred in 1558, when the patriarch of Constantinople—Joasaph II—sent a deacon, Demetrios Mysos, to Wittenberg to "gather first hand opinions about the faith, worship, and customs of the Reformers." Melanchthon befriended Mysos, and "they worked together on the Greek version of the *Augsburg Confession*."[60] Melanchthon wanted the patriarch of Constantinople to have a clear understanding of the faith of the reformers; thus, he and Mysos went to great lengths to create an accurate translation that emphasized the true catholicity and genuine orthodoxy of the reformers. In a letter sent via Mysos, Melanchthon tried to assure the patriarch of Constantinople that "all new inventions in the church come through Latin monks."[61]

Mysos started his long return trip to Constantinople via his native Serbia. When he arrived in Serbia, he began plans to translate certain writings of the reformers into the Slavic language—showing his real attraction to Protestantism. This move got him into trouble with local peasants who were zealous in their Orthodoxy, however. They thought he had proven himself a traitor to true Orthodoxy, and they murdered him. The result of this episode was that "Melanchthon's letter and the translation of the Augsburg Confession never reached Constantinople."[62]

The next major contact occurred in 1573—thirteen years after Melanchthon's death—when a delegation of Lutheran theologians from Tübingen University in Germany traveled to Constantinople to hand-deliver a Greek translation of the *Augsburg Confession* to Patriarch Jeremias II. The Lutheran travelers "hoped to initiate some sort of Reformation among the Greeks." One of the Germans wrote in a letter that the Orthodox "must join us and embrace our teaching, or else perish eternally!"[63] Thus began a correspondence that would last from 1574 to 1582 and would bear little fruit.

Elected to the Patriarchate on three occasions, Jeremias II led the Orthodox world between 1572 and 1595. He is an Orthodox hero of sorts, famous for the following three important decisions he made:

1. Refusing to accept the Gregorian calendar in 1582 (thus remaining with the Julian calendar)
2. Raising the metropolitan of Moscow to the rank of patriarch (thus inaugurating the "Third Rome" in 1589)
3. Refusing to join the Protestant Reformation[64]

Jeremias "surrounded himself with learned men who were steeped in Greek and Latin thought." He was an academic-minded man and established the first publishing house in Constantinople. When the Lutheran delegation met him on October 15, 1573, they were "impressed with Jeremias' erudition" as well as with his physical stature. They described him as charming, robust, and tall, and he carried a "black patriarch's staff." The Lutheran delegation returned home after much discussion and genuine hospitality from the patriarch. They returned two years later, in May 1575, to exchange more writings and to make more overtures to the Orthodox in hopes of continuing what seemed to be a constructive relationship.[65] Patriarch Jeremias promised that he would give thoughtful deliberation to the Protestants and provide an official response in due course.

Jeremias wrote *The Three Answers of Patriarch Jeremias to the Lutheran Scholars in Tübigen* in the years 1576, 1579, and 1581. In his letters, he "adhered strictly to the traditional Orthodox position and showed no inclination to

Protestantism." Lutheran theologians responded to his first two *Answers*, but the third was essentially a farewell letter since there was little sign that the relationship would bring the two entities any closer on matters of theology.

One of the key problems was that the Lutherans accepted the *filioque* clause in the Nicene Creed—that the Holy Spirit proceeds from the Father "and the Son." Orthodox Christians always have been and even still remain deeply offended by this Roman Catholic interpolation, which the Lutherans simply assumed. Thus, in the final letter, Jeremias wrote: "Go your own way, and do not write any more on doctrinal matters; and if you do write, then write only for friendship's sake." The patriarch's misgivings were mainly on the topics of free will, grace, Scripture and tradition, the sacraments, prayers for the dead, and the invocation of the saints. It was a courteous exchange, but ultimately unproductive.[66]

In many ways, the reformers and Orthodox could have benefitted from each other. But Patriarch Jeremias was a theologian with a deep and profound respect for the history of the church as well as the Orthodox tradition. It would have been shocking for him to compromise on theology for the sake of political opportunity.

Also, there can be little doubt that Patriarch Jeremias saw the Protestant Reformation as merely an internecine quarrel between Rome and its rebellious northern European churches. In the Western world, it is common to think of Roman Catholicism and Protestantism as opposite ends of a spectrum, but to Orthodox Christians they are merely "two sides of the same coin." Put another way, in the words of Orthodox theologian Timothy Ware, "Protestantism was hatched from the egg which Rome had laid."[67]

In conclusion, we could say that while Luther had limited interactions with Orthodox Christians, Melanchthon and others saw hope for cooperation. Ultimately, the overtures failed, however, due to the deep convictions of both parties that they were right. The Orthodox Christians were every bit as convicted in their truth as Luther was in his "Here I stand" speech. But their convictions came from different places. Jeremias's fortitude had fifteen centuries behind it. Luther and his reformers were in the midst of a recent struggle, and they were going to fight to the death to keep their movement afloat, despite terrific odds.

The reformers persisted, strengthened by the memory of their fearless leader, Martin Luther, who throughout his truly astounding career persuaded them that they were on the side of God. And the gates of hell would not prevail against them. It was this profound courage, irrepressible confidence, and intense conviction that caused Luther's most cherished ideals to live on beyond his earthly demise. Now we turn to Luther's final years and death.

Notes

[1]Heiko Oberman, *Luther* (New Haven: Yale University Press, 1989), 294.

[2]Hartmut Lehmann, "The Quincentenary of the Protestant Reformation in Germany," *Lutheran Quarterly* 30:3 (Autumn 2016), 329–335. For the quotation, see Lehmann, 334–335.

[3]There are many renditions of the poem, as Niemöller recited various versions of it in many different places. This version is from the website for the United States Holocaust Memorial Museum. See: https://www.ushmm.org/wlc/en/article.php?ModuleId =10007392.

[4]Luther was aware of these expulsions and seemingly approved of them. See *On the Jews and their Lives* in *Luther's Works* 47, 266 and 272. See also Harry Loewen, *Ink Against the Devil: Luther and His Opponents* (Waterloo, ON: Wilfrid Laurier University Press, 2015), 229.

[5]See for example Brooks Schramm and Kirsi Stjerna, eds., *Martin Luther, The Bible, and the Jewish People: A Reader* (Minneapolis: Fortress Press, 2012), 3. They argue that "to absolve Luther as simply a man of his times" is a view that has been "jettisoned."

[6]Schramm and Stjerna, 5–6.

[7]Martin Brecht, *Martin Luther,* vol. 3 (Minneapolis: MN: Fortress Press, 1993), 334.

[8]See Denis Janz, *The Westminster Handbook to Martin Luther* (Louisville, KY: Westminster John Knox Press, 2010), 76.

[9]Brecht, 335.

[10]Schramm and Stjerna, 6.

[11]Ibid.

[12]See Scott Hendrix, *Martin Luther: A Very Short Introduction* (Oxford: Oxford University Press, 2010), 89.

[13]Schramm and Stjerna, 7.

[14]Lowen, 228–229.

[15]Ibid.

[16]Oberman, 295.

[17]Schramm and Stjerna, 7–8; Loewen, 228.

[18]Loewen, 230.

[19]Martin Marty, *Martin Luther* (New York: Penguin, 2004), 173.

[20]Brecht, vol. 3, 341.

[21]For this list of seven see Christopher Probst, *Demonizing the Jews* (Indianapolis, IN: Indiana University Press, in association with the United States Holocaust Memorial

Museum, 2012), 49. Probst's summary is based on the text of *On the Jews and Their Lies*, vol. 47, 267–292.

[22]Probst, 50. This book's title has also been translated *On the Tetragrammaton and on the Geneaology of Christ*. See Denis Janz, *The Westminster Handbook to Martin Luther* (Louisville, KY: Westminster John Knox Press, 2010), 77. Janz, however, argues that *On the Jews and Their Lies* is actually the harsher of the two books. See Janz, 77.

[23]Janz, 76.

[24]Oberman, 294.

[25]Marty, 173.

[26]Hendrix, 86.

[27]Sarah Henrich and James Boyce, "Martin Luther—Translations of Two Prefaces on Islam," *Word and World* 16:2 (Spring 1996), 252.

[28]Adam S. Francisco, *Martin Luther and Islam: A Study in Sixteenth-Century Polemics and Apologetics* (Leiden: Brill, 2007), 97.

[29]See Francisco, 98, and Hendrix, 87.

[30]Janz, 75.

[31]Henrich and Boyce, 255.

[32]Ibid., 263.

[33]Adam S. Francisco, "Luther, Lutheranism, and the Challenges of Islam," *Concordia Theological Quarterly* 71:3/4 (July/October 2007), 91.

[34]Marty, 168.

[35]Loewen, 250.

[36]Janz, 75.

[37]Francisco, "Luther, Lutheranism," 292.

[38]Ibid.

[39]Loewen, 250.

[40]Janz, 74.

[41]Francisco, "Luther, Lutheranism," 290.

[42]See Janz, 74–75.

[43]Francisco, "Luther, Lutheranism," 289.

[44]Henrich and Boyce, 256.

[45]Loewen, 256.

[46]Marty, 166.

[47]Loewen, 249.

[48]Hendrix, 88.

[49]See Henrich and Boyce, 252.

[50]Francisco, "Luther, Lutheranism," 289.

[51]Janz, 75.

[52]Loewen, 243, 246.

[53]Henrich and Boyce, 253, 255–256.

[54]Brecht, vol. 3, 351.

[55]See Berthold Korte, "Early Lutheran Relations with the Eastern Orthodox," in *The Lutheran Quarterly* 9:1 (Feb. 1957), 53–59. The quotation is on 53.

[56]Ibid., 53.

[57]The letter is dated 22 February 1543. See Peter Fraenkel, *Testimonia Patrum: The Function of the Patristic Argument in the Theology of Philip Melanchthon* (Geneva: Librairie E. Droz, 1961), 123. For more details on Eparchos, see Korte, 54.

[58]Korte, 54.

[59]Ibid.

[60]John Travis, "Orthodox-Lutheran Relations: Their Historical Beginnings," in *Greek Orthodox Theological Review* 29:4 (Winter 1984), 303–325. For quotations, see Travis, 304.

[61]Korte, 55.

[62]Ibid., 56.

[63]Timothy Ware, *The Orthodox Church* (New York: Penguin, 1993), 94.

[64]See Ken Parry, "Jeremias II," in *The Blackwell Dictionary of Eastern Christianity* (Oxford: Blackwell, 2001), 263.

[65]Travis, 305–306.

[66]Ware, 94.

[67]Ibid., 2.

20

Luther's Last Years and Death

As his life was coming to a close, Luther was increasingly convinced that the end of human history was near. Scholars often refer to this as an apocalyptic outlook. Luther believed the expansion of the Turks would soon overtake Germany and perhaps all Western Christendom, as it had done in the East. He was also frustrated by what he perceived to be the slow pace of reform in the churches. Although the Reformation's success by this time was truly impressive, Luther was depressed by what he thought was its glacial progress. That Luther viewed it this way is curious. It sheds light on his amazingly high level of confidence in the movement he founded. After all the years of quarreling with Rome, with other reformers, and even with those in his immediate circle, Luther was nonplussed that people disagreed with him. In his mind, he was always on the side of truth, and he seems to have believed that his detractors would eventually come around and realize how correct he really was.

Luther's writings give us a good sense of what he was thinking and feeling during his final years. Scholars of Luther have speculated much on why he grew so cantankerous. Whatever the cause, it was a reality. Whether it was because of his impatience with the progress of reform, his failing health, his belief that the end was nigh, or his own self-righteousness, virtually all biographers of Luther notice an increase in his strident tone. He could become peculiarly cruel at times: "He lashed out at his enemies—real and perceived—with a vitriol that eclipsed the language of some of his earlier work. . . . He saw no reason for moderation or compromise and he eagerly dismissed his critics as imbeciles or demons."[1]

Writings during His Final Years

Luther was not the only one who was impatient and stubborn. So was the Roman Catholic Church and its leaders. Contrary to what Luther might have thought, they did not take most of his views seriously. They did, however, finally take his *movement* seriously, and in the 1530s, Pope Paul III (ruled 1534–1549)—the last pope Luther would have to deal with—began to take steps toward organizing a massive council. These steps ultimately led to the great Council of Trent that lasted from 1545 to 1563 and has gone down as one of the most important councils in Christian history.

The Council of Trent was supposed to shut down Lutheranism, giving Catholics a chance to reinforce their claims on the truth while discrediting the various Protestant movements running riot in northern Europe. Trent was also a chance for the Catholic Church to evaluate the *cause* of the Reformation and determine how they could prevent such wholesale hemorrhaging from the church based in Rome. Pope Paul III was an intelligent man, a man of the world (he fathered five children before becoming Pope), and at first he seemed to show a willingness to at least hear from Luther and the German princes who supported him. He sent out nuncios to invite various Protestant leaders, but as time went on, he became more obstinate in his rhetoric and less congenial to Protestants.[2]

It soon became clear that the huge council Paul III had in mind would have to wait several years. Instead, he opted to call a smaller one to test the waters to see how the Protestants might react or to determine whether they would show up at all. Thus, in 1536, Pope Paul III announced a more humble council to meet in Mantua, Italy, in 1537. Many Protestant rulers dismissed the requests to attend, figuring they had no real reason to trust Rome anymore. Luther struggled over whether he should attend, especially since the pope sent a very high-ranking official directly to Wittenberg to invite him personally. Pietro Paolo Vergerio was chosen for the task because of his successful career in law and ecclesiastical service. If anyone could coax Luther to the gathering, they believed it was him.

Vergerio arrived at Wittenberg in November 1536 and was treated like royalty by the city's officials. Luther realized the significance of the event and dressed in his finest clothes to put the best face possible on the movement he had founded. He admitted later that he wanted to appear youthful and virile to the nuncio. This explains why he bragged about having fathered five children with his much younger wife. Vergerio was not impressed, however. He seemed to think himself intellectually superior to the earthy Luther—who only spoke German during their meeting—and he made it clear that he had a low opinion of Wittenberg, especially compared to the sophistication of Rome, the eternal city. Their exchange became heated, but in the end Vergerio's mission was successful. He persuaded Luther to attend. Luther knew he faced a risk. He was quite familiar with John Huss's fiery end despite safe passage guaranteed by the pope.[3]

By the late 1530s, however, Luther was a valuable person for the German nobility to have in their corner. When the elector of Saxony—John Frederick I—found out that Luther had committed to attend the council, he reacted negatively. His opinion was that any Protestant who might attend would be deemed a heretic and shamed publicly, if not killed publicly. Nevertheless, he wanted to honor Luther's decision to go and fight for the cause of reform, so he asked Luther to prepare a definitive statement of Protestant belief that he and his colleagues could discuss to determine whether they should make an appearance in Mantua. Once Luther finished, he was to present the document to the other princes in the Schmalkaldic League for approval and acceptance.[4]

Luther complied. His finished product was entitled *The Schmalkaldic Articles*—a statement of faith revered today as "an authoritative statement of essential Lutheran doctrines."[5] However, the articles were not immediately endorsed by the Protestant leaders assembled in the German town of Schmalkalden in 1537. Several key players, notably Philip Melanchthon and Martin Bucer, had misgivings about them. Melanchthon believed the *Augsburg Confession* of 1530 was sufficient for explaining the core tenants of Protestant theology. What need was there for yet another? By this time, Melanchthon was taking his place as the key leader in the movement, so in the end, the princes listened to his recommendation, and "Luther's articles were not adopted."[6] Oddly, Luther soon published his *Schmalkaldic Articles* with an explanation that they had been "adopted unanimously." The statement was patently false. It is possible that Schmalkalden participants successfully hid their decision from Luther, perhaps to protect his deteriorating health.[7]

The Protestant gathering at Schmalkalden in 1537 included thirty-eight Protestant theologians, princes, and reformers, from eighteen territories and cities.[8] Their purpose was twofold: to discuss the state of Protestantism and to determine whether they should attend the papal council in Mantua now scheduled to convene in only three months. It was also a final opportunity for the princes to meet with Martin Luther, whose health was beginning to fail. All in all, they enjoyed a productive conference characterized by a relatively high level of ecumenism and mutual respect. While they did not adopt Luther's articles, the gathering did give them an opportunity to think through their theology in a context of trust and mutual support.

More than anything, the gathering at Schmalkalden served to cement a common Lutheran identity. They decided not to attend the Catholic council in Mantua. By going, they had nothing to gain but much to lose. Luther disagreed with his colleagues on this issue, thinking that if they traveled to Italy, they would enjoy a rare opportunity to justify themselves right in the front yard of the Roman Catholic Church. The Protestant princes, however, distrusted Rome now even more than Luther did. They saw the Mantua council as a death trap, and they were not willing to go to Italy and put their heads into the noose, as had happened before in ecclesiastical history.[9]

First Signs of Illness

Luther became extremely ill while traveling to Schmalkalden. He had been fighting heart trouble for months already, but just before the meeting he developed a case of debilitating kidney stones. He arrived to the gathering in tremendous pain and in overall very poor shape. He suffered diarrhea early in the conference, and soon found himself unable to urinate. Luther figured he was nearing death and wrote to Katie. She wrote back urging him to drink almond broth, as well as a mixture of garlic and raw manure. Luther wrote back to Katie, complaining they had made him drink copious amounts of liquid, as if he were "a big ox," to help his body pass the stones.[10]

Luther's health was much too poor for him to be a major player at the Schmalkalden assembly in 1537. He did prepare his articles and share some remarks during discussions, but it was clear to all that he was in no shape to dominate proceedings as he had always done throughout his career. When he failed to urinate for a week, "people began to fear for his life."[11] Luther desperately wanted to get back to Wittenberg because he did not want to die in a foreign city without his family and close friends. Melanchthon insisted that Luther wait one day. In his mind, it was inauspicious to travel on the night of a new moon. When they eventually loaded a wagon to head to Wittenberg, Luther made the sign of the cross and stated to those gathered around him, "The Lord fill you with his benediction and with hatred of the pope."[12]

All who witnessed his departure on February 26, 1537, assumed that his days were nearing an end.[13] On the bumpy ride home, Luther was in such excruciating pain that he wished aloud that "a Turk was there to kill him." However, during the jolting around on the path back to Wittenberg, the kidney stones somehow became dislodged and suddenly he was able to urinate.[14] Immensely relieved, he wrote to Katie that night that he felt he had been "born again."[15]

They stopped in the town of Gotha for five days, since Luther was far from well. Believing himself about to die, Luther "decided to dictate a last will and testament" to his close friend Johannes Bugenhagen. He then spoke to his traveling companions about the faithfulness of his wife and asked them to look after his children. He asked everyone there for forgiveness if he had sinned against them. He confessed and received absolution from Bugenhagen. He let them know that he felt ready to die, but he hoped he could make it to Pentecost—about half a year away—so that he could see his family and beloved Wittenberg and be with his congregation a while before passing. It was 1537, and Luther seemed ready to pass on to be with his God. No one present that day would have imagined that Luther had nearly a decade of life ahead of him.[16]

On the evening of March 1, Luther was dealing with "weakness, indigestion, vomiting, and insomnia" when suddenly he passed six stones in his urine, one of them the size of a bean.[17] He instantly felt a huge relief, and he began to recover. His companions decided the way was clear for them to get him back to Wittenberg. Meanwhile, Katie, Melanchthon, and several others had been notified that Luther was close to death in Gotha, so they hurried to him. Utterly relieved he had taken a turn for the better, they joined him for the last days of the journey. They arrived home on March 14.[18]

A New Lease on Life

With the breakdown of health behind him, Luther felt he had been handed a new lease on life, and he began to write—as furiously as ever—scathing attacks against his enemies. Typically, these came in the form of published pamphlets, Luther's preferred method of provocation. Luther's writings now were acerbic broadsides into the institution of the papacy and its claims to supremacy. He openly insulted the pope in a critical essay on the *Donation of Constantine,* a forged document from the Middle Ages that was used by the medieval church to "prove" that Emperor Constantine had granted supremacy to Pope Sylvester I during his reign in the fourth century (314–335). By Luther's time, it was a known forgery, but Luther used it anyway to provide yet another example of rampant corruption in the Roman Catholic Church. His sole purpose in writing documents such as these was, admittedly, to "annoy the devil and his papacy." When the pope retorted with claims that anchored his authority on the Chair of Saint Peter, Luther responded with sarcastic questions such as asking what Peter, the poor fisherman from Bethsaida, had to do with the politics of world supremacy.[19]

After Luther returned from the precipice of death in Schmalkalden, he resumed his incredibly busy schedule of writing, preaching, and lecturing. In 1537, he preached fifty-two public sermons; in 1538, sixty-three; in 1539, thirty-nine; in 1540, thirty-three; and in 1541, only ten.[20] Luther was also tasked by Elector John Frederick to take a leading role in ordaining competent pastors for the now-Lutheran churches. The elector had discovered that "persons unfit for parish ministry were being accepted without having their competence evaluated." So Luther spearheaded the initiative to train and ordain hundreds of ministers to fill pastoral positions all across Germany. Luther presided over the first ordination at Wittenberg on June 24, 1537. By the time of Luther's death in 1546, he and his Wittenberg colleagues had ordained 740 men for ministry.[21]

During Luther's last decade of life, he wrote militant treatises against Islam and Judaism, as discussed in the previous chapter. He continued to write aggressively against the papacy, and he demanded that pastors associated with the Protestant movement "condemn vehemently the papacy and its adherents." In 1539, he published *On the Councils and the Churches*, a document written in "provocative and abusive style." He wanted to show "once for all" that Lutheranism and Rome would never reunite. Some pastors in Germany—known as "expectants"—still hoped that the ecumenical council that was brewing might lead to a united church once again. Luther was adamant, however, that the Roman Church was corrupted beyond repair. He demanded that all his pastors must either choose to follow Rome or reject it forever as wicked and corrupt.[22]

Luther's last polemic against the Roman Catholic Church was published in 1545, the year before he died. The title reveals its contents: *Against the Papacy at Rome, Founded by the Devil*.[23] This work "gave Luther the opportunity to return to the themes that had defined his career and encapsulated his life's work: The pope could not be head of the Church."[24] It has been described as "the most intentionally violent and vulgar writing to come from Luther's pen."[25] One last anti-Catholic tirade—against the (very Catholic) theological faculty at Louvain in Belgium—was in the making when Luther died, but he was unable to finish it due to what would prove to be his last trip.[26]

Luther could be harsh with his own people, too. In 1539, he penned *An Admonition to All Pastors*. In that work, he "declared that the threats both from the Turks and from the pope were God's punishment on the Evangelicals for their evil lives and neglect of Word and sacrament."[27] Luther was feeling the heat of the Turkish threat, as was all Europe. And he realized that the Protestant princes must go to war alongside the troops of the (very Catholic) Emperor Charles V to have any hope of victory. Thus, Luther gave his support to Protestant troops joining the Catholics in a battle against the Muslims. To join up again with Catholics was not an ideal situation, but Luther felt that even in death "God will be able to find his own." For Luther, fighting alongside a Catholic was bad, but allowing Christian civilization to be snuffed out by Islam would be even worse.[28]

This was a dark time for the Holy Roman Empire. Not only was the Ottoman advance seemingly unstoppable, but in 1536, King Francis I of France allied himself with Suleiman the Magnificent against Emperor Charles. Now, a major section of Christendom had joined forces with the

Turks. By 1542, "the Turks were in Hungary seeking permission to cross Poland in order to invade Germany."[29] Luther was forlorn, and he interpreted these political developments in decidedly theological ways. Thus, in his mind, it was time to stand up for Christ and live faithfully for him. In his treatise *An Admonition to Prayer against the Turks*, he exhorted all Protestant soldiers who proclaimed Christ to pray more, to listen to the Word of God more carefully, and to partake frequently of the Lord's Supper. Children at home should become more fervent in learning the catechism, Luther insisted. Only then would God come to the rescue—unless he allowed the End of Days to happen first.[30] Indeed, when the Turks were making such massive gains on Europe in the 1540s, "Luther was convinced that time was running out for the German people to amend their wicked ways and recover their trust in God."[31]

In the 1530s, publishers began to produce Luther collections, bound in large, stout volumes. They were published in Latin and directed to scholars.[32] It was clear now that Luther's written corpus had become something of a staple for Protestantism, almost like a collection of classic works—yet even while he was alive.

Furthermore, Luther's supper guests, usually students, were busy recording his dinner conversations during his last years. This "treasure trove" of off-the-record comments from Luther was collected and published in 1566 as *Table Talks,* and it has been in print ever since.[33] For many decades, these words "were read in every home" that supported the Lutheran cause.[34]

Luther's Last Years at Home

Luther's home was like a Protestant hub during his final years, stuffed with his own children, orphans, "at least ten nieces and nephews," widows, travelers, and of course dozens of students who lived with him free of charge. The Luther home came to be known as "more of an inn than a family residence."[35]

Luther was never accused of being niggardly. He offered his time, money, and indeed, virtually everything he owned with impressive generosity. In later years, Luther's iconic and trusted status in Germany meant that he often had to settle disputes, whether between couples, business disputants, or political leaders. He interceded for people in court. Recognizing these roles that had been entrusted to him, he commented, "I do not intend to be a new pope . . ., but I grant that I am obligated to give my counsel and help to those who need it."[36]

Despite the fact that he made a good income, money often was tight around his house. Luther "never demanded royalties" for his books. He viewed book publishing strictly as a way for him to get his message across and not as a source of income.[37] In addition, the cost of maintaining the Luther household was "substantially more than he earned." Indeed, the Luther homestead—the former Augustinian cloister—was a "money pit," requiring constant maintenance. "Much of their reserves went toward remodeling the house from cellar to roof and installing a new bathroom with a tub." Luther was also "not infrequently . . . deceived into performing acts of charity and lending money." His mind was rarely distracted by these earthly concerns: "He considered himself poor but was not greatly concerned about it."[38]

A tribute to Luther's character was his willingness to pay his fair share of tax, even when he did not have to. For instance, in 1541, Suleiman the Magnificent's forces "crushed the German forces . . . and placed much of Hungary under Turkish control." The 1542 Diet of Speyer required all Germans to pay a special "Turkish tax" designed to "field a massive army that would defend Germany against the Turks." Luther was exempted, but he decided to pay his share nonetheless.[39]

Throughout the 1530s, Luther scaled back his public preaching, although he did continue to preach often to the small crowds staying in his home. By the early 1540s, he rarely was found in the church pulpits of the town. He preached publicly only once in Wittenberg in 1542, and only four times in 1543. Surprisingly, in 1544, he turned this pattern around and found it in himself to handle a substantial preaching load—forty times that year. In 1545, the year before his death, he preached an impressive thirty-three public sermons.[40]

Luther remained a pastor to the end, and he was a capable comforter to the people in his care. When at a parishioner's bedside, he spoke with his usual conviction but also with sweet tenderness. He accompanied many people in their dying moments and truly excelled as a pastor when praying them through their final breaths. His profound memory of the Scriptures encouraged many as they walked into their own valley of the shadow of death.

Truth be told, Luther was ready to leave this earth. In 1544, the measles virus came through Wittenberg and struck all four of Luther's children. One child, Margaret, struggled with a high fever for ten weeks. Luther commented that he would not blame God if he were to take her. Luther thought the world had become truly awful, dominated by Satan. He began telling friends that he was tired and weary and ready to depart.[41]

In his final years, Luther was losing sight in one of his eyes. This would have been difficult for him to bear, not just because he was a scholar who depended on his sight, but also because his eyes were perhaps his most recognized physical quality. Throughout the years, so many people—both friends and foes—had commented on his eyes.

- Cardinal Cajetan called Luther a "beast" with "profound" eyes.
- In 1524, Swiss observers at the Black Bear Inn commented that Luther's eyes "were a deep black and twinkled like a star."
- Melanchthon described Luther's eyes as "bright and joyful like the eyes of a lion."
- Two different observers described Luther as having "the eyes of a falcon."
- Enemies said Luther's eyes were "demonic" and "glistened like the eyes of one possessed."
- The papal nuncio Vergerio thought Luther's eyes were "frenzied as if he were possessed."[42]

Luther had tasted death already, his health was bad, he was blind in one eye, and further, he was sick of Wittenberg. He felt like it was a city of "filth" that was "destroying his hard and faithful work." He confided in Katie that he wanted to move to Zöllsdorf because Wittenbergers had become lax and lazy in their faith. They openly violated the Ten Commandments, cheated, whored around, were greedy drunks, and practiced too much superstition.[43]

Luther's Death

Virtually all biographers of Luther discuss his frequent illnesses and complaints of ill health: "constriction of the chest and heart . . . phobias . . . extraordinary nervousness . . . dizzy spells and pains from gall-stone."[44] He always carried a tremendous workload, however, so it is difficult to gauge the seriousness of those afflictions. What is fairly well established is that he was close to death due to heart trouble in 1527 and then nearly passed away during his kidney stone attack at Schmalkalden a decade later. But Luther lived a lot longer than he thought he would.

In January 1546, Luther—age sixty-two—was called upon to arbitrate a decades-long financial and land dispute between several important counts in Mansfeld, where he had grown up. They arranged to meet twenty miles away in Eisleben, the town of his birth. Luther always kept an eye on his home region and had gained many supporters there. Led by a troop of mounted escorts commissioned by the counts of Mansfeld, he set out in the depths of winter, knowing that his precarious health could potentially fail him on the journey. He brought with him two close friends—John Aurifaber and Justus Jonas—along with his three teenage sons: Hans (19), Martin (14), and Paul (13).[45]

While the weather was dreadful, Luther's letters to Katie show flashes of humor and warmth: "A huge female Anabaptist met us with waves of water and great floating pieces of ice; she threatened to baptize us again, and has covered the [whole] countryside." He wrote to Katie in a letter that they opted not to try crossing the river since "the Devil is angry at us, and he lives in the water." Luther also noted that just before they arrived in Eisleben, they passed through a Jewish village, giving Luther the opportunity to blame them for the bad weather. On a more sinister note, Luther remarked that when he returned to Wittenberg, he would "start expelling the Jews." He railed against Jews in his last four sermons—all preached in Eisleben—charging that they "knew the art of poisoning someone so that they die instantly." Luther's spiteful anti-Semitic sermons in Eisleben show plainly his view that they were evil due to their persistent blasphemy against Christ. In these same letters, Luther also took the opportunity to apologize to Katie that he was no longer able to make love to her, but he would if he could.[46]

Luther became very ill during the trip to Eisleben. Upon arrival, they put him in the home of Dr. Drachstedt, an important miner with long connections to the Luther family.[47] Luther was recovering his health fairly well because he is reported to have had "a jovial disposition," ate well, drank well, and entertained many old friends who gathered to see him.[48] His frequent letters back to Katie are full of fun and tenderness, but they also reveal that Katie may have realized Luther's end was in sight. He urged her to relax: "I am worried that if you do not stop worrying about us, the earth might open up and swallow us."[49] Death was on his mind. He told his companions that if he were to go back to Wittenberg, he would "lie down in a coffin and give the maggots a fat doctor to eat." He also declared that he was ready to return his "miserable body . . . to its home in the ground and be consumed by worms."[50]

During his stay, Luther and his associates gathered each evening for a communal meal. Promptly at eight o'clock, Luther would go to his room to pray. His companions would eavesdrop, and they were amazed by the earnest nature of his prayers. After praying, he would return to visit with his friends for a bit and would then retire to bed. Luther's friends reported that he talked about death often during that time, and on one occasion he said, "We old ones have to live so long that we see into the backside of the Devil, and experience so much evil, faithlessness and misery."[51]

On the evening of February 17, 1546, Luther enjoyed supper with his friends. They talked about the resurrection and whether the dead would recognize one another in glory. Luther was confident they would. Afterward, he went to his room with his two younger sons. Suddenly, he became febrile and complained of chest pains. Friends rushed in and applied hot cloths on him. Someone brought him a narwhal tusk—they all believed it was from a unicorn—and grated some of it into a powder and mixed it with wine, as this was considered a powerful curative agent. At nine o'clock, Luther lay down to nap for an hour. He then awoke and asked those keeping watch whether they wanted to go on to bed.[52]

While Luther was walking to the toilet, someone heard him pray the words of Psalm 31:5, "Into your hand I commend my spirit; You have redeemed me, O Lord God of truth." He returned to his room, shook hands with everyone present, wished them all good-night, and made some comments about the Council of Trent that had begun the previous year and was considered the launching of Catholicism's Counter-Reformation. He urged everyone to pray that the "evil Pope" would not succeed against the gospel. At one in the morning, he complained of more pain in his chest. He went to the toilet again and repeated his earlier words commending his spirit to God. Luther knew he was dying, but he refused last rites on the grounds that extreme unction is not a true sacrament. He spoke a final prayer of thanks to God for revealing the truth of Christ to him. Once more, he denounced the "accursed Pope."[53]

More medicine was tried and more hot cloths were applied. Luther then recited several passages of Scripture. First, he recited John 3:16: "For God so loved the world that he gave his only begotten Son, that whosoever believes in him will not perish but will have everlasting life." Then, he recited the Christmas prayer from Simeon (Lk 2:29): "Lord, now let your servant depart in peace." And finally, he recited Psalm 31:5 three more times, very quickly, in Latin: "Into your hand I commend my spirit; You have redeemed me, O Lord God of truth." Then, suddenly, he was silent.[54]

His friends worked to revive him to no avail. One close friend shouted loudly, "Reverend father, are you ready to die trusting in your Lord Jesus Christ and to confess the doctrine which you have taught in his name?" Luther replied, distinctly, "Yes." He then began to turn pale. His feet and nose grew cold. And finally, at 2:45 A.M. on February 18, Martin Luther took one last deep breath and gave up his spirit. One of the doctors present administered an enema in an attempt to revive him again, but it was futile.[55]

Luther had uttered his final words, but they were not necessarily his last, for when they searched his pockets, they found a little scrap of paper that read, "No one can think that he has tasted the Holy Scriptures thoroughly until he has ruled over the churches with the prophets for a hundred years. This is true: We are all beggars."[56]

To the last, Luther's most important belief—that each of us receives salvation as a gift—remained closest to his heart. The gospel is the great equalizer. In the presence of God, we are all beggars. No one can earn salvation. It is given to us.

The Aftermath

Luther's friends immediately sent word to the elector of Saxony via courier. They composed a comprehensive account of Luther's death to prevent mischievous claims that he might have died a painful or otherwise horrible death. A good death was vital in the medieval world; it proved whether someone was right with God. At the crack of dawn, Luther's friends sent for a painter to depict the great reformer in repose. The first one was unsatisfactory, so they requested a second painter.[57]

So how did Luther die? Ostensibly he suffered heart failure, but several theories were offered at the time. The physicians who tended to him in Eisleben disagreed on the diagnosis. One thought it was a stroke (apoplexy), while the other blamed Luther's weak heart. Luther's doctor in Wittenberg—using the now discredited medieval "humorism" theory of bodily fluids—surmised it might have been the moisture (humors) in Luther's legs that worked their way to his chest, thus constricting his heart.[58] Another observer speculated that Luther choked to death due to inflamed nasal passages.[59]

Luther biographer Johannes Cochlaeus, a fierce enemy of Luther and all Protestants, claimed that "after [Luther] had taken his supper in public with others—a supper where they had eaten plentifully and which had been cheerfully lengthened with jokes—on that same night he died."[60] Cochlaeus was insinuating that Luther died from gorging himself. Luther was noticeably overweight, and this theory would have played marvelously well into the Catholic perception of Luther as having given himself over to gluttony and to the desires of the flesh. Many other tales emerged about Luther's death in the years and decades that followed. Of course, the Protestant versions were hagiographical, and the Catholic ones were most malicious. Luther was at once hero and devil throughout his career, and this ambivalent reaction continued for centuries.

"In death, Luther was treated like an emperor, the rituals mirroring the honors paid a major prince."[61] After much viewing and mourning in Eisleben, his body was sent back to Wittenberg for burial via the city of Halle. The famous "death mask" that was purportedly made after Luther's death was taken from a "life-sized effigy . . . early in the 1600s." It is unlikely that a death mask was made from Luther's corpse.[62]

Once back in Wittenberg, on February 22, 1546, Luther's body was dressed in a white shirt and displayed in a tin coffin at the Castle Church in Wittenberg, where Luther had courageously nailed the *Ninety-Five Theses* nearly three decades before. There was "a procession such as had never been seen at Wittenberg."[63] Luther's close colleague and pastor, Johannes Bugenhagen, preached the sermon before a crowd of thousands.[64] Melanchthon provided a eulogy wherein he famously referred to Luther as "the Charioteer of Israel"—drawing on the story of Elijah in the Old Testament who was taken up to heaven.

Melanchthon's point was unmistakable: Luther was a prophet. In his speech, he pointed out what by now everyone knew—Luther was an imperfect prophet, but a great one nonetheless. Although he could become overly caustic in his writings, his intentions were godly, and his clear understanding of the gospel was a great gift to the world. Melanchthon's reflections were published in 1546—less than a year after Luther's death—and are among the earliest biographies of the great reformer.[65] Other addresses were given for the occasion as well.[66] In the end, his casket was buried in the Castle Church, near the front, just below the raised pulpit where he had preached so many times. It has remained there ever since.

Great adulation came from Protestants, while bitter jeering came from Catholics, but of all responses, the one closest to home is perhaps the most important. Katie, Luther's beloved wife, was devastated by the death of her "precious and beloved man." She "could not eat or drink or sleep" for some time and became "utterly disoriented."[67] She was distressed that she had not been there to comfort him when he died. She was deeply grieved that her four living children—ages 19, 14, 13, and 11—had lost their father, a man who so deeply loved them and cherished their presence in his life.[68]

Notes

[1]Larry Mansch and Curtis Peters, *Martin Luther* (Jefferson, NC: McFarland, 2016), 193.

[2]Ibid.

[3]Ibid., 194.

[4]Martin Brecht, *Martin Luther,* vol. 3 (Minneapolis: Fortress Press, 1999), 179.

[5]See Kurt Hendel, "The Smalcald Articles," in *The Annotated Luther,* vol. 2: *Word and Faith* (Minneapolis: Fortress Press, 2015), 422.

[6]Brecht, vol. 3, 184.

[7]Hartmann Grisar, *Martin Luther* (Westminster: The Newman Press, 1950), 443.

[8]Brecht, vol. 3, 183.

[9]Mansch and Peters, 198.

[10]Brecht, vol. 3, 185. See also Mansch and Peters, 197.

[11]Grisar, 441.

[12]Brecht, vol. 3, 185–186.

[13]The date comes from Scott Hendrix, *Martin Luther* (New Haven: Yale University Press, 2015), 253.

[14]Brecht, vol. 3, 186–187.

[15]Hendrix, 253.

[16]Brecht, vol. 3, 187–188, and Hendrix, 253.

[17]Brecht, vol. 3, 188.

[18]Ibid., and Hendrix, 253.
[19]Brecht, vol. 3, 189.
[20]Ibid., 249.
[21]Hendrix, 254.
[22]Grisar, 443–444.
[23]Richard Friedenthal, *Luther: His Life and Times* (New York: Harcourt Brace Jovanovich, 1970), 525.
[24]Andrew Pettegree, *Brand Luther* (New York: Penguin, 2015), 301.
[25]Hendrix, 282.
[26]Ibid., 283.
[27]James Kittelson, *Luther the Reformer* (Minneapolis: Fortress Press, 1986), 279.
[28]Ibid.
[29]Hendrix, 271.
[30]Kittelson, 279–280.
[31]Hendrix, 274.
[32]Martin Marty, *Martin Luther* (New York: Viking, 2004), 162, and Friedenthal, 525.
[33]Mansch and Peters, 191–192.
[34]Grisar, 485.
[35]Mansch and Peters, 187, 190.
[36]Brecht, vol. 3, 7.
[37]Hendrix, 273.
[38]Brecht, vol. 3, 18, and Hendrix, 273.
[39]Hendrix, 273.
[40]Brecht, vol. 3, 249.
[41]Hendrix, 281.
[42]Ibid.
[43]Ibid., 282.
[44]Grisar, 564.
[45]Hendrix, 283.
[46]Lyndal Roper, *Martin Luther* (London: The Bodley Head, 2016), 398.
[47]Ibid., 399.
[48]Grisar, 568.
[49]Kittelson, 295.
[50]Marty, 184.
[51]Roper, 400.
[52]Ibid.
[53]Ibid., 400–401.
[54]Ibid., 401. See also Marty, 186.
[55]Brecht, vol. 3, 376.
[56]Kittelson, 297.
[57]Grisar, 573–574.
[58]Roper, 403.
[59]Grisar, 573.
[60]Elizabeth Vandiver, Ralph Keen, and Thomas Frazel, *Luther's Lives* (Manchester: Manchester University Press, 2002), 346.
[61]Roper, 404.
[62]Hendrix, 284.

[63]Roper, 404.
[64]Kittelson, 298.
[65]Roper, 405.
[66]Grisar, 579–580.
[67]Marty, 188, and Kittelson, 299.
[68]Brecht, vol. 3, 377, and Hendrix, 286.

21

Conclusion: Luther's Legacy

Few individuals have changed the course of history—especially during their lifetime—to the extent that Martin Luther did. As he looked around in his final years, he saw his teaching "spreading like wildfire" throughout Germany, Switzerland, Scandinavia, England, France, Austria, Poland, and even parts of Italy, such as in Venice and Naples.[1] However, this amazing progress did not last. In July 1546, just a few months after Luther's death, a yearlong war broke out between the Schmalkaldic League and the Holy Roman Empire. The Catholic forces of the Empire triumphed, and Luther's former protector, Elector John Frederick (the Steadfast)—that great champion of the Reformation—was captured, as was Philip of Hesse.[2] Wittenberg fell into Roman Catholic hands in 1547.

Holy Roman Emperor Charles V—a lifelong opponent to Luther—stood over Luther's grave in victory and considered whether he should exhume the reformer and desecrate his remains. He decided against it, only because of the trouble it might have caused him as he strove to get Lutheran territory back under his control. His famous quote at Luther's grave was: "I war not with the dead, but with the living."[3] Emperor Charles had ruled the Holy Roman Empire since 1519, and Luther had been a constant thorn in his side. So, rather than exhume, he chose to punish the Protestants severely.[4]

The emperor lived another decade, but even with his victory over the Schmalkaldic alliance, he could not erase the theological and ecclesial gains made by Luther. Although he required Protestants to submit to the Roman Catholic Church, so many defied him that it soon became clear he would never achieve his dream of total annihilation of Luther's legacy. Most Protestant pastors refused to submit, although some compromised on certain things, resulting in a splintering in the Lutheran family. Hundreds of resisters were imprisoned, some were executed, and many fled to England, Holland, Switzerland, Poland, Bohemia, and elsewhere. Within just a couple of decades, it was clear that many different versions of Lutheranism were being birthed, such as the Gnesio ("genuine") Lutherans and the Philippists, followers of Melanchthon's more moderate stances.[5]

In 1555, one of the great treaties of church history was signed: the Peace of Augsburg. It ended the war between the Holy Roman Empire and the Schmalkaldic League and ushered in that famous dictum that precipitated the concept of religious freedom: *Cuius regio, eius religio*, Latin for "Whose realm, use his religion." In other words, princes and rulers could choose either Lutheranism or Catholicism for their domain, and other political powers were bound to respect their decision. It was a major victory for Protestantism. It was now official. There were two recognized religions in the Western world. Official persecution of Lutherans was over, at least in theory.

In 1580, Lutheran scholars put together the important *Book of Concord* as the official standard for orthodoxy. It is a compilation of several documents: the *Apostles' Creed*, the *Nicene Creed*, the *Athanasian Creed*, the *Augsburg Confession* (1530), *Apology of the Augsburg Confession* (1531), Luther's *Schmalkaid Articles* (1537), Melanchthon's *Treatise on the Power and Primacy of the Pope* (1537), Luther's *Small Catechism* (1529) and *Large Catechism* (1529), and the *Formula of Concord* (1577). The *Book of Concord* remains to the present day the official doctrine and authoritative standard of the various Lutheran denominations around the world.

Protestantism proliferated greatly in the years after Luther, diversifying into various families, or major worldwide Protestant fellowships.

- Lutherans (explicitly identify with Martin Luther): around 70 million members[6]

- Reformed/Presbyterians (rooted in John Calvin): around 80 million members[7]
- The Anglican Communion (rooted in Church of England): around 80 million members[8]
- Baptists (rooted in English Puritanism): around 50 million members[9]
- Methodists (rooted in John Wesley): around 80 million members[10]
- Pentecostals (rooted in global Protestant revivals): around 280 million members[11]

Each of these movements includes dozens of denominations. The Anglican Communion is unique in that the archbishop of Canterbury (UK) serves as a symbolic head of the associated denominations. The others have no such central figure.

Experts at Division

This large variety brings up one of the obvious criticisms of Martin Luther. In his long career, he failed to create an institutional structure that might prevent infighting and division. While he was an expert de-constructer—critiquing the authority of the papacy at every turn—he was negligent in creating something that might take its place, whether it be a council or some other form of ecclesial mechanism that might prevent Protestant churches from constant schism. Alas, he never offered anything, and Protestants have excelled at division. Some estimates identify more than thirty thousand different Protestant denominations in the world. Of course, it depends on how one defines a denomination, but the criticism is valid. Protestants, like their founding father, are excellent at protesting, but they are far less adept at preventing division. Like Luther, many Protestant leaders have inherited his "Here I stand" mentality, with little room for negotiation. My way or the highway. Again, they come by it honestly.

In the world today, nearly two and a half billion people consider themselves Christian—about a third of the planet's inhabitants. Protestants account for about 40 percent of the whole. Catholics comprise around half of the world's Christians, and the Orthodox are at around 10 percent. Having existed for only five centuries, Protestantism has made impressive gains, with no signs of this upward surge abating. Christianity is growing mightily in Asia and Africa, and Protestantism has drawn the lion's share of those converts.[12]

Catholics in Luther's time realized only too well that a schism was tearing apart the church. This sudden loss of members, privilege, and money was one reason the Catholic Church considered the gains of millions of souls in the New World to be such a blessing. God had preserved his church. As Protestantism expanded north and west, Catholicism expanded south into Africa and across the Atlantic into the Americas. History shows, however, that the Protestants, too, would realize great gains in the Americas, mostly in the north. They would also—several centuries later—begin to tap into Asia and Africa for new converts, taking a lesson from the Roman Catholic playbook.

The Catholic Church's response was one of "too little, too late." A year before Luther died, they finally managed to convene the Council of Trent. Instead of wooing back Protestants by softening on certain teachings, that two-decade-long council drew a deeper line in the sand. It reaffirmed all the major teachings that had motivated Luther in the first place.

- *Sola Scriptura* was rejected; both Bible and church tradition are authoritative.
- The number of sacraments remained at seven.
- Transubstantiation in the Eucharist was retained.
- Purgatory was reaffirmed, and indulgences were declared perfectly legal.
- Members of the clergy were to remain celibate.
- Priesthood of all believers was outright rejected.
- The Roman Catholic hierarchy was affirmed a divine institution.
- The Mass is a sacrifice.
- The authority of the pope was enhanced; now clergy were required to take oaths of obedience to him.
- Luther's idea of "faith alone" was rejected. Salvation came from faith *and* good works.

After the Council of Trent, there was no going back for the Roman Catholics. It signaled the end of any hope of Protestant-Catholic reconciliation.

But I suppose Luther would be happy with the division formalized at Trent, that is, if the Roman Catholics were going to persist in their ways. Luther truly considered them to be in error on all manner of things, and he was unwilling to compromise his convictions. The Council of Trent displayed a similar disposition on the part of the Catholics. Thus, a third form of Christianity was born: first was Orthodoxy; the Great Schism of 1054 led next to Roman Catholicism; and third came Protestantism. Some scholars have argued that Christianity splits about every five hundred years. In the fifth century, the Council of Chalcedon split the Orthodox in two. In 1054, the Roman Catholics broke from the Orthodox. Then, in 1517, the Lutherans broke from the Catholics. What comes next? Another five hundred years have now elapsed. Should Christians expect yet another massive break?

Luther's Impact on the Christian Faith

Luther's impact is complicated. Some lament his life's work and others consider him to have brought Christianity back to its fountain of purity with his "Scripture alone" declaration. What is clear for all to see is how Luther changed Germany in the years following his death. Almost endless rounds of Protestant-Catholic hostilities tell only part of the story. Luther's legacy has another side.

His impact on music has been profound. The music of Bach was unmistakably indebted to Luther, and as a result, so was the music of the other German masters: Mozart, Beethoven, and Mendelssohn. The world of art was influenced by Luther, most notably by the Wittenberg school, led by Lucas Cranach, the pivotal artist who did more than anyone to create a lasting iconography of Luther and his movement. Albrecht Dürer—Germany's great master painter and a contemporary of Luther—was most certainly sympathetic to Protestant ideas.[13] Luther's portrait was all over the Lutheran world: life-size pinups, ubiquitous portraits in virtually every church and Lutheran publication, and on many other material objects such as Luther medals and earthenware such as Luther beer jugs.[14]

Luther's impact on the global church is undeniable. From basic beliefs about salvation to whether congregants should sing during worship or whether clergymen can be married, no part of Christianity has gone untouched by Luther.

More than anything else, Luther got people reading the Bible. The German Bible was "Luther's most lasting achievement."[15] Cranach provided the woodcut images to help people better understand what they were reading. Luther's introductions to each biblical book provided his interpretation, the only interpretation that really mattered, he thought, since it was true and the others were not.

Luther was from another time. He was a medieval man. He prayed "for hours a day," about anything and everything.[16] In an age without real medicine, a world lit only by fire, a sky touched only by cathedral spires, and an intellectual climate dominated by theology, Christianity was the only game in town. Thus, a lot was riding on Luther's interpretations because they touched every sphere of life. There was no secularity. Everything was religious. That's why Luther's ideas mattered so much. He was laying an axe to the root of everything known to mankind.

Luther's axe destabilized not only the church, but all reality. Today, we think of Luther ushering in modernity, human agency, autonomy, democracy, and that great catchword of our time—freedom. And there is something to all of that. But Luther did not see it that way. He saw himself as unleashing the gospel for a people who had been impoverished by a corrupt church. Luther believed he was doing a great service to humankind by putting the Bible into the hands of *the people*. Luther believed his theology was not just for the clergy but also for *the people*. Thus, he became the theologian—yes, truly a hero—for *the people*. He walked with them, lived with them, ate with them, and wrote for them. This was no ivory-tower person. Earthy and crass, Luther was readily available to anyone who came to Wittenberg to see him. His house was open for anyone who needed a place to stay. Come in and visit, sit at his table, drink beer with him, ask him questions, get to know his children, share in his life. This was behavior not often associated with famous theologians, clergymen, and monks. Luther upended all of that.

No wonder many Catholics through the years have viewed Luther as a man who undermined everything religion is supposed to represent. Jesuit scholar Hartmann Grisar (1845–1932) studied Luther's life more carefully than perhaps anyone in history. He wrote many works on Luther, including a massive, carefully researched, six-volume biography. Ultimately, however, Father Grisar rejected Luther's life and work as defiant and destructive.

> This very defiance which would assail heaven, the very quality of "superman," induced many admirers to refer to Luther as a great historical phenomenon. Most of them, however, base their admiration upon something quite different. Luther's courage has begun to gain that unrestrained spiritual liberty which they desire to enjoy. Luther destroyed for his adherents the authority of the old Church. It is this destructive phase of his activity which makes him so important to our modern age. The freedom of the intellect which he won by his struggles, we are told, must be extended.[17]

Indeed, Father Grisar alludes here to something that scholars today often affirm: Luther ushered in the great age of secularization. When Lutheranism split from Catholicism, no longer was a particular religion required. Consequently, Europe began to split: into two, then into three (Calvinism), then into four (Anabaptism), then into five (Anglicanism), then into six (Methodism) . . . and on and on.

Thus, Luther represents the death of an era. Due to this fracturing of Christianity—this near-death blow to the authority of the church—the lasting political consequences mean that Western Christianity is probably fractured forever. Luther's "stand" in many ways was a "stand" against a unified Christendom.

In the conclusion of his magnum opus biography, Father Grisar's final words warn all those who follow in Luther's wake: "It is possible to deliver a scathing indictment against the ever-increasing ranks of his admirers."[18] Grisar admired Luther in many ways, but he realized that the Catholic monk who forsook his vows of obedience ultimately destroyed much more than the unity of the Catholic Church. He destroyed Christendom, a reality that sustained Western civilization for over a thousand years. And I think Grisar was prescient in his ability to see decades beyond his own life and recognize one of the more inauspicious implications of Protestantism: that its tendency to protest, critique, and de-construct may in the end prove to be its worst enemy. Make no mistake, Protestantism is a protest movement. And when a movement is defined by protest, how can it ever achieve unity, or even taste peace?

"Burn My Books"

We have no way to know for certain why Luther "insisted that at his death all his books and writings should be burned and 'the children of God not be called by my name.'" Perhaps he had "a fairly low opinion of himself," evidenced in his self-effacing and pitiful declaration: "I am but a stinking bag of worms."[19] But whether he approved, his writings have lived on and inspired many for different reasons. While until recent times, he was simply dismissed as a heretic by Catholics, in Protestant circles he has been variously associated with a number of large, cultural movements.

In seventeenth-century Germany, Luther's ideas were credited with launching the important Pietist movement. In the eighteenth century, his ideas were hailed as ushering in the European Enlightenment. In the nineteenth century, Luther acquired a unique aura as "the quintessential German, the hero of German history." However, in the twentieth century, due largely to the work of German theologian Ernst Troeltsch, he was condemned as "nothing short of a catastrophe" for Germany due to his "conservative-patriarchic worldview" and as the one who almost ruined the Christian ethos of German society. By the late twentieth century, his reputation was being rehabilitated by Tübingen theologian Karl Holl's writings, leading to a sort of "Luther Renaissance."[20]

Luther's reputation was further restored in the twentieth century by the Danish theologian Sören Kierkegaard, who died in 1855 but whose writings became standard theological fare for seminarians and philosophers much later. Kierkegaard must be considered today one of the most influential existentialists, and he gave much credit to Luther: "Oh, Luther is, after all, the master of all masters."[21]

The United States of America received many waves of Lutherans from Germany and Scandinavia in the eighteenth and nineteenth centuries, leading to a robust network of Lutheran churches, although they tended to remain as ethnic enclaves for decades. "Not until the twentieth century did a series of mergers bring about Lutheran ecclesiastical bodies in the United States that transcended the various European ethnic backgrounds."[22]

In 1706, overseas Protestant missions began with the work of two German Lutherans, Bartholomaus Ziegenbalg and Heinrich Plütschau. They traveled to India to proclaim the gospel to those who had never heard of Christ, and they set the bar high for Protestant missionaries in the ensuing generations.[23] Protestant Christianity has gone global over the last three centuries and is making an impact in Asia, Africa, and Latin America. Interpretations of Luther are quite different in the Global South, possibly because "there exists a certain similarity between Third World countries and the situation prevailing at Luther's time: economic misery, low literacy, lack of liberty, oppression by the rich, etc." Luther's theology gets reinterpreted in these contexts. For instance, Luther's notion of justification by faith "leads to participation in God's reign with the aim of transforming evil social structures." Luther is being reinterpreted by the poor and alienated, rather than only by wealthy westerners, and the results can be as liberating and motivating today as they were in sixteenth-century Germany.[24]

That's not to say that Luther has lost his relevance in the West. Indeed, Luther's name lives on in the United States, most notably with the great American Baptist pastor and civil rights leader Martin Luther King Jr. The activist was born in 1929 with the name Michael King Jr. However, after his father traveled to Germany at the age of thirty-five, he was convicted to change his own name to Martin Luther King Sr. In 1957, the son, Michael King Jr., also changed his name—to Martin Luther King Jr.[25]

In the United States, Martin Luther King Jr. is forever linked to the German reformer for many reasons. This is especially the case in the black Protestant churches, which see great and meaningful parallels. While Martin Luther was the Moses of Protestantism, leading his people out of the Babylonian captivity of the church, Martin Luther King Jr. was the "Moses of the civil rights movement, leading his people out of bondage to segregation and racism."[26] Both men are seen as prophets, as ushering in a new era and taking radically courageous stances for human freedom. Indeed, the word "eleutheria"—adopted by the German reformer when he changed his name from "Luder"—is the Greek word for "freedom," and both of these stalwarts embody the power represented in that term.

The centennial Lutheran commemoration of the origin of the Protestant Reformation occurred on Friday, October 31, 1617. It was celebrated all over Protestant Germany and was a time of great thanksgiving for the man who rediscovered the true gospel. Some communities celebrated for several weeks. Plays were performed about Luther's life, special prayers were distributed, congregational processions were common, children were presented with medals of achievement for memory work, many important sermons were preached, and everything was planned with care, "down to the last detail." A "true evangelical jubilee," it was considered "an enormous success."[27] Protestantism had survived its first turbulent century and had established itself, seemingly against the odds.

However, the battle had not been won, for within a year the tranquility was shattered by "a long and destructive war that at times seemed once again to threaten the survival of Luther's church."[28] The Thirty Years' War (1618–1648) was the deadliest European war in history, resulting in eight million casualties. It was very much a Protestant-Catholic war. Luther would have been amazed to observe the wreckage. His theological reforms at Wittenberg had settled deeply into people's hearts and had antagonized many others, and these big ideas—whether you were for or against them—were worth killing and dying for. Eight million lives were given to sort out whether Luther's followers, a century later, even had the right to exist.

Fast forward to 2017, another celebration of Luther occurred—the quincentenary of the beginning of the Protestant Reformation.[29] Planning for the celebration and events began as early as 2008. Sixty European cities linked variously to the Reformation agreed to host festivities. Great exhibitions were shown, festive church services were held, and many activities for young people were organized. Federal funding allowed for magnificent renovations to the original sites in Wittenberg, Eisleben, and other cities.

Ample reasons existed, however, to protest the celebrations. First, the major church service was scheduled for May 28 and not October 31—when the Reformation began—to avoid conflict with federal elections. Second, Catholics and Protestants disputed whether to "celebrate" or "commemorate." The Catholics felt they could "commemorate" but had grave misgivings about "celebrating" Luther. Third, disputes arose over whether the event should celebrate "freedom." Catholics were offended by Protestant intimations that Luther ushered in "freedom" over "captivity"—as if Catholics were less likely to support human liberty. Catholic Germans argued that they had been equally, if not more, supportive of freedom in the modern era.

The 2017 commemorations also revealed intra-Protestant misunderstandings. "Why did the Evangelical Church of Germany not attempt to include other churches of the Reformation, for example, representatives from the Reformed churches?"[30] Furthermore, of the twenty-four members of the Academic Advisory Council—convened to assist in the quincentenary—only one was a non-German, causing one historian to ask sarcastically: "Is the memory of the Reformation an exclusively German property?"

Many Lutherans outside Germany are aware that Germany is not really the bastion of Lutheranism it once was. In 2017, only 27 percent of Germans were Protestant, while 29 percent were Catholic. However, 34 percent were non-believers, and 6 percent (and rising as fast as the migratory trends into Germany) were Muslim. Among Protestants, less than 5 percent declare themselves as active church members anymore. Catholic participation is better, at 10 percent. And Lutheran church membership continues to plummet. In 2017, Luther's beloved Wittenberg saw only 10 percent of its population declare itself as belonging to *any* church. No longer known for religion, Luther's base is now a museum devoted to a past when people *were* religious.[31]

A notable absence in the planning of the 2017 celebrations was the virtually complete snub of Baptists, Pentecostals, and any of the Free Churches in Germany. Luther hated the Anabaptists—the progenitor of the Baptists—and had few qualms with supporting the active persecution of them. He was no friend to these groups, and this fact seems to be reflected in the planning of the quincentenary.

And, finally, it has been extremely problematic for many to hold up Luther as an icon in the aftermath of the Holocaust. Having Martin Luther at center stage was "a most problematic decision" for some.[32] Anyone who studies the events leading up to the Holocaust becomes painfully aware that the Nazis adopted and appropriated his most slanderous writings against the Jews, especially his work *On the Jews and Their Lies*. Even the pastors of the Lutheran churches were complicit in the violence, with comparatively few rising in opposition, causing historian Diarmaid MacCulloch to declare that Christianity is "fatally implicated" in the murder of six million Jews.[33] German historian Hartmut Lehmann has argued that while American Lutherans "unequivocally" distanced themselves from Luther's anti-Semitism in 1994, their German counterparts did not do the same until 2015, a decision that he insists came much too late.[34]

But perhaps we could say that *humans* are "fatally implicated," period. I think Luther would agree with that assessment. He often asserted that we humans have made a mess of things, and collectively, we are beyond repair.

In the earlier years of his reforms, he seemed to hold out hope that the church could repent and make all things right again. By the end of his life, however, he had become jaded in many ways. But perhaps this callousness was a decision he reached honestly. Perhaps Luther knew his own foibles as well as anybody, and rather than having confidence in his own abilities and accomplishments, he found refuge in the grace of his savior—and in God's great provision. Indeed, Luther's last message to us was the handwritten words on that note found in his pocket: "We are beggars, this is true."[35]

Notes

[1]Richard Friedenthal, *Luther* (New York: Harcourt Brace Jovanovich, 1970), 522.

[2]Lyndal Roper, *Martin Luther* (London: The Bodley Head, 2016), 407.

[3]Larry Mansch and Curtis Peters, *Martin Luther* (Jefferson, NC: McFarland, 2016), 207.

[4]Roper, 407.

[5]Ibid., 410.

[6]See The Lutheran World Federation, located at http://www.lutheranworld.org/content/about-lwf (accessed 4 June 2014).

[7]See World Communion of Reformed Churches, located at http://wcrc.ch/our-story/ (accessed 4 June 2014).

[8]See Anglican Communion, located at http://www.aco.org/tour/ (accessed 4 June 2014).

[9]David Bebbington, *Baptists Through the Centuries: A History of a Global People* (Waco, TX: Baylor University Press, 2010), 3. See also Baptist World Alliance, located at https://www.bwanet.org/ (accessed 4 June 2014).

[10]See World Methodist Council, located at http://worldmethodistcouncil.org/about/member-churches/ (accessed 4 June 2014).

[11]See "Global Christianity—A Report on the Size and Distribution of the World's Christian Population," *PewResearch*, 19 December 2011, located at http://www.pewforum.org/2011/12/19/global-christianity-movements-and-denominations/ (accessed 4 June 2014).

[12]See the extensive statistical work in three of my previous books, *To Whom Does Christianity Belong?* (Minneapolis: Fortress Press, 2015); *The Changing World of Christianity* (New York: Peter Lang, 2010); and *Church History: Five Approaches to a Global Discipline* (New York: Peter Lang, 2012).

[13]It is said that as early as 1521, Dürer heard that Luther might have been killed at the Diet of Worms, and he wrote in his diary: "Oh, if Luther is dead, who will henceforth expound to us the true gospel?" See Hans Hillerbrand, "The Legacy of Martin Luther," in *The Cambridge Companion to Martin Luther* ed. by Donald McKim (Cambridge: Cambridge University Press, 2003), 227–228.

[14]Roper, 412–417.

[15]Ibid., 421.

[16]Ibid.

[17]Grisar, 584.

[18]Ibid., 585.

[19]Hillerbrand, 227.

[20]See Hillerbrand, 232–235. The quotations are from Hillerbrand, 234–235.

[21]Ibid., 238.

[22]Ibid.

[23]See Dyron Daughrity and Jesudas Athyal, *Understanding World Christianity: India* (Minneapolis: Fortress Press, 2016), 34ff. A good resource here is Ingemar Oberg, *Luther and World Mission* (St. Louis, MO: Concordia Publishing House, 2007).

[24]Günther Gassman, "Luther in the Worldwide Church Today," in *The Cambridge Companion to Martin Luther* ed. by Donald McKim (Cambridge: Cambridge University Press, 2003), 298.

[25]Peter Hodgson, "Luther and Freedom," in *The Global Luther*, ed. by Christine Helmer, (Minneapolis: Fortress Press, 2009), 42.

[26]Ibid.

[27]Andrew Pettegree, *Brand Luther* (New York: Penguin, 2015), 308–311.

[28]Ibid., 311.

[29]For this discussion of the 2017 celebrations, see Hartmut Lehmann, "The Quincentenary of the Protestant Reformation in Germany," *Lutheran Quarterly* 30:3 (Autumn 2016), 329–335.

[30]Ibid., 333.

[31]Statistics are from ibid.

[32]Ibid., 335.

[33]This quotation is from volume 6 of MacCulloch's BBC film series *A History of Christianity* (New York: Ambrose, 2009). See also Harvey Hill, "Diarmaid MacCulloch's 'A History of Christianity: The First Three Thousand Years,'" *Anglican and Episcopal History* 81:4 (Dec 2012), 465–466.

[34]Lehmann, 335.

[35]Martin Brecht, *Martin Luther,* vol. 3 (Minneapolis: Fortress Press, 1999), 375.

MORE BY DYRON DAUGHRITY

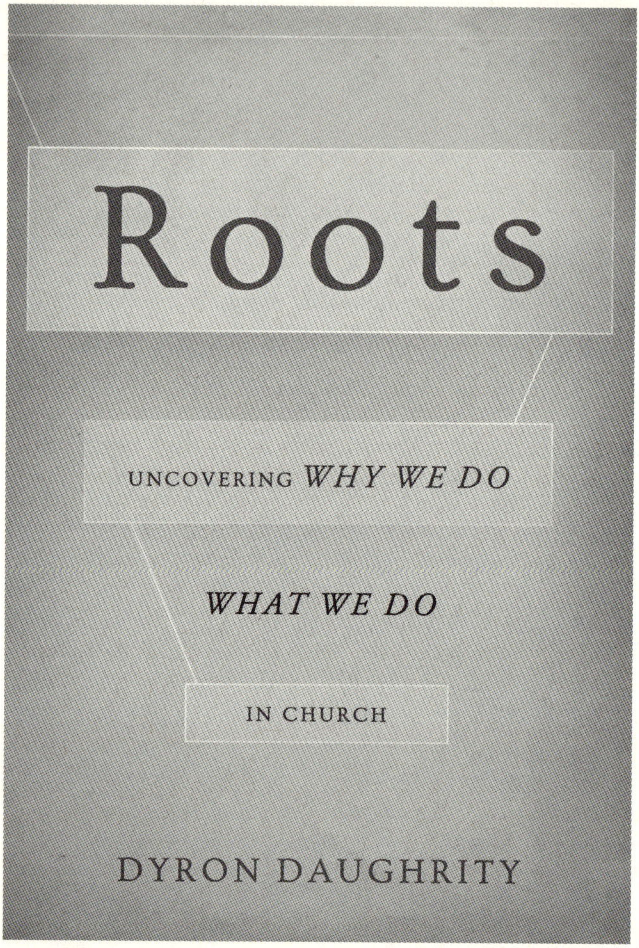

"Only when you delve a little further can you realize just how smartly Daughrity identifies and confronts the key questions facing all denominations. *Roots* offers its readers deep and wide-ranging scholarly resources. An enjoyable read throughout.

—**Philip Jenkins,** Distinguished Professor of History, Institute for Studies of Religion, Baylor University

Abilene Christian University Press

LEAFWOOD PUBLISHERS

www.acupressbooks.com
www.leafwoodpublishers.com